Welcome to Putingrad

by
Franz J. Sedelmayer

with John Weisman

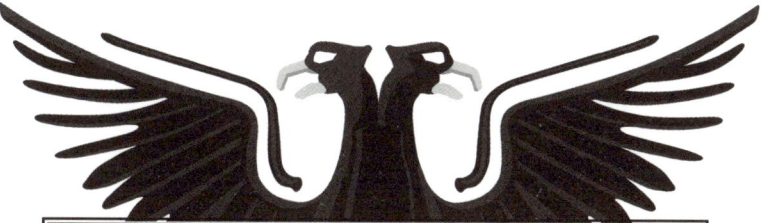

To Jack, you better enjoy this read!

Privately Printed First Edition of 1000 Copies

Welcome to Putingrad

The Incredible Story of the Only Man to Collect Money from Vladimir Putin

by

Franz J. Sedelmayer

with John Weisman

Copyright © 2017 by
Welcome to Putingrad LLC™
All rights reserved.

Publisher: Welcome to Putingrad LLC™
Editor: Richard Koestler
Assistant Editor: Daniel Sedelmayer
Cover Design: Esther Schenk Panic
Illustrations and Interior Design: Esther Schenk Panic
First Edition 2017

Hardcover Edition: 2017
Softcover Edition: 2017
Digital Edition: 2017
Audio Edition: 2017

Printed and bound in Poland
ISBN 978-0-9990783-0-3

All rights reserved. No part of this book may be reproduced in any written, electronic, recording, or photocopying form without written permission of Welcome to Putingrad LLC™.

This book is available in print, electronic and audio editions. Direct all inquiries, including distribution, purchase orders, special sales and foreign rights to the publisher by email:

info@welcometoputingrad.com
FJS@welcometoputingrad.com
www.welcometoputingrad.com

Welcome to Putingrad LLC
10001 LILE DRIVE
LITTLE ROCK, AR 72205
USA

Dedicated to
Vlada, Corinna and Danushka,
and to
all the men and women
of Kamenny Ostrov

*"Oh, East is East, and West is West,
and never the twain shall meet"*
— Rudyard Kipling

That will change, and still in our lifetime, because the young cannot be contained!

Acknowledgements

My special thanks goes to my friend and co-author John Weisman, who selflessly dedicated himself to this project. I have learned a great many things from him about the literary world. It is a wonderful experience to work with a man of wisdom and same sense of humor. Many thanks to artist and designer Esther Schenk, editor Richard Koestler, assistant editor Daniel Sedelmayer and lawyer Mary Ann Wymore. Without them there would be no book!

Dima and Tanya, my in-laws, and my parents Franz Sr. and Ingrid, deserve all the praise for their wonderful and passionate support.

Over the last five decades I benefited tremendously from wise men and women who went to great length to teach me about life. Many of them are no longer with us. I will never forget what you have done for me, Hans and Anna Absmeier, Walter Steininger, Tom Church, Stanley Olchovik, Okan Merzeci, Hans Geburek, Adnan Munlu, Salim Dervisoglu, Charles Kym, Jack Gaffigan, Anton Goldes, Gerd Beetz and Venjamin Fabritzky.

I was very, very lucky in having the finest lawyers, experts and scholars on my side when the talking stopped and a regular legal dispute turned into a 20-year conflict on many fronts. I will always be grateful to Wolfgang Heinicke, Edith Kaindel, Sandra Huber, Stefanie Solotych, Mike and Candy Johnson, Dag Wersén, Jonas Löttiger, Mikael Stöhr, Hans Forssell, Reiner Heyer, Craig Galle, Bruno Simma, Rudolf Geiger, Andreas Paulus, Burkhard Hess, Ulrich Magnus, Bill Burnham, Thomas Wälde, Said Mahmoudi, Patrick Lucke, Karel Schweiss, Erich Waclawik, Ove Bring, Matthias Bender, Brigitte Schmidt and Jörg Dehnhardt.

I was blessed and would like to express my heartfelt thanks to all my friends and colleagues who I have had the privilege and pleasure to work with over the last 30 years from Russia to Europe, from the Middle East to the Americas. It was great fun!

All the events in this book took place. I have, however, in certain instances altered places, events and details and in order to protect certain individuals' anonymity have changed names, characteristics, and physical descriptions. My conversations I have recreated as accurately as possible, given that many of them took place more than two decades ago.

F.J.S.

Part One

Go East, Young Man

CHAPTER 1

Welcome to Putingrad

"The KGB has one little sister—the police.
 Unfortunately, she's a whore."
 – KGB Joke

Sept. 2nd, 1993: Stone Island Company Headquarters, Stone Island, St. Petersburg.

My friend, Vladimir Putin, is arriving.

He jumps out of the car, shakes hands with Russian dignitaries, waves at the cameras, heads my way and bids me a good day in perfect German, then makes a quick escape up the stairs leading into our headquarters building where I hurry to catch up with him. The TV camera crews and journos in the reportorial free-for-all are still outside. They have problems keeping up with Putin. He's just too fast for them.

I guide him to our dining room. Today, it doubles as the photoop-location for the official launch of the GRAD counter terrorist SWAT team that Putin, St. Petersburg's Deputy Mayor, suggested that I conceive, build, and train for the Leningrad office of the FSB, Russia's new domestic counterintelligence service and successor to the KGB's 9th Directorate.

We've got about 300 guests attending. It's a warm, late summer day and the sun is shining. Our headquarters is a huge log and stone chalet on Stone Island—*Kamenny Ostrov* in Russian—one of three islands sitting in the delta where the mouth of the Neva River meets the Gulf of Finland.

The place is buzzing with reporters and local brass all trying to get a glimpse of the FSB's newest counterterrorist team, as well as get some face time with Putin, St. Petersburg Mayor Anatoly Sobchak's chief foreign affairs advisor, and since June, the head of the Mayor's powerful Committee for External Relations. It is Putin's responsibility to encourage foreign investment, register business ventures, and promote St. Petersburg's international relations. Putin has other functions too—shadowy assignments I hadn't known about when we first met the previous year.

But these days he's a friend and a supporter. He takes a seat facing Vladimir Schulz, the FSB general for whom I built the team. Directly behind Putin stands Igor Sechin, Putin's gatekeeper, handing out the transfer documents. They'll be signed by Putin for the city, and Gen. Schulz for the FSB. Putin executes his signature and immediately turns to the TV cameras at the far end of the table. The Deputy Mayor thanks me for the equipment and training my company has given the new unit, and reminds us that the Goodwill Games will be held in St. Petersburg next year. His expression growing serious, Putin stresses that with the GRAD unit now in play, the city is ready to deal with any terrorist challenge.

"And *that*," he emphasizes to the cameras, "is something that you will understand when you see GRAD's capabilities for yourselves."

Putin wishes General Schulz lots of success. Then, we all shake hands and head for the courtyard, where the demo will take place.

Within minutes, sirens go off and the shooters demonstrate their tactical skills rappelling down a building, assaulting a target, and evacuating victims. Squad cars do wheelies and perform a felony stop. Most, but not all of the tactical gear is on display. Still, it's a pretty good show. Everyone seems to have fun and I've made sure that copious quantities of free beer is flowing.

One of the journalists volunteers to play a bad guy. Boy, does the team have fun with him. After tackling him, they grab his head to restrict any movement, then yank his arms as high as possible—it's an old KGB technique known as the Chicken Wing—lift him up and toss him into the back of a paddy wagon like a sack of potatoes.

Not exactly what we were training for, but it looks impressive. The poor reporter puts on a brave smile even though he's probably going to be in pain for days. But who cares? The video crews are eating it up.

We didn't know it that morning, but six years later—August of 1999, to be exact—when Russian president Boris Yeltsin would name Vladimir Vladimirovich Putin prime minister of Russia, the photos and videos taken that day on Stone Island would blanket the Russian media, visual evidence buttressing Putin's forward-thinking, hard-edge commitment to counter-terrorism.

Until that time, Putin had been largely invisible to the Russian public. He was ex-KGB, one of those unremarkable 'grey men' who make good spies. But by 1996, he'd gone from being a bureaucrat—a politician's aide and fixer—to a Kremlin insider. So, the Stone Island video made him look tough: the kind of strong leader Russians admire. Indeed, those videos burnished the bare-chested, black-belt, tall-in-the-saddle Marlboro Man persona Vladimir Putin has encouraged until today. Certainly, they helped cement his image as the new prime minister in 1999. And, they reinforced his aggressive nature: a couple of months later in October, when the same footage played a vital agitprop role as Putin launched the second war in Chechnya.

But in September, 1993? No one—probably not even Putin—had any idea that he'd go so far so fast.

I certainly didn't.

My introduction to Russia was accidental. In the mid-80s, after service in the German Army Airborne and college in the U.S., I joined my family's Munich-based defense products business, where I handled NATO sales. But it didn't take me long to become convinced that counterterrorism was about to become a growth industry, and that we should get in early. In Germany, we had the Red Army Faction; Spain and France had ETA Basque separatists; Italy had the Red Brigades. Palestinian and Iranian-sponsored terrorism were expanding exponentially in Europe—and police departments were not prepared. So, I started a line of counterterrorism equipment for police—the sorts of supplies American SWAT teams and elite hostage rescue units like the German police unit GSG9, the American Delta Force, and SEAL Team 6 were using. What we could not manufacture we sourced from other producers, most of them located in the United States.

In early 1989, an officer in the Bonn-based Federal Border Patrol Command told me that the Leningrad Police Department was looking for supplies and training for its ill-equipped and under-trained force. I made inquiries. For whatever reason, German government bureaucrats declined to follow up on the Russian request. But they were delighted to pass the Leningrad police contact on to me.

It was a real opportunity: Gorbachev's introduction of *perestroika*—restructuring—not only gave the Soviet people a rather limited degree of economic freedom, but also contributed to a burgeoning crime epidemic that many local police forces could not handle. Within a couple of weeks, I visited Leningrad. Within a few months, I had a toehold there and built a successful business as a security consultant.

In 1991, at the age of 28, I started the Stone Island Company. And by 1992, I'd built it into a successful full-service tactical equipment and training enterprise, a joint venture with St. Petersburg's police department—the GUVD.

That's when things got sticky.

I'd invested heavily. I spent a lot of cash obtaining specialized police and SWAT vehicles, rehabbing the shabby office space in the run-down chalet we used as our headquarters-cum-training center, and stocking a wide range of expensive tactical equipment. And then? Then it was like being dumped into the middle of a "*Sopranos*" episode. My company became the target of a takeover initiated by a corrupt GUVD deputy chief. A bully and a gangster named Leonid Pinchuk.

It was classic Mafia. First, Pinchuk tried to insinuate his people into Stone Island Company's management so he could juggle the books and skim the cash. When that didn't work, he tried to replace me as president. And when *that* did not work, he had the company headquarters invaded, assaulting my staff, trying to take physical control and arrest the management—that would be me—all because he wanted to gobble up the assets for himself.

Pinchuk's assault on Stone Island—it was a total fiasco and I'll explain why in a bit—took place on April 29, 1992. A couple of days later, I heard from Stew Swanson, a Foreign Service Officer with the U.S. Consulate. Stew and I stayed in touch because Stone Island was a U.S. registered corporation. Of course it was: most of our equipment was "U.S.-made."

I gave him a sit-rep about Pinchuk's intentions. "You should meet with Vladimir Putin from the mayor's office," Stew said. He gave me a wry wink. "I hear he has a soft spot for Germans."

Asking Putin to help fix the situation hadn't occurred to me. I'd seen his signature on our company's registration certificate. And I knew he was responsible for foreign commercial relations for St. Petersburg. But I knew very little about him, and said so.

Obviously, Stew knew more. "Definitely worth a call. He's well connected politically—and very, very close to Anatoly Sobchak." Stew rubbed his two index fingers together. "Very, very close."

I thought, hmm… well-connected politically and an intimate of Mayor Sobchak. Maybe Mr. Putin could fix things.

❖

The St. Petersburg city hall is located in the Smolny district, in a building complex that once housed the Russian Empire's Institute for Noble Girls. In 1918, it was turned into a government building by Lenin. Putin's office was on the ground floor and access was tightly controlled by his beefy, scowling doorkeeper, Igor Ivanovich Sechin. Sechin would go on to greater things. Today he is CEO of Rosneft, Russia's largest publicly traded oil company. But even so, he is still sometimes referred to as Putin's *eminence grise*.

Before entering Putin's office, I had to pass a reception room featuring lounge chairs: and a huge wooden glass case displaying souvenirs and gifts, memorabilia, predominantly presented by international socialist organizations like the Communist Party of the United States. Igor's desk was located on the right-hand side of Putin's office door and no one, absolutely no one, could bypass him. He never seemed to leave Putin's side, was a very well-organized bureaucrat, cordial, quiet, and always maintained a stoic face. I only learned later that Igor could actually smile, possessed a good sense of humor, and, because of his background as a military translator who'd done tours in Africa, spoke fluent French and Portuguese.

Once I had gained entrance, Putin came around his big desk and offered me and my translator seats at a small four-person conference table in the middle of the room. He is not a very tall man. And he never smiled during our conversation—not once—coming across as pale and formal, his thinning hair styled in a very 1980s style comb-over.

Still, he had a firm handshake and did his best to dominate the situation by displaying an unsettling façade: a mélange of implied power tinged with self-important arrogance. He also worked hard to create the illusion of how pressed he was for time, as if he had far better things to do than talk to me.

In other words, he came across like every typical German bureaucrat/civil servant I'd ever met—and thus not very Russian at all.

It was, I decided, an act.

My suspicion was reinforced by what I saw on Putin's desk. At his right elbow sat a small cluster of telephones. In those days, you could tell the standing of a bureaucrat in the Russian hierarchy by counting the number of telephones on their desk. In the Soviet Union, multi-line telephones were unheard of. Each phone connected to its own network. The more phones an apparatchik possessed, the more networks they could access. The other indicator was phone numbers. The shorter the phone number, the more important that network was. The Kremlin network, for example, had two digits, FSB and GUVD had three, and other, less important agencies four or five. I couldn't see the numbers, but Putin's desk held nowhere near the number of phones I'd seen on high-ranking Russian bureaucrats' desks.

I began to state my case in English, pausing after each phrase as my translator put it into Russian. Putin sat and listened, cold as a fish. Then, after a couple of minutes, he impatiently raised his arm and cut her off—"*Stoy!*"—stop!

Then, he turned and addressed me in perfect German.

It blew me away: he *was* a German civil servant!

But it also helped. We'd gone from speaking through a translator to a conversation only Putin and I understood.

In a 15 minute monologue, I told him how I'd entered into a joint venture with the St. Petersburg police nearly a year before, invested heavily in terms of money, vehicles, office space, and tactical equipment, only to find myself the target of a corporate raid by a totally corrupt deputy GUVD chief.

"I'm committed to being here," I told Putin. Which is why, I explained, it would be in the city's best interest to help avoid such ugly incidents for the future by helping me now.

It was my hope, I said, that Putin could talk to the GUVD brass and settle this unnecessary dispute once and for all. After all, wasn't city hall doing its utmost to attract foreign investors? Wasn't the St. Petersburg government embarrassed by the negative publicity? Indeed, hadn't the abortive GUVD takeover already made the nation's primetime television newscasts?

When I finished, Putin was blunt. "I have no intention whatsoever of interfering in a commercial dispute. I'm busy enough trying to keep the peace between city hall and all—*all* the executive departments for Mayor Sobchak."

He paused and fixed me with a stare. "Besides, what have *you* ever done for the city?"

My answer was, "Quite a lot, Mr. Deputy Mayor."

My rationale? In those days there were only 150 private joint ventures operating in the St. Petersburg area, and most of those were owned by Russians who had emigrated under communism. The Stone Island Company was not only a Western-registered joint venture that brought outside capital to the region, but one of the larger ones in terms of assets. Its future growth would bolster the local economy.

Besides, I pointed out, we'd already done a lot for St. Petersburg. We'd invested greatly, created a good number of jobs, introduced new know-how and products, and moreover we consistently acted in compliance with the laws of the land. "All I expect is that city hall not to treat us worse than any Russian national. How can city hall ignore strong-arm tactics by a corrupt individual just because he happens to be deputy chief of the GUVD?"

Putin's answers grew evasive. He deflected. He was oblique. He obviously didn't want to comment on my accusation. It made me wonder for a fleeting second if our meeting was being recorded. And then, he suggested my problems could be solved if I'd strike a deal with the GUVD, specifically with Leonid Pinchuk.

I told him flat out I'd never do that. I knew enough about corruption in Russia to understand that trying to pay my way out would open a door that could never, ever be shut. Pinchuk was corrupt. Worse, he was greedy. He'd destroy my company—suck every bit of blood out of it and then leave me with the corpse.

And so, the meeting was over. Putin shook my hand. His expression told me he didn't expect to see me again.

But I wasn't about to concede. I told him, "Mr. Deputy Mayor, you will soon realize the city needs the Stone Island Company and the people who run it. We are true friends of St. Petersburg. Don't worry—I'll be back in touch soon."

He stared at me in total disbelief.

No, I hadn't received his support. But I left his office wiser than I'd entered it. I left the meeting convinced Putin was afraid of crossing swords with the GUVD.

The question was, why. After all, he was KGB. And GUVD? It was the police—part of the Interior Ministry. And for decades, the KGB had 'lorded it' over the Interior Ministry and its police units. Insiders called GUVD the KGB's "Little Sister." It wasn't a compliment.

That same day, I started digging. And it didn't take me long to discover that Putin's real job was to protect his boss, Mayor Anatoly Sobchak—and Mayor Sobchak's considerable assets.

Here's a little modern Russian history for you. From the time of Gorbachev until the present, Anatoly Sobchak is widely credited throughout Russia as having been a true anti-Stalinist and Democrat; an individual who did great things for the City of St. Petersburg and for Russia as a whole. Tall, charismatic, a powerful speaker, Sobchak gained fame when he took a stand against the 1991 Kremlin putsch, which ended the existence of Soviet Union. And he would become the co-drafter of the new Russian constitution in 1993.

Sobchak's second wife, Lyudmila Narusova, was a Parliament member of Russia's Supreme Soviet—it was later renamed the Duma for many years. Their child Xenia became a prominent TV journalist and talk show host, and actually managed to annoy Putin and the Kremlin insiders so much that they started a tax case against her, making sure she never went on the air again. (These days, Xenia has found her new home as a presenter on the Internet. She's known to sympathize with the Kremlin's opposition and is considered Russia's answer to Paris Hilton.)

In 1997, under investigation for financial crimes, Sobchak fled Russia. He returned in 1999, just after Putin became prime minister and was able to quash the charges against his old boss. Sobchak died under mysterious circumstances in 2000 during a visit to Kaliningrad, a campaign trip he made at Putin's request.

What I quickly discovered after my meeting with Putin was that there was another and much more sinister side to Anatoly Sobchak. He was corrupt. Through and through corrupt. And of course, being a crook, he had to make sure that the local authorities—GUVD and Leonid Pinchuk—turned a blind eye to what he was doing. Maybe even pay them off.

Which was why Putin did his utmost to maintain good relations with the Big House, which was the nickname for GUVD headquarters. The pre-war building (it remained unscathed during the brutal 872-day German siege of Leningrad because the Russians kept captured German officers on the top floor) is located on Liteyny Prospekt next to the Neva river near a huge drawbridge. The front door leads to GUVD headquarters. The KGB's separate entrance is just around the corner.

There's even a Stalin-era joke about the place they still tell: "What's the tallest building in Leningrad?"

"It's the Big House."

"Why is that?"

"Because from the basement, you can see all the way to Siberia."

So, here's how Sobchak was getting rich, and there was no telling how deep Vladimir Putin, the former KGB officer, was involved.

Yes: he was most certainly involved.

Why? Because with the turmoil going on in the USSR under Gorbachev, the Communist establishment had become increasingly nervous. "*Glasnost*", Gorbachev's mild form of democratic progress, not only brought more openness to the Soviet society, but also threatened the influence of the organs of power, namely the KGB and the Communist Party.

And so, from the mid-1980s on, the spooks and the Party started to privatize state assets, passing them on to their friends and taking a cut under the table. They also "parked" loyal operatives inside Soviet enterprises, government agencies, new political parties and movements, universities, trade unions, and other nonprofit associations and, once they'd started allowing them, joint ventures.

This was the situation Lieutenant Colonel V.V. Putin found in 1990, when he came back from his KGB assignment in East Germany. Like many former officers, Putin remained active even though he'd officially left the KGB.

And why not? After all, in the intelligence business, retirement is often just another form of cover.

And so, newly retired KGB officer Vladimir Vladimirovich Putin's first assignment in Leningrad was to assist the tall, charismatic university professor, legal scholar, and aspiring democrat politician Anatoly Sobchak. I have heard conflicting accounts of Sobchak's role in and for the intelligence services, and have never—even to this day—been sure whether or not the mayor was the KGB's asset, or the KGB's pawn.

But one thing is certain. It made perfect sense for the KGB to place Putin close to Sobchak. After all, you cannot leave a charismatic democrat unsupervised, especially if he ends up running the city government. There's too much money at stake.

In 1991, Leningrad became St. Petersburg. A new name, but the city's problems remained. The KGB was also renamed. Its foreign intelligence branch became known as the SVR, while KGB's domestic intelligence branch was now the FSB—although it was certainly a case of no new tricks for either of those old dogs.

Little Sister GUVD, of course, never changed a single letter!

Putin must have been a valuable asset when Sobchak started to profit from his newly won position as Leningrad's mayor. And as it was Putin's real full-time job to cover up his boss's under-the-table dealings, perhaps Putin was benefiting as well. All of this, of course, would be known to the GUVD.

Which is precisely why Putin didn't want to ruffle GUVD's feathers. Because doing so would affect Sobchak's profits.

Of course: that's what Putin meant when he'd told me his job was keeping the peace "between city hall and all—*all*—the executive departments."

That was the essence of what I discovered in the days following my visit to Putin's office. Not that I was a trained investigator, but one of the necessities when running a business in what at times can be a hostile environment is knowing how to obtain good intelligence.

For example, soon after I arrived I'd made it a point to cultivate an FSB officer named Alexander Sibarov. Alex was a chain-smoking, leather-skinned, prematurely grey guy who looked ten years older than he was—he was in his early 50s when we met but he looked late 60s.

He commanded the Bodyguard Department of the newly established Russian Ministry of Security (formerly known as the KGB's 9th Chief Directorate) in St. Petersburg. His department was responsible for the physical safety of all Russian and foreign dignitaries residing or traveling the region. We became drinking buddies, and then friends.

Which is why in April of 1992, Alex showed up at Stone Island, a worried expression on his face. I took him into my office and I poured us a couple of beers.

"I hear you've got problems with the GUVD."

"Word travels fast."

"Pinchuk is planning to raid you."

"I've heard rumors."

"They're more than rumors. He's been bragging about it all over the Big House."

"And?"

"Look, Franz, Stone Island is currently guarded by OMON."

"Affirmative." OMON was the St. Petersburg riot police unit. I paid them a monthly fee to protect our headquarters and equipment. But ultimately OMON came under GUVD's authority. Which meant Leonid Pinchuk pulled their strings.

Alex's expression grew serious. "What are your contingency plans when Pinchuk shows up?"

"That's the million-dollar question, Alex. Look—my guys are reliable. But OMON is subordinate to GUVD. To be honest, I'm not sure how they'll react. If they take our side, someone will get into trouble. If they fold, Pinchuk wins and I'm out of business—he'll loot the place."

"I have a proposal for you. You know I'm in charge of the FSB's protection force. Moscow hasn't paid my guys in more than six months. But here's the thing: we're allowed to moonlight. If you want, we can take over your security. That's what we do and we are very good at it. This is good for you, for me, and the money will help my boys no end."

"Alex, you just made my day!"

After Alex left I called the OMON commander and invited him to Stone Island. Over a couple of drinks, I explained that we'd no longer be needing the services of his men and thanked him for the good work done. The look on his face told me everything I needed to know. A huge weight had been lifted from his shoulders. Of course: he knew all about Pinchuk's plans. I could literally see how he relaxed upon receiving the news.

He told me he knew about my problems with Pinchuk and told me I shouldn't worry about OMON becoming involved. Best of all, he assured me of his warm feelings for me and my staff.

I appreciated that. We'd developed a great working relationship over the previous two years. I liked his guys and he was a true gentleman to the end.

The biggest laugh I had, though, was when I learned that the OMON commander had never bothered to report back to the Big House that OMON no longer provided security for Stone Island.

Pinchuk tried to conceal his intentions by scheduling a board of directors meeting on the day he planned the raid. Of course, he broke security and bragged about his brilliant plan, which meant I had plenty of notice. So, on the day of the 'meeting', my wife Vlada and I decided to visit Peterhof, a fabulous palace initially built by Peter the First and finished by Catherine the Great, just outside St. Petersburg.

Pinchuk showed up with a dozen cops and a lady lawyer in tow, demanding entrance. First, the raiders discovered FSB personnel instead of OMON troopers. Even better, when Pinchuk called the OMON duty officer to request backup, he was told no one would come to Stone Island as there were no criminals to arrest, only innocent employees. He went apoplectic.

Pinchuk pounded at the gate. The speaker next to it came to life: a very polite voice said, "I am very sorry, comrades, but I am not authorized to let anyone in. Franz Sedelmayer instructed us not to open the gate to anyone until he returns from his business trip."

Pinchuk started to scream and ordered his guys to break down a small entry gate off to the side of our main gate.

It took them a while, but they got through.

But not far. Alex Sibarov had sent us two of his best FSB officers. There was Misha, a young guy in his early 20s, about five feet 11, 160 pounds, and an experienced hand-to-hand fighter, and a second chap by the name of Seriosha, in his early 30s, about 7 feet tall with hands the size of dinner plates. Both were well-trained, well-prepared, and loved a good brawl.

So, when the little gate eventually gave in to the blunt force, Pinchuk's sidekick Nefiodov tried to force his way in by pushing Seriosha, eventually punching him.

Big mistake. Seriosha grabbed him by the chest, tossed him into the scrum of GUVD cops, and slammed the gate shut in Pinchuk's face.

That's when all hell broke loose. The GUVD guys broke through the gate and the two FSB men took them all on. In the confusion, a couple of cops managed to slip past Misha and Seriosha and headed for the main building, Pinchuk right behind them. The rest of the GUVD cops were busy trading kicks and punches with our two-man security force—and losing badly.

Inside the main house, Pinchuk attacked one of my employees, a retired naval officer we called Eduardovich, knocking him to the ground. Then he got hold of a phone and requested backup from OMON, which of course never came.

Pinchuk wouldn't use his radio. Of course not: he wanted no one at the Big House knowing how badly things were going—or worse, anyone at FSB headquarters, which routinely monitored GUVD transmissions.

Within minutes, Seriosha and Misha made it back to our main building. It didn't take them long to "convince" the last few GUVD raiders it was time to leave Stone Island.

By the time my wife and I returned later in the day, we found the company headquarters safe and our people largely unharmed. Eduardovich seemed a little traumatized, but he said he was OK.

Seriosha and Misha just smiled. Of course they did: they'd had a ball. Over the next couple of days, the staff who had seen anything sat down and wrote detailed reports, which our lawyer took to the public prosecutor's office. Filinenko, the prosecutor, immediately issued a restraining order against the GUVD.

Then Pinchuk did the stupidest thing imaginable: in reaction to the prosecutor's restraining order, Pinchuk held a press conference. He whined about how badly GUVD had been treated by the FSB's brutal security forces (he didn't say, "All two of them"). Officer Nefiodov even took off his shirt to display the black-and-blue imprints of Seriosha's hands, while other GUVD officers showed off their "war wounds" to the cameras.

The local news media covered the story. It came and went. I visited Putin's office and he turned me down. But then, in the following weeks, something incredible happened. The footage of my appearance on a TV show named *600 Seconds* was very favorable to me, and Pinchuk's press conference, for which he received negative reviews, got picked up by Russia's mainstream media: TV, newspapers, magazines. They went viral.

St. Petersburg's GUVD became a laughing-stock. The stories ridiculed Pinchuk—rhetorically asking whether a corrupt cop trying to take over a law enforcement and security company was the brightest bulb on the Christmas tree.

And, about two weeks later, Slava Butin, an undercover FSB operative and close Putin associate, came by my office. Over a glass (or two, or three) of good Bavarian beer, he reported that both city hall—by which he meant Putin and Mayor Sobchak, and the Big House (the FSB)—were laughing their heads off. His comment made me smile: the law of unintended consequences had worked for me by giving Putin and his boss Mayor Sobchak some juice over the Little Sisters at GUVD.

Because within weeks, the GUVD started investigating the FSB, and the

FSB opened an investigation of the GUVD.

And Putin, who'd initially refused to intervene on our behalf, realized that not only were we in St. Petersburg to stay, but we had value to him and to his boss Mayor Sobchak. And so, like the good intelligence officer he was, Putin became my fixer and my friend. He was a regular visitor to Stone Island, where we'd trade gossip over cold beer or long dinners. Indeed, it was Putin, who, over one of those evenings, suggested that I cement my relationship with the city by equipping and training a new FSB SWAT team in time for the 1994 Goodwill Games.

By the time I put GRAD in play the following September, he made sure it was his face the cameras focused on as he shook my hand.

Little did we know on that September day that GRAD would go on to play a key role in preventing the turmoil, caused by the unsuccessful Moscow White House revolt in September and October of 1993, from spilling over to St. Petersburg. Or, that a few weeks later, GRAD would take out the group of rogue snipers who had indiscriminately shot and killed civilians from the roofs surrounding Russia's parliament.

Almost overnight, GRAD became a serious tactical asset in a volatile society. It was also Vladimir Vladimirovich Putin's first huge political success as St. Petersburg's deputy mayor—something he took credit for and let no one forget. Little did I imagine that the relationship I'd have with Putin would become a metaphor for the path Russia has taken into authoritarianism, corruption, and kleptocracy.

Welcome to Putingrad.

CHAPTER 2

Show me the Chow…
Show me the Money

"If you chase two motorists, neither one will grease your palm." — Russian Traffic Police Proverb

Whenever I think about what Russia was really like in 1989, I don't think about the first time I crossed the border, which was in the spring. I think about a return trip from Munich I made in the winter. I was driving my rented Volvo on the highway from Vyborg to Leningrad. I was perhaps an hour past the Finnish border control shack—it was still just a shack in those days, not the multi-lane border crossing it is today—with the guards in their fraying, patched uniforms. The road was completely icy. Of course it was: we're talking about Soviet winter and in case you missed "Dr. Zhivago", everything—*everything*—that far north is covered in snow. There was virtually no traffic—a couple of trucks was all. Certainly there were no snow plows. Basically no one on the road but me.

Then, all of a sudden, I came up fast on this poor guy. He's on skis. He's mushing in the snow. Mush-mush-mush on the right shoulder of the road. Going home? Probably. To his *derevnya*—some tiny village. Wherever that may be.

Who knew how much further he had to go.

Probably miles.

On skis. Because there was no public transport out here.

It dawned on me I hadn't seen another private vehicle since I passed the last Vyborg checkpoint.

I glanced at him as I drove past.

Mush, mush, mush. Trudge, trudge, trudge. Covered in snow.

He didn't even look up at me.

And then, he was in my rear-view mirror. A figure from another century. Bundled up like some peasant named Boris in a *Dostoevsky* novel.

And then—cue the balalaikas—he faded into the distance. Mush, mush, mush. Trudge, trudge, trudge.

That's when it hit me. Boris—that poor guy on skis—was the perfect metaphor for the empty husk that was the Soviet Union. The vaunted worker's paradise of Lenin, Stalin, Khrushchev, Brezhnev, Andropov, and Chernenko? Coming apart at the seams. They bragged about socialist utopia? In truth it was moribund, corrupt, and bankrupt. Trudge-trudge-trudging, mush-mush-mushing toward implosion.

But right now? Now there was Gorbachev. Whose introduction of *perestroika* (restructuring) in 1986 and *glasnost* (openness) in 1988, was encouraging entrepreneurs like me to head toward what was fast becoming known as *dikiy dikiy vostok* (The Wild, Wild East). It was *perestroika* and *glasnost* that had drawn me here—to the possibilities those concepts offered. I'd seen evidence in the past few months that after seventy years of totalitarian government, the Russian people were ready for a change. Certainly, I'd already seen that Gorbachev's new programs encouraged the people—for example the little guys who weren't getting paid—to speak out.

And it was evident—certainly inside Russia it was evident to me, even if much of the international press missed it—that the Communist Party was falling apart. I remember vividly a coal miner's strike, a strike that they actually showed on television, which would have been a complete no-no before

Gorbachev. And in one sequence, there was video of some local secretary or other Communist Party functionary trying to convince the strikers to go back to work because that everything would be better; that the problems with pay, food, transportation, heating, were just temporary and they'd fade away. But the people just didn't want to listen to his BS anymore.

And there was this one striker—he was so angry, and he starts screaming at the communist apparatchik, "We don't care what you say, we just want our *shratz-i-den'gi*," which translates as chow and money.

That was it. *Shratz-i-den'gi*. Chow and money.

Nothing else would do.

Not anymore. No more empty promises, no more lies.

Just chow and money. Ante up.

And it was at that instant on that snowy highway I realized—that I could do something the communist apparatchik on TV could never do.

I could provide anyone and everyone who worked for me exactly what they wanted: chow and money. And I'd make money in the bargain.

That particular televised strike would take place later in the year. So, I'm getting ahead of myself. Let's start at the beginning: the spring of 1989. I was on my way from Munich to Leningrad, a young man mirror-imaging Horace Greeley by going East. Bright-eyed and impatient to bring commerce, innovation, and my Western business skills to rescue the dead-on-its-feet Soviet economy—and make a lot of money in the bargain.

I couldn't wait.

Of course not. I saw myself as the perfect trailblazer. I was 26. Looking for adventure and expanding my own business—law enforcement supplies and training—and Russia seemed to be the answer.

I'd worked in my family business, which was located in Munich, forever.

Literally forever. I started sweeping corners when I was 12. I started machine-tooling when I was 13, even before I was a student at Munich International School. I know how to do metal work—just about everything, I think, except for welding. I know how to build a vehicle. I know how to distribute weight. I know what a crane has to look like and how it's got to be mounted.

But after the Army and some college in the United States, I decided to go out on my own. I spent just over a year in the U. S. in the mid-1980s and decided that law enforcement and special operations—stuff like SWAT teams and counterterrorism—were trending upward, and that supplying special ops equipment and training could be profitable.

My first opportunity came in 1987. I was in the U.S., and an American acquaintance in Washington D.C. told me that Ulrich Wegener, the head of GSG-9, West Germany's premier police border guard counterterrorist-slash-hostage rescue unit, was heading to Saudi Arabia as a private contractor. "You're German—and you sell special operations equipment to law enforcement. You should get in contact with GSG-9 and Wegener. Maybe there's something in it for you."

As luck would have it, I had family friends working in the Bundesnachrichtendienst—West Germany's Federal Intelligence Service, known as BND. Like the CIA, BND gathers intelligence on potential threats to German interests and collects and assesses information across a wide variety of areas, including organized crime, human trafficking, terrorism, weapons and drug trafficking, money laundering, illegal migration, weapons of mass destruction proliferation and illegal transfer of technology. The agency worked both the civilian and military side, because in those days, Germany didn't have a dedicated military intelligence apparatus.

I spoke to one of my BND family friends and asked if he could help. He called someone in Bonn and about a week later, I met with Wegener and his chief of staff. Bottom line: we ended up doing some business in Saudi.

The project ended embarrassingly for Wegener—who was unceremoniously deported from the Kingdom at one point. But ultimately things, in Saudi worked out well for me—providing me not just contracts, but contacts with movers and shakers with some of whom I'm still in touch, individuals like HRH Prince Mohammed Bin Nayef, who is the current Crown Prince of Saudi Arabia, and highly involved in that country's counterterror programs against Al Qaeda, ISIS, and other extremist groups.

After Saudi, I did business in South and Central America, and in Turkey. I got burned a couple of times, but also gained valuable experience. I learned that being an optimist isn't a bad thing, but that one has to become a wary, open-eyed optimist if you're going to succeed in business in the third, fourth and fifth worlds. In other words, I learned how to dot my 'I's' and cross my 'T's.' I also learned that arrogance gets you nowhere, that your word may be your bond, but it's best to get everything down on paper, and that sure, opportunity may knock—but when it does, you've got a much better chance at success if you go proactive.

The knocking part of opportunity took place early in 1989, when I got a call from a friend who was working for the command unit of the Border Patrol Staff/West, which was Ulrich Wegener's old command.

"Franz, something's come across my desk that might interest you."

"Shoot."

The Interior Ministry got a call from someone representing the Leningrad Police Department—they're known as GUVD..."

"...And?"

"And GUVD wants German help with technical support, equipment, and training. Basically, it sounds as if they're floundering. But our shop can't have any direct link with a Soviet police entity—that's Foreign Ministry business."

His comment brought a wry smile to my face. His shop, like all Federal Police units in Germany, belonged to the Ministry of Interior. Which was oil to the Foreign Ministry's water. After all, the term "German Bureaucracy" is probably the original oxymoron. "Got it. So?"

"So we can't help them—and the Foreign Ministry? Screw them. But you sell that kind of stuff, and you have training resources available to you. Maybe the Ministry of Interior would hand the GUVD thing over to you. It's certainly worth a call, and I can give you the name and number of the guy who called me."

It was worth more than a call. I went and talked to the guy at Interior Ministry face to face. He gave me a name and a Leningrad phone number.

I called. The individual who picked up the phone was named Sayid Shubber. He started in Russian, but quickly switched to English because he didn't speak German. When I told him Sayid didn't sound like a Russian name, he laughed and explained he was Iraqi—an exile. The short version: his father had been an advisor to Saddam Hussein, fell out of grace and was executed. Sayid and the rest of the family fled Baghdad, ending up in Spain. Then he went to university in Leningrad—hence his fluent Russian. He told me he was in his 50s, had a Russian wife, a college-age daughter, and knew a wide range of contacts.

And how, I asked, had an Iraqi exile come to be the point of contact for the Leningrad police?

It was, Shubber said, all because of Gorbachev's *glasnost* and *perestroika*. When he saw there was potential for business, he'd decided to come back to Leningrad where he'd gone to school. He wasn't exactly a business person, but he had contacts. He knew people—lots of people with different backgrounds. And he had languages.

I got it: he was a fixer. That's a good thing. I'd learned in Saudi Arabia and Turkey, and places like Panama and Colombia, that outsiders and newcomers need people to help insinuate them into the local culture, facilitate introductions, and expedite bureaucracy. Good fixers are worth their weight in gold.

So, we spent some serious time on the phone. Shubber said he was convinced he could help me. All I had to do was show up. He'd make sure I got a great room at Leningrad's best hotel. We'd drink vodka. The police department needed equipment and training—that it was like a slam-dunk. But he'd make other introductions for me. They'd be lining up to meet me. I'd make deals. I'd make a lot of money. And he'd get a piece of the action.

The ghost of Horace Greeley was whispering in my ear: "Go east, young man…" It all sounded good to me. We set a date.

The die was cast. I planned my trip, and, looking at the map, I thought it best to fly into Helsinki, then take a rental car to cross the border and make my way to Leningrad. The distance wasn't bad—just under 400 kilometers, or about 240 miles. In the U.S., 240 miles would have been a breeze—like driving from New York City to Washington D.C. But as I soon discovered, things in the Wild, Wild East were different.

I left Helsinki easily enough, but reaching the border was hard because there were no signs pointing me toward Leningrad. The Finnish signs all said Pietari, which is, of course, a completely different word.

But, I finally got things straight and showed up at the Finnish/USSR border crossing. Where about 20 uniformed people were running around. Some worked for Customs, some for Immigration. Others—who knew? Most didn't really know what to do. Many looked like draftees, not like officers. The guy in charge of the Command Post who handled Immigration was an elderly gentleman—he looked about 60 and actually spoke some German, which was very nice.

I held a Business Visa and another permit that allowed me to drive. So, the guy in charge of the Border Post eased my way through Customs, was very helpful, and sent me on my way. Only later did I realize that actually I was in what they call the "Border Zone." It is a strip of land about 40 kilometers between the border post and the city of Vyborg, which is about a quarter of way to Leningrad.

In those days, Vyborg was a very sleepy little place. It was predominately occupied by people working in the wood manufacturing and shipping industry. There was a road heading south—the shortest route to Leningrad. But that road was closed to foreigners and people without a special permit. So, I took a more obscure route.

Before you enter Vyborg, there's a bridge. And just before the bridge was a checkpoint with a liftgate. I was stopped and my passport was checked. Actually, at that point in time, there was quite a lot of passport-checking in the Soviet Union, because there were a huge number of checkpoints. It was, I guessed, a way of employing people who otherwise wouldn't have anything to do.

So, I started crossing the bridge. On the other side was a military depot with 50 or so artillery pieces, and trucks, and storage facilities for ordnance, ammunition, and so forth. The narrow bridge had three guard posts. One on each end and one in the middle. Each held a single guard—border guard draftees from the look of them. The bridge was cratered with massive potholes—huge, deep potholes—we're talking maybe two feet deep. I slalomed around them carefully, because these were real axle-breakers.

My first thought when I looked at the military depot, was that I was getting my first up-close look at the weapons and supplies with which the vaunted Red Army would invade the West if it ever came to that. But that vaunted Red Army was going to have one hell of a time rolling into Finland if it had to cross the Vyborg Bridge. Wasn't gonna happen. Not with those potholes.

I passed through Vyborg, got lost again, ran into a dead end, finally discovered a newly constructed highway, but travelling at about 140 Kilometers an hour I nearly collided with a huge pile of sand put there to demonstrate impressively where the new road ended. So, I spent some more time finding another alternative route.

Finally, I found myself on the edge of Leningrad. I knew I was getting close because of the traffic police checkpoints. All major crossroads in Russia—right up until today—have traffic police checkpoints. They have the right to stop any car, inspect any cargo, inspect anything or anyone. They have the power to take your driver's license away. More ominous, they have the power to take your car away. They also have the power to detain you—even if they don't see any immediate reason.

Now here's the good news, at least so far as I was concerned: back in 1989, the traffic police didn't screw with foreigners. They were more concerned about catching locals. Why? Because it was kind of a game. They weren't enforcing the law so much as they were angling to make a little money on the side for letting people go.

It took me a while to figure out, but what it came down to was that traffic cops didn't make a living wage. So, they supplemented their meager salaries with bribes and handouts from the folks they stopped. So many rubles would get you out of a bogus speeding ticket, so many more for an 'illegal' left turn, and so on.

It didn't take me long to understand that those checkpoints are one indicator about what makes a democracy and what does not. Example: when the Baltic Republics—Estonia, Latvia, and Lithuania—became independent, the first thing they got rid of were their traffic police posts. They just abandoned them. Then you could actually see, 'ah ha, people are driving around without being extorted.' It was a sign of the move from totalitarian police state to democracy and freedom.

Today, unfortunately, the opposite is true in Russia. The traffic police are still extorting money. In fact, in the early nineties, the Chief of Police in Leningrad issued a written order to the traffic police giving them the right to shoot at any cars that didn't stop. That was because most of the traffic police were on foot and the poor Russians would just drive away. In order to compensate, the chief said, "Okay—now you're allowed to shoot them."

My Russian friends tell me that the order to shoot is still in effect. Which means that Russian traffic police are still in the extortion business.

Spring, 1989. I worked my way into town from the north, driving past Russian buildings called *Khrushchyovkas*, which were boxy, pre-fabricated concrete structures that ran for blocks and blocks; cookie-cutter buildings that sang—loudly—every verse of "Back in the USSR." You can still see these apartment blocks today all across the Russian Federation. They're called *Khrushchyovkas* because, of course, they were first built during Nikita Khrushchev's time. In the 1960s, *Khrushchyovkas* were very popular as they helped families in the big cities escape their overcrowded communal apartments. But building *Khrushchyovkas* continued all the way into the nineties. All the older cities are still surrounded by neighborhoods of *Khrushchyovkas* —which I always call "sleeping quarters for the working population."

Once I left the *Khrushchyovkas* behind, I drove through another older section of Leningrad, where there were dozens of gorgeous old villas. Real eye candy—stuff that had been kept intact more or less since the days of the Revolution. Within a few months, however, I began to realize how much of Russia is a façade—a Potemkin Village. Sure, to the eye of the first-time beholder, it's really a majestic city. You've got these wonderful houses, and an old part of town where you find beautifully built palaces.

But when I toured some of these buildings, I discovered that the rooms had been split into *kommunalkas*, which means they split up each floor into an apartment of eight, nine, ten rooms that used to house, in the old days, one family. But now, it would be one family to each room. With one toilet between them all. One bathroom.

I mean, the most distinct picture I still have in my mind about *kommunalkas*, is that the people who lived there—most of them—would carry their own toilet seat with them. They'd bring it from their room to the toilet so nobody else would sit on their stuff.

But from my first day in Leningrad, I fell in love with the city. You have the river, the Neva, which makes the place look a little bit like Amsterdam or Venice. There's lots of Italianesque architecture, because that's what Peter the Great and his descendants liked to build. He brought in architects, most of whom were Italian, French, with some Germans thrown in, and a few Dutch for the canal work. And even after the horrors and destruction of World War II, you can still see the structural footprints that Peter's architects left behind.

I finally found my hotel, which was on the river Neva, at about 2 p.m. It was called the Hotel Leningrad, probably the best hotel in the city in those days. It was right downtown, not far away from the Big House—the headquarters of the police and KGB—and directly across from the *Aurora*—the battleship that, so the legend goes, fired the first shot of the Bolshevik Revolution back in 1917.

(There's a joke about the Aurora. It goes, 'Do you know why the Russian Battleship Aurora is the most powerful warship in the world? Because it fired only one shot and yet the whole country was destroyed for seventy years.')

Judging from its shoebox, *Khrushchyovka* style of architecture, the Leningrad Hotel was probably from the sixties. It had six, maybe seven huge entrance doors. In Soviet fashion, all but one were chained shut. The remaining door was guarded by a bouncer-sized guy with a mouth full of golden teeth—he looked like photos I'd seen of World War II Russian generals.

His nametag read Sergei, but instead of saying, "*Pajalsta*, Herr Sedelmayer, *Zakhodite*" ("Welcome, Herr Sedelmayer, come on in,") he stood blocking the doorway his muscular arms crossed, and interrogated me.

He spoke only Russian—which of course I didn't understand.

But the gist was unmistakable. So I answered—in German, which he didn't understand.

He gave me a dirty look. "What's your name?"

"Herr Sedelmayer."

He flexed his arms. Obviously, he spent a lot of time on the weight rack. "Why do you come here?"

I looked him straight in the eye. "Because I have a reservation."

His lip curled. "That is no reason."

So did mine. "It's reason enough for me."

His eyes narrowed. "You don't want to come here. What's your name again?"

I was having none of it. "It's Sedelmayer, you idiot—and I have a reservation."

We went back and forth three or four more times, because it took me that long to realize what Sergei was up to. He was a doorman—like at a club or something. Bottom line: he wanted a bribe to let me in.

Problem was, I wasn't about to give him a bribe. So we went back to Russian and German for another few minutes, until he finally gave way and I headed for the desk. Sayid Shubber had arranged super accommodations for me—a suite on the ninth floor overlooking the old city, the Neva, and the *Aurora*. I went upstairs. By the time I unpacked it was mid-afternoon—and Sayid showed up. He knocked at the door, introduced himself, and suggested that we head for the bar upstairs, which also looked out over the Neva.

Great idea. As I locked the door, I thanked Sayid for getting me such a great suite.

"It was nothing," he told me. "In fact it was easy."

"You know the people who run the place?"

"*Of course.*" He smiled. "I live here, too, Herr Sedelmayer." He explained that he was separated from his Russian wife and as opposed to getting his own flat, he'd moved into the Leningrad. No fuss, no muss, plus daily maid service and prostitutes.

He probably worked for them as a fixer, too. He certainly was typecast. Sayid Shubber looked a lot more like someone out of Baghdad or Amman than Leningrad or Smolensk: dressed in a sport shirt and slacks, dark hair, olive complexion and what appeared to be a permanent five o'clock shadow. We climbed the flight of stairs that took us to what turned out to be one of Leningrad's few decent bars, which was on the hotel's tenth floor.

Once we'd sat down and he'd asked how the drive had been, the second thing that came out of his mouth wasn't "OK, Franz, let me tell you about the Leningrad Police Department, but, "Do you like vodka?"

I wasn't much of a hard-liquor drinker in those days, but I said, "Sure," and what he ordered tasted pretty damn good. I'd always thought they served vodka icy cold in Russia. But no—the Russians drink it straight from the bottle at room temperature. It was served with pickles, and pickled garlic, and leeks and sour cream. And, of course you could get black caviar either with blinis or without. When we moved from the bar to the restaurant, the food got worse, the vodka stayed good, but because of its sheer quantity any discussion about my deal with the GUVD was drowned by alcohol. And if that wasn't bad enough, from the restaurant we moved to the night club. That's where Sergei, the gold-toothed bouncer, was drinking. There was, of course, more vodka. Now that I had a translator, Sergei was all smiles. He insisted that we arm-wrestle—and despite the fact that he was in his sixties, he won. Turns out he'd been on the Soviet Olympic Team as a weightlifter—taken a Silver Medal in the 1970s. By then I was more than ready for bed—I'd been driving and drinking most of the day.

❖

I woke up with a tremendous vodka and pickled garlic headache. How bad was it? So bad that I was afraid my head wouldn't fit through the bathroom door. But hung over or not, Sayid Shubber had scheduled a full day of meetings.

My first was with a fascinating character by the name of Venjamin Fabritzky. Tall and aristocratic, with mane of white hair combed straight back, he was the Leningrad City Architect. We would become very good friends. He was the darling of the Communist Party, and because of this, Venjamin was able to design the sorts of innovative things that no one else was allowed to touch. His wife was an opera singer with an international reputation. He was a truly talented artist, although his plans and designs were often so ornate and expensive that very few people could afford to hire him. Fabritzky was connected not only to the Communist hierarchy, but also to the firebrand reformer Anatoly Sobchak, a law professor and political activist who was probably going to become Leningrad's next mayor. Venjamin knew a lot about what was going on in the city, and probably more than anyone else in those first weeks in Leningrad, he would help me to understand the warp and weave of the situation on the ground. Sayid Shubber could get me to GUVD. Venjamin could get me to Leningrad's movers and shakers.

After Fabritzky left, I finally asked Sayid about GUVD. After all, it was the Leningrad Police who'd brought me here in the first place.

His answer wasn't very satisfactory. The bottom line was, that, yes, he'd been contacted by the police because they needed equipment and training. But there was one slight wrinkle.

"And that is?"

He hemmed and he hawed. Finally, not looking me in the eye, he said, "It might be the case that they may not have exactly the budget to do everything they want, Franz."

"What kind of budget do they have?"

He stared at the floor. "It's sort of restrictive."

"How restrictive?"

Shubber shrugged. "I think they were hoping that the German government would give them a grant or something."

Was he nuts? He'd mentioned none of this. On the phone he'd suggested that the GUVD deal was a slam-dunk. "You mean they're looking for a handout?"

Shubber's guilty look told me I'd answered my own question.

Fuck me. Another unforeseen welcome to the Wild, Wild East.

Well, you know what? This could be dealt with. I poured myself a vodka and reached for the pickled garlic. Nothing's perfect. This was just a bump in the road. Or—since I was in Russia—a pothole on the bridge.

Screw it: I'd make it work.

CHAPTER 3

Welcome to the Russian Free Market

"Business is like sex: if it's good, it's really good;
if it's bad, it's still good." — Early 1990s Russian proverb

So, there were probably a hundred or so Western businessmen and Russian émigré entrepreneurs trying to make deals in Leningrad when I arrived. And every one of them was a peddler. By which I mean they were all trying to do a quick deal—sell bananas today, auto parts tomorrow, ball joints the day after, and computers the day after that. Anything to make a fast buck. No one but I had a specialty or saw the prospect of a longer term investment. Even more significantly: there was nobody from Siemens, nobody from Volkswagen, nobody from *any* of the multinational companies, European or American. They'd arrive, but they hadn't when I first showed up.

And, thinking back on it now, Sayid Shubber probably thought I was just another peddler. Because every day, starting at about nine in the morning and going on until about three in the afternoon, a line of Russians would form outside my hotel room. One by one they'd be escorted in by Shubber, and they'd pitch me on money-making schemes, or try to hawk their gadgets, devices, or inventions.

Like what? One of the first was a first responder from the 1986 nuclear disaster at Chernobyl. He tried to sell me the rights to a portable

Geiger counter that looked as if it had been stolen from the set of a 1930s science fiction movie. Another guy showed up—he'd worked in one of the military goods factories—with ten rubber-coated wire mesh penises in an assortment of sizes. He explained that the dildos were his groundbreaking answer to erectile dysfunction and we'd make a million rubles selling them. A Kazakh brought samples of titanium ore and titanium sponge—the porous form of the metal created during the first stage of processing. All I had to do was to buy the mine and its processing facilities and start exporting. Yeah, right!

And these meetings didn't just involve coffee. Coffee was during the day, but at night we had a more exclusive category of prospects show up. And when you get into this level, you've got the vodka-drinking crowd, some of whom used to be connected to the State, or maybe still are, or who just want to freelance and make some fast cash. It was a diverse group in the evenings. There were ex-military, ex-KGB—even politicians. That's how I met the Governor of the Leningrad Region and his bag man. And they all had schemes: "I've got access to scrap metal. You can sell it in the West. You'll make millions." Another guy said, "I've got a ship for you. It doesn't quite work but we'll tow it wherever you want."

There were even people from the prisons. The Soviet prison system produced a huge number of goods although the materials and workmanship were uniformly bad. The lacquer used on some of the furniture, for example, contained so much arsenic and formaldehyde that the finished product was chemically toxic. It was Alfred Hitchcock surreal: not only were the goods produced by slave labor, which put them off-bounds from the get-go so far as I was concerned, but you could actually be killed by your own dining table and chairs.

Judging by the large number of dead-wood possibilities, what Sayid had no doubt done was tell all his contacts to tell their friends, "Yo, *tovarich*, there's a new sucker in town—a German guy and he's sitting on a pile of cash." And to top it off, he set me up with a translator who charged me $60 an hour to deal with all the Russians, and the Kazakhs, and the Uzbeks, and the Georgians, and the Ukrainians, and the Turkmens who showed up.

Plus, given that they all spoke Russian, I thought $60 an hour was a bit expensive. I did some checking. It turned out the translator was paying Sayid $50 of the $60 as a kickback. He was happy to make $10.

Lesson learned. Kickbacks were commonplace in the Wild, Wild East.

Another lesson I learned was to keep my floor matron happy. In those days the Soviets had a desk on every hotel floor. And behind those desks sat women—the floor matrons. Working in shifts over 24 hours, they were like hall monitors on steroids. They kept a log of who came and who went, and at what time, and in what condition, and if they were in conversation, what the conversation was about. And there was no doubt in my mind that they were reporting all of this to the KGB.

But like most Russians, my floor matrons were interested in making a little hard currency whenever possible. They had access to the State stores as well as some of the local farmer's markets that were beginning to spring up under Gorbachev. And so I cultivated them. At first with a smile and some polite small talk and Mars Bars, and then with U.S. dollars. In return, they'd bring me fresh cucumbers, tomatoes, pickled garlic, and homemade *smetana* (sour cream) from one of the roadside markets, as well as cans of cod liver, *salo* (bacon) and Krakau style smoked and cured sausages.

They'd also give me gossip. Like confirmation that, yes, my room was indeed bugged, but that since every room was bugged, there were far too many tapes to be individually checked anymore, so not to worry. And they let me know there were plainclothes police all over the hotel.

Of course there were. I'd already made friends with the cops who manned the small police station inside the hotel. They were from the GUVD, and their function was to keep the riff-raff out so the hotel could engage in the newly-allowed free enterprise—in other words, the prostitution—that Gorbachev was encouraging under *perestroika* (restructuring). Simultaneously, however, in that same 1989-1990 time frame, that same riff-raff developed their own version of *perestroika*, which involved encouraging free enterprise by paying off the GUVD.

Which, I realized, was why there were so many prostitutes at the Hotel Leningrad.

When I asked, one of the GUVD cops put it to me this way: "We're not here to fight crime. We're here to control crime."

Let me translate that for you in *perestroika* terms: "If an '*entrepreneur*' pays us, he can run as many prostitutes in this place as he wants. And if he chooses not to pay us, that's okay too. But if he doesn't pay, we will arrest him and all his prostitutes to ensure that he does not engage in free enterprise."

Within days of my arrival, Sayid took me over to visit GUVD. The Leningrad Police was headquartered on the Neva in what was known as the Big House, and it shared quarters with the KGB. I was introduced to the chief, General Voshinin, and the chief deputy, a GUVD general named Mikhail Ivanovich Michailov, as well as the officer in charge of organized crime. I also spent time with the colonel running the crime lab, a woman named Lyudmila Bystrova. And with the chief of OMON, which was the riot control squad of the Interior Department. I spent the most time with a colonel named Gennadi Kolbasov, who was Leningrad GUVD's head of intelligence. He'd more or less been assigned to me as a caretaker by GUVD General Mikhail Ivanovich Michailov.

Kolbasov was an English-speaker. I'd actually met him on my second day in Leningrad—the same day I met Venjamin Fabritzky. Like Venjamin,

Gennadi was a sophisticated, well-connected individual. Tall, with blondish hair and horn-rimmed glasses, he looked like a Russian version of John Hurt playing George Smiley in the movie "Tinker, Tailor, Soldier, Spy." Unless we were going to some sort of official function, he dressed in a civilian 'uniform'—a grey suit, white shirt, and dark tie. He was hugely well-connected to the KGB and, while I soon hired him to work part time for me as a fixer, translator, troubleshooter, and coordinator, I always remembered that first and foremost, he was an intelligence officer. He served other masters and was probably writing reports on me, which led me to believe that Gennadi's GUVD nickname, "The Snake", might be well-deserved.

But certainly, he was helpful. At one point I had to make a pitch to the political entity—the local parliament, which was called the City Soviet. Before I spoke, Gennadi talked for about 15 minutes explaining the benefits of cooperation with me and my proposals, and we ended up with a unanimous 'yes' vote. He also accompanied me to Moscow on several occasions so we could speak with the bureaucrats at the Ministry of Interior and ensure that we could actually do what we wanted to do—and most important, get them to sign off on paper that the proposed joint venture between me and the GUVD was legal.

Of course, I didn't just rely on Kolbasov. I made contacts at the German Consulate, and also at the Consulate of the United States, where I became acquainted with the Consul General, the resident economics officer, and the Consulate's security officer.

It didn't take me long to see that the Leningrad GUVD was in much worse shape than Sayid had described. Their equipment—what there was of it—was outdated and poorly maintained. And, of course, they had no money and no budget for training or equipment.

I discovered a possible path to funding during a conversation at the Big House. As it turned out, the Soviet Ministry of Interior was the largest industrial complex in the Soviet Union with the exception of the armed forces. The prisons around Leningrad (they called them working colonies) manufactured just about everything—metal goods to wood products to agricultural items. You need furniture? You go to Colony 5, where they built it all from movie theater seating to the nice stuff you'd find in some Commissar's office. You want beehives, you go to the largest producer of beehives: the prison colony in Karelia. You want tank components? You go a little farther afield to the metallurgy working colony in Ekaterinburg.

Between them all, there had to be a way to work exchanges—barter—so that GUVD, part of the Interior Ministry, could finance the procurement of what it needed. All I had to do was learn how to understand the subtext of what I was being told, and discover a *modus operandi* allowing me to work within the Russian framework.

Subtext? Well, yes. The people I was going to do business with had been living under a totalitarian system of government for more than seventy years. The state controlled everything: food, drink, commerce, the economy. Everyone had a job—the state saw to that. Everybody got paid. Not as much as they might have liked, but at least enough for the occasional bottle of vodka and tin of cod liver. But full employment was a big part of the problem. Because everyone was guaranteed a job and guaranteed a paycheck, the vast majority of workers would show up—but not give a damn about the quality of their work. If you ran a factory that made tractors and you had a quota of 100 a month, you made 100 tractors. Whether they worked or not was someone else's problem. Your box, the 100 finished tractors per month box, had been checked.

So, why should Russians actually work hard? Under Communism, it didn't matter. There was even a joke about it. "We pretend to work; they pretend to pay us" was the line you'd hear in the factories.

And the working colonies. The prisoners worked there, too. And the money they earned helped support their families—after, of course, the prison authorities skimmed most of the cream off the top.

In 1989, the Gorbachev era, with *glasnost* and *perestroika* underway, Russians were being given a taste of free enterprise. But they'd never done business before, especially business with Westerners.

It didn't take me long to realize that the Russian 'art of business communication' was pretty much determined by the fear of looking stupid. That was to be expected. I was dealing with a people who were very proud. Proud in the sense they would never admit that they don't know something. So, when I'd ask a question like, "Do you know what a letter of credit is?" They'd say "Of course, we know." Except: they had no idea what a letter of credit was. They'd never seen one in their lives. How could they? In the old days, there was no commercial foreign trade. Hell, in the old days it had been forbidden even to communicate with foreigners.

There'd been no freedom under Communism. And if the Russians did get some freedom under Gorbachev, it still was limited. Most had no experience traveling abroad. Most had no experience in commerce, or commerce with import/export companies, all of which were still a state monopoly.

Another problem was that it would often turn out to be impossible to purchase Western goods because nobody had any *valuta*, which was the Russian term for dollars, Swiss francs, Deutsche marks, French francs, British pounds—any of the hard currencies with which to make the purchase. Instead, most often, you'd get an offer of something in trade.

An example. Let's say you are Marina Popova, the warden of Prison Colony No. 5, just outside Leningrad. And you need spare parts for your wood-milling machines. The machines were made in Canada perhaps 25 years ago and they've broken down, and broken down, and broken down so often that finally not one of them is working.

Marina needs parts. But there's no real money for parts—no *valuta*. So what can Marina do? It occurs to her that she could export some of her furniture in exchange for hard currency, and then buy the spare parts. Except no one in a hard currency country wants her furniture, because the lacquer that's used on it is, as I just mentioned, heavy on the arsenic and formaldehyde.

Then, it strikes Marina that since Colony No. 5's furniture is made from birch, aspen, and Scots pine—all marketable furniture-grade woods—perhaps she could sell logs in the West, get valuta, and buy the machine parts she needs. The wood arrives at Colony No. 5 debarked, in six-meter lengths. It would be simple to sluice off a couple of thousand cubic meters, cook the books, and sell it for *valuta*.

Marina checks with a friend, who has a friend, who has a friend in Sweden, and the Swedish guy is in the furniture business with Ikea, and he's always looking for a source of good wood. So, Marina calls him. He's interested, but he says he needs logs that are twelve meters in length, not six.

"Easy," says Marina. She goes to the prison colony that harvests wood and talks to her colleague Ivan. Ivan's willing to cut twelve-meter logs. But he wants a piece of the action. Marina doesn't even blink. No problem. How much? Ivan says, "How about 20 percent? They're my logs, and I have to fiddle with my books too."

Well, it's the cost of doing business, so Marina agrees. All she has to do now is export the logs and she'll get the spare parts, her partner will get a cut, and the assembly line goes back into business.

And then Marina hits a roadblock. She needs an export license to move the logs to Sweden. So, she checks with the Interior Ministry and finally gets the name of a guy named Anatoly who is in charge of Leningrad's only import/export company (it's the only one because im/ex is a state monopoly).

So, she calls Anatoly, who's happy to help—for a cut. Of 30 percent.

So now, if Marina needs a thousand dollars' worth of spare parts, she has to sell two thousand bucks worth of wood, because she's going to lose half of it in bribes. And if Marina's going to put any *valuta* in her own pocket, she'd better sell three grand of wood.

Welcome to the Russian free market.

And, incidentally, I learned pretty quickly that what I've just described was more or less how the whole Soviet system worked—even for the big shots. When you were in the upper ranks of the Soviet system, say a police chief, or a politician, you got a very modest salary. But you received a free apartment, a dacha—all state owned, of course—and a whole assortment of other goodies. So you behaved. You protected the system. Why? Because if you didn't, and you lost your job, you also lost your apartment as well as all those other perks: the food that came from a special store where there were no lines, the cases of vodka, the vehicles, the free gasoline, lumber and on and on. The Soviet term for all these bribes-cum-perks was *kruglak*. And guess what all those VIPs did with their *kruglak*? They bartered it of course, or sold it on the black market.

Which is how and why Communist Party apparatchiks lived so much better than the Lumpenproletariat over whom they ruled, but loathed.

Worker's paradise? Horse puckey. The Soviet Union was a corrupt society from top to bottom. And yet, I had to find a way in which to work—sell my products and market my training—without engaging in bribery, kickbacks, or *kruglak* of any kind.

After all, I was operating under different rules. Because most of my equipment was manufactured in the United States, I'd formed and incorporated my company in the USA—St. Louis, Missouri to be precise—and hence came under U.S. law. Which included the Foreign Corrupt Practices

Act of 1977. Which basically said it was illegal to bribe my way to success with the GUVD or any other Russian entity. No under-the-table money, no kickbacks, no nothing.

❖

Late in 1989, the GUVD finally approached me with the idea of a Joint Venture—a deal in which they and I would form a company. The agreement would give me a firm base in Russia, and GUVD would get the benefit of what I could provide. The deal made sense because, first, they had no western currencies available, and second, they hardly had any ruble budget available for training, police cars, crime lab equipment, even uniforms. GUVD looked like a fourth-world police force. Their uniforms were old and mismatched. They didn't have enough winter boots, or even batons and handcuffs to go around. Their policing skills were minimal.

A few months passed. With a deal in the offing, I suggested, "Why don't you come to Munich and have a look at what we do in Germany?" And GUVD accepted.

I called ahead. I set up appointments for the Russians with the Munich police, the Bavarian SWAT team, and other law enforcement units. It was all done unofficially because in those days, there were no diplomatic ties between police organizations in Russia and the West. In fact, it was the first ever visit of a Soviet police delegation to Bavaria. My German subsidiary would pay for the GUVD's tickets, hotel, and food. It was legal, and besides, they had no budget for travel.

They sent four officers, picked by the GUVD brass, and a colonel. We'd stay a week. The head of the delegation was a colonel named Frolov. Frolov was one of GUVD's deputy chiefs, and had been put in charge of negotiating the joint venture with me. White-haired, in his sixties but physically fit, three fingers missing from one hand because of an accident cutting wood at his dacha, he looked exactly like what he was: a hard-ass prison boss. Indeed, Frolov ran most of the working colonies in the Leningrad area. GUVD's head of intelligence, Gennadi Kolbasov, who came along as my interpreter, told me that Frolov was so tough on prisoners that when they went on strike, they'd sometimes actually sew their lips shut with a needle and thread as a way of protesting.

The GUVD cops were so excited about the trip, they arrived at Munich airport dressed in their Soviet police uniforms. This did not sit well with the German border guards. In fact, Frolov and his men had to change into civilian clothes before they were allowed to pass through immigration.

Despite Frolov's cold personality, it was a super week. The Russians were wide-eyed by the sophistication of what our German law enforcement units had, and what they could do. More important, I showed them my company's capabilities and what we could do. I showed him who we trained and who we equipped.

At the end of the week, Frolov came to me. We were on a first-name basis by then: he called me Franz, and I called him Colonel.

"Franz, we must sit down and negotiate a formal agreement."

I was delighted and told him so. "But frankly, Colonel, I'm happy with a handshake deal until we get back to Leningrad."

Frolov's head wagged negatively. "Let's do a proper Protocol of Intent so we know where we stand and I have something to show to my boss."

The light bulb in my head went off. Frolov's boss, General Voshinin, was an elderly guy, close to retirement. He was very much a bureaucrat; afraid to make waves, especially when it came to any kind of business decision. So Frolov needed something substantial, quantifiable, physical, to show the boss. That way, the Voshinin box could be checked and we could get on with the deal.

In Russia, the box must always be checked.

Besides, the idea of a formal agreement signed in Munich made perfect business sense to me. GUVD had been talking about a Joint Venture for months—and nothing had happened. Now we'd have something on paper. I could push forward. After all, I needed a compound to achieve my goals. A big compound. Venjamin Fabritzky had taken me to Kamenny Ostrov, Stone Island in English, an island at the mouth of the Neva River on which sat dozens of fabulous old mansions and big properties.

We'd even looked at one, a huge place that belonged to the Trade Union. If I was able to get a long-term lease, it would have been perfect. Venjamin set up a meeting with one of the trade union officials, a guy named Snetkov. Snetkov seemed interested, but asked for a second meeting in a couple of days. When I showed up, Snetkov was accompanied by some of the local Mafiosi, who wanted $300,000 a year rent.

I told them, "I may have been born at night—but it wasn't yesterday night." No way was I about to do any business with organized crime.

Still, I needed space. I'd need a showroom, an office, an additional venue I could use for entertaining, and a living area. I wanted ample room for training—classrooms and somewhere we could do force on force—even with vehicles. I'd have to have space for warehousing supplies and equipment. I wanted safe storage facilities for arms and ammunition. And a defensible perimeter with fences and gates. I'd need a security team too.

And guess what: GUVD owned a big compound on Kamenny Ostrov. The house, a classic Russian log chateau, dated from 1904, and it was located right next to the mayor's residence. GUVD even let me stay there one night just to let me have some idea about the place.

It wasn't perfect. I'd want a 25-year lease for the building and the land, giving me stability. And stability was critical because the main structure, as well as the outbuildings, would need a lot of refurbishment, because the most recent renovation had been done sometime in the 1960s. But if the GUVD hierarchy wasn't opposed to it—and they weren't, so far as I could tell—Kamenny Ostrov was the answer. It would be perfect. And it could become a reality once we had a signed protocol. Plus, for providing me workspace and security, I could repay the police in kind with training and equipment.

So in Munich, on July 21, 1990, Colonel Frolov and I signed a protocol of intent.

Among the items we agreed to were:
- Importing police and production equipment,
- Developing new law enforcement products,
- Establishing a police training facility in Leningrad, also for foreign, private, and government security organizations, and
- Organizing a private and armed security agency for the protection of individuals and objects, as well as the transport of valuables.

Problems solved. Now all I needed to do was as we got back to Leningrad was finalize the arrangements on the Kamenny Ostrov property. I was elated. The colonel and I were seeing eye-to-eye about how business is done.

Or so I thought.

On GUVD's last night in Munich, I took them out for drinks and dinner. At the hotel bar, we were met by an old friend from the local police, one of the German officers who'd been showing the Russians around. And he brought them all gifts: Zippo lighters engraved with the dates of their visit and the Munich Police insignia. It was a thoughtful touch. With reason: the Frolov delegation was truly historic: the first visit ever of a Russian police unit to Bavaria.

He made a big presentation of it, with toasts, and then he presented the lighters individually to each of the delegation.

I was sitting on the far side of the group, watching. And then I saw

Frolov. He stuck out his hand and he motioned with his fingers as if he was saying 'come here,' and he said *"dajdajdaj,"* which in Russian means "Gimme-gimme-gimme." And without another word, the rest of the delegation handed their lighters to Frolov, and Frolov dropped them all in his pocket.

What incredible fucking chutzpah.

I slid off my chair and walked over to Gennadi Kolbasov, the intelligence guy and my GUVD 'handler'.

"Gennadi, what the hell just happened?"

Gennadi's expression told me to STFU—shut the F-word up. "Not now," he whispered without moving his lips.

Maybe half an hour later, I was able to corral Gennadi where we wouldn't be overheard. "Okay—tell me what went on in there."

"It's how things work," he said. "Frolov's the boss. In Russian, the boss is referred to as a *nachalnik*. If you're *nachalnik*, everything belongs to you."

"So basically, Frolov thinks, 'it's my delegation and anything anybody gives us—gifts, trinkets, souvenirs, anything like that—it's all mine because I'm *nachalnik*?"

Gennadi's head wagged up and down. "*Tochno*. Precisely."

He continued later, over a drink. "It's all about attitude. You call it the *nachalnik* syndrome. In Russia, being *nachalnik* is comparable to being the Pope. *Nachalniki* can say no wrong, can do no wrong. When a guy has gotten to a particular level, when he's stepped into a certain hierarchy, you can no longer question his actions."

Gennadi looked up from his drink and gave me a 'this is a no-shitter' stare. "And that, Franz, is how Russia is these days. Get used to it."

It was a hugely valuable piece of information. The concept of *nachalnik* is totally foreign to Westerners—the closest parallel would I guess be a Mafia boss like Tony Soprano. And yet, the *nachalnik* syndrome would affect everything I did in Russia. Because in Russia, the *nachalnik*—the boss is an animal beyond control. Which means they can get away with about anything, just so long as what they do doesn't offend a higher ranking *nachalnik* in their chain of command. Whatever the *nachalnik* says or does is right; it cannot be criticized. The *nachalnik* has absolute immunity. He can say, "I'm in a position where I can fuck with whomever I please." And because of that, *nachalniki* can—and do— act with total impunity. Chutzpah on steroids.

So far as I'm concerned, the best *nachalnik* story ever took place in 2005. Robert Kraft, the owner of the New England Patriots, was visiting Russia. At a reception for visiting American businessmen in St. Petersburg on June 25, a group of Fortune 100 moguls including Kraft, Fox and SkyNews owner Rupert Murdoch, and Citigroup's Sanford Weill, met with President Vladimir Putin. They were making pleasantries and taking photos when Putin noticed Kraft's huge diamond-encrusted Super Bowl ring, which Kraft was displaying to Murdoch, sitting in the Patriots owner's hand.

Putin asked Kraft if he could try the Super Bowl ring on.

The Patriots owner said something to the effect of, "Sure, Mr. President."

What happened next Kraft told the *New York Post* in 2013.

"I took out the ring…and he put it on, and he goes, 'I can kill somebody with this ring.'"

"I put out my hand and he put it in his pocket, and three KGB guys got around him and he walked out."

Putin had taken Kraft's $25,000 Super Bowl Ring. Just walked off with it.

And in Putin's eyes, he hadn't done anything wrong—at least not in Russian society. Why? Because Vladimir Vladimirovich Putin is *nachalnik*. In fact, he's the *über-nachalnik*. He runs the bloody country. What he did that day is neither more nor less than any other *nachalnik* would do in the same circumstances.

In Putin's mind, he was entitled to Robert Kraft's ring the same way Colonel Frolov was entitled to his GUVD delegation's Zippo lighters.

I'm *nachalnik*. *daj-daj-daj*—Gimme-gimme-gimme.

And this was the surreal environment I'd chosen to operate in. To build a business in. I'd thought—from Munich, from the outside—that *glasnost* and *perestroika* would ever so surely morph the Russians toward entrepreneurism, perhaps even capitalism. But that wasn't the way things seemed to be going. Gorbachev's restructuring and openness weren't making things better, they were creating a new criminal class, many of whom had been mid-level to high-ranking KGB officers and Soviet functionaries.

Russia was ever so surely morphing, alright. But into a kleptocracy.

CHAPTER 4
It's a Long Way to Volzhskiy
"The road may be icy and the bar may be far but I will walk carefully." — Old Russian proverb

In 1990s Russia, even checked boxes sometimes didn't mean much.

I was ready to get my business started and commence renovations on Kamenny Ostrov right after the Frolov delegation got back from Munich. General Voshinin? Not so much.

"I've got to wait for permission from the MVD," he said. "Be patient." I was many things. But patient wasn't one of them. First of all, I wanted to move into Kamenny Ostrov because I was living out of a hotel. And not even the Leningrad Hotel anymore. The Leningrad had burned down while I was on a quick trip to Kazakhstan. It was a bad fire, too: sixteen people died, including nine firemen. Luckily, I had most of my business documents with me and didn't lose as much as I could have. After the fire, I lived for a while at the Oktyabrskaya, close to the train station and a real dump, and finally, at the Pribaltiyskaya, which was located on Vasilyevsky Island and looked out on the Gulf of Finland.

But I needed a permanent base. The Pribaltiyskaya had a guarded parking lot and some storage facilities. But none of them were as secure as I wanted.

I wanted Kamenny Ostrov. I knew it needed work, but the site was perfect. The chalet itself had three stories. There was space on the top floor for bedrooms; there was an adjacent structure that could serve as a banquet hall, although the reception room on the second floor of the main house could probably hold more than a hundred people. There was a separate sauna house—*banya*, they call them in Russian—with a lounge, a toilet, and an attached massage room that had originally been built for Yuri Gagarin, the Russian cosmonaut, who, in April 1961, was the first man to orbit the earth.

Just beyond the *banya* was a little lake. You could sit in the sauna, then run out to a wooden deck and jump into the cold water. There were lots of guard houses, and an outhouse for the guards. The only real bathrooms were in the main house, the banya, and the banquet hall, because in the true spirit of Marxist-Leninist equality ("To each according to his abilities; to each according to his needs"), the guards had been forbidden to use bathrooms and were stuck with the outhouse. There was also a fenced perimeter, operational gates—the whole package.

We agreed that since the police had no cash, I'd pay for all the renovations. In return, I'd get the whole compound—the house, the outbuildings, the guard shacks, everything—for 25 years. At which point, Mr. Murphy of Murphy's Law, stuck his nose into my business. General Voshinin, who'd signed the letter of guarantee allowing me access to Kamenny Ostrov, was replaced by an old communist investigator by the name of Arkady Kramarev. Kramarev, according to my contact Dr. Andreev, the Chief Pathologist of St. Petersburg, was "a very good investigator but a very bad *nachalnik*."

Another wrinkle: during the transition from Voshinin to Kramarev, some of the people in the Procurement Department of the GUVD—their Russian acronym was HAZO—thought that in the time vacuum between the old *nachalnik* and the new *nachalnik* they could insinuate themselves into the Kamenny Ostrov deal and perhaps get a little taste of all that money I was reportedly going to invest in refurbishing the compound.

I made sure that Gennadi Kolbasov passed a strong message to HAZO. Basically, it went, "You people can do what you want, but I'm going to stick to my plan because I have a signed agreement. And since we've got the Frolov protocol and my Letter of Guarantee from General Voshinin, I don't want additional partners. So if you try anything, I'll pull out and take my business elsewhere." Bluntness worked. HAZO's scheming came to a halt.

With HAZO quiet and the new general settling in, I asked Gennadi to set up an appointment with him. And so, at the end of January, 1991, we sat down for a face to face. Unlike Voshinin, who was basically a cautious, reticent apparatchik, Kramanev was a pleasant individual. Nutshell discoveries: he liked to smoke, he liked to drink; he was what they call in Missouri a good ole boy with an easy sense of humor. But he was no rube. You could see he had a real 'police thing' in his eyes. As the meeting progressed, I sensed that the guy was actually interested in what I was doing. He was sharp; he had good antennae.

So, we got along just fine. He scanned General Voshinin's Letter of Guarantee and told me, "You know what? Don't worry. It's good as gold. Voshinin's signature and stamp are on it and Colonel Kolbasov was there as a witness. So far as I'm concerned, you can go live there until we get this company off the ground—no problems. Is that alright with you?"

Yes, sir, indeed, sir. No problems.

I'd already done a detailed walk-through. Most of the 1960s equipment was functioning. But it wasn't operating efficiently. For example, there were four gas furnaces heating the three main buildings. They'd been installed in 1914. It took eighteen people to run the boilers, working shifts 24 hours a day because GUVD was afraid the ancient devices would explode if they weren't continuously supervised. There were drafty, uninsulated guardhouses the size of a telephone booth—like the single-occupant guardhouses I'd first seen on the bridge in Vyborg—guarding the gates. And the resident staff? It was roughly thirty or so, mostly hanging around but doing an occasional sweep of the ragged carpets or checking the perimeter.

They sure weren't GUVD's best and brightest. Not by a longshot. The site Commandant, a female, was in charge. Every time I came over to explore, she'd call headquarters and give them a running commentary. But deal with any of the real problems at Kamenny Ostrov? Fuggedaboudit. Let me put it this way: I took a flashlight and made my way down the stairs to the basement, where I discovered a couple of inches of standing water. I asked but no one knew how long it had been standing there.

Bottom line: the place was going to take some work. Which meant money out of my pocket. And so far, nothing had been coming in. I was in the hole well into the six figures, with money going out and nothing coming in.

Luckily, I already had a deal—my first major one in Russia—in my pocket.

But there is a God, and He is not only merciful, but generous.

Shortly after we got back from Munich in November of 1990, I'd had a visitor. Fedor Kuzmin was the Deputy Mayor of a small but important industrial city called Volzhskiy, which sits just north of Volgograd, on the Volga River, about 650 or so miles southeast of Moscow.

And Deputy Mayor Kuzmin said, "If all goes well, I'm going to introduce you to my chief of police. His name is Aparin. He'll sit down with you and the two of you will draw up a plan for equipment and training. The reason is that we have a real Mafia problem in our little city and we have to get it under control. I'd like you to design, equip, and train a police unit to deal with the Mafia..."

I looked at Kuzmin. He seemed like a serious individual. "What you want is a SWAT team."

He nodded. "Yes—we call it *gruppa zahvata* but that's what it is: a SWAT team. But a big SWAT team."

"I can do that, Mr. Deputy Mayor. I can do it start to finish."

I was delighted. First, because this was the first time a police SWAT team, equipped and trained to Western standards, would be formed in Russia. It was an incredible opportunity for Volzhskiy—and for me. Not only would they need vehicles—police cars and SWAT trucks and a mobile crime lab—they'd need enough tactical and ancillary equipment to outfit a SWAT team of 30 officers, and all the training that would go with it.

We could even do some of the training during the trip from Munich. After all, we'd have to move everything from Munich all the way to Volzhskiy—a distance of some 3,000 kilometers, or just over 2,000 miles overland—not counting the ferry ride from Travemünde, Germany, to Helsinki, Finland. And on the way, of course, we'd start instructing—basic driving skills, working with the equipment, and team-building could all be accomplished on the road. There'd be lots of time to play with the new equipment hands-on.

Plus, I had great trainers. My lead instructor was a retired Special Forces colonel named Stanley Olchovik, whom I'd known since I met him through a mutual acquaintance at Fort Bragg, North Carolina, in the mid-1980s, shortly after he retired from a 36-year career in the military. Born in Czechoslovakia, Stanley'd been interned by the Germans as a teenager. He escaped, and somehow joined the French Resistance. After the war and the communist takeover in Czechoslovakia, he escaped again, this time to West Germany, where he became involved in American intelligence operations.

He finally emigrated to the United States and joined the Army in 1950. By 1955 he was an officer; by the 1960s he had passed the infamous, grueling Q-Course and was a Special Forces officer. He'd worked in Taiwan, Vietnam, and Thailand, among other places. From 1976-1981 he'd been the commanding officer of Special Forces Detachment Alpha, an undercover Army unit that worked in Berlin as part of the intelligence community's covert action programs in that region. SF Detachment Alpha also served as the only U.S. counterterrorist asset in continental Europe in those days.

Stanley had worked with GSG-9 and the SAS, and with any number of U.S. police SWAT units. Between his language skills (he spoke Turkish, Russian, Ukrainian, Polish, Czech, and Slovak among others), we'd be able to teach Deputy Mayor Kuzmin's officers without interpreters, which is always the best way to instruct. I had other instructors, too—some from Missouri, others from California, all of whom had long experience in police special operations.

The Deputy Mayor broke into my reverie. "It will be a big order," he smiled. "And we have money. Money is no object."

"*Money is no object.*" Those words set off all sorts of alarms. Because I'd heard them before. More often than I'd like.

In Russia, when someone tells you "*money is no object*", they're probably going to try to scam you.

Damn it. This was probably just another smoke-and-mirrors Russian game. It'd happened a dozen times—maybe more.

Here's how it worked. I'd be making a presentation. Let's say it was to a police department in a major city like Yekaterinburg, which has a population of close to a million and a half people. I meet with the chief and the chief says, "I need helmets for 500 motorcycle officers."

That's not an unreasonable number given the size of his department. So, I do the math and tell him how much it'll cost.

The chief shrugs and says, "Sounds good to me." Then he says, "And can I have maybe a dozen now for T&E?" T&E stands for testing and evaluation, and passing out samples for T&E is common practice in the U.S. and all over Western Europe. Nothing out of line, and I've probably got a couple of dozen samples from four or five different helmet manufacturers with me, so I say it would be fine, hand them over, and get a receipt.

Then I ask about payment.

The chief says, "Well, how would you like to get paid?"

I tell him, "Well, ideally, 30 percent down and 70 percent by letter of credit against the shipment before it leaves our facility, which will either be in Germany or the United States.

And the chief smiles and says, "Great—money is no object. I can have the 30 percent for you in two weeks."

And so, I call ahead to the helmet manufacturers and make sure everything's set to go as soon as the chief decides which helmet he likes best and the down payment and letter of credit arrive. And then I wait. When I don't hear from the chief I call him. But now he's not available.

So I call the chief again, and then again and again. But he doesn't call back.

And then I wait some more and call some more with no result.

And about a month later when the chief finally takes my call, he says that he couldn't find the funding, and he's oh, so very sorry, but he lost all the helmets.

And then I realize that it's all a scam. The chief had no money. He never intended to buy anything. What he needed were a dozen helmets for his favorite motorcycle officers. And now he had them.

For free. Simply by promising me a big deal. And so I shred his receipt because there's no way I'm ever getting my sample helmets back.

Fool me once, shame on you. Fool me twice? Shame on me. So, when Deputy Mayor Kuzmin told me that money was no object, the dollar signs danced right out of my head and a klaxon horn in my brain started going *oougah-oougah, dive, dive, dive!* Because this was Russia. All that equipment, all that training was going to cost money. Real money. Hard currency money. *valuta*. And now I was going to hear some typical Russian smoke and mirrors about 'we'll trade you tractors', or what about a dozen shotguns to T&E, or something similar.

But Deputy Mayor Kuzmin never mentioned bartering, or asked for samples. He said, "You tell me what it's going to cost and I'll send you the money."

I said, "The normal deal is 30 percent down and 70 percent by letter of credit against the shipment."

He paused. I thought, now is when he's going to ask me for freebies.

But he didn't. What he said was, "I don't mean down payment and balance. I mean the whole thing—all your money."

"*What?!*" I was thunderstruck. "How come? I mean—"

He waved a hand at me. "Look, if I don't spend it now—this year—I'm going to have to give it back."

Now I was puzzled. "Give it back? To whom?"

Kuzmin gave me a sly look. "Well, as it turns out, we have several companies in our little city and they're all involved in export in one form or another. Consequently, we have access to *valuta*—to hard currency."

My expression didn't change, but all of a sudden I, was wary again. I knew the Russian system by now, and one of the most basic rules of that system was that no company gives up its *valuta*. After all, *valuta* is the most important thing a company can have. *Valuta* buys you machinery. *Valuta* buys you the ticket to export your stuff. I mean, it's nothing you give away, especially to your Deputy Mayor. Maybe it was still a scam—just a more sophisticated one.

So, I said, "That's amazing. But how did you get this done?"

Kuzmin shrugged. "Yeah, well, we have a company that manufactures tires, they export. We have a company that makes abrasive materials that you need for manufacturing wood merchandise or metal works, and they export. Then we have the electricity company that runs the dam across the river Volga—it's several kilometers wide which provides water and power for all the local companies."

He paused. "So, I went to them and I asked if they could help me out because we need equipment for our police force so that we could build a *gruppa zahvata* to fight the Mafiyosi, and they of course, said, 'Sorry, we have no money for you. We have not enough money for ourselves. How could we even entertain such a thought?'"

He shook his head as if to say 'what idiots'. And showed his teeth. "So then I told them, 'As Deputy Mayor I can cut off your water line, I can cut off your electricity. I can cut off your garbage disposal services. And I will. I'll do whatever I can do to ruin your businesses if you won't contribute. Why? Because we have to fight organized crime. Face it—if the Mafiyosi take over your business, you won't have any *valuta* left.'"

"And all of a sudden, they all say 'Fedor, what a brilliant idea. We absolutely agree, and we volunteer to pay whatever you need to improve our police capabilities.'"

He grinned. "And that's how I obtained *valuta*. We can pay in full. Transfer the money to your account within ten days. No problem."

I liked this guy. For his ingenuity alone I would have made him a really, really good price. And, of course, the deal would be good for us, too because it would help me establish business in the Russian heartland.

We signed a contract, I went back to negotiating with GUVD, and about a week later the money landed in my corporate account in Munich. Every *pfennig* of it.

We were in business. And, I did sit down with Kuzmin's police chief Aparin—after a few vodkas I started calling him 'Aspirin', but he didn't mind at all—and I learned precisely what he needed and started constructing the training package that would allow him and his people to do their jobs professionally and with cutting-edge U.S. equipment.

❖

The good news was that I had a major contract, and permission to move into Kamenny Ostrov. The bad news was that my negotiations on the Joint Venture with the Leningrad GUVD were dragging on…and on…and on.

The reason lay in that basic element of the Russian soul: *vranyo*—the little (or big) white lie. It's a way of life stretching w-a-a-y back into the pre-communist, tsarist Russian culture. In point of fact, the worst problem I encountered in Russia in my early days was that I was being lied to on a constant basis. There are two variations of *vranyo*. There is the intentional lie, to see how far the liar can dupe you into spending your money, telling you things like, "I've got a ship to sell," or "You're looking for a house? I've got the perfect house to sell you." Except there is no ship, and there may be a house, but it belongs to a State entity and just happens to be empty.

Those are the obvious scams, the fraud stuff, and unless you're a total idiot, you'll pick up on them quickly because the liar will simply disappear with your deposit or take your suit to a nonexistent dry cleaner—you get the idea.

Vranyo becomes more problematic when you're trying to establish yourself in business and trying to get to the right people, make business decisions, and obtain straight advice. Real answers are hard to come by because people tend to tell you what they think you want to hear. It's a holdover from Soviet days, when you never knew who was listening. There's even an old Soviet-era joke about it: "You lie to me and I know you are lying to me, but you keep lying anyway so I'll just pretend to believe you."

I understood it intellectually. The Soviet system was inherently corrupt top to bottom. The government lied to the people, and the people lied to each other. And the people lied to the government, and the government lied to the government. Sure it did: remember all those photographs from the May Day Parade in Moscow during the Stalin era, in which individuals who'd been standing next to Stalin or one of his flunkies were suddenly airbrushed into nonexistence when they fell from favor? But emotionally, *vranyo* is incredibly draining, because it is so ingrained in every facet of Russian life, and virtually every Russian with whom you deal, that it simply grinds you down day after day after day.

I moved into Kamenny Ostrov in April of '91. We didn't have the contract signed yet, but because General Kramarev had accepted my letter of guarantee from General Voshinin, the gates opened for us—literally! It was kind of an ad-hoc move, with some staff working out of the hotel, others working from their homes, and others on Stone Island, a situation that wouldn't be solved until the fall. And, I certainly wasn't going to move any of my stock from Munich until I'd signed a full contract with GUVD and there was full-time, effective security. But the good news was we had a permanent headquarters and I could begin creating a customer base.

The staff was small. I had a core of about twenty people. Most of them were GUVD, like Gennadi Kolbasov. There was one GUVD officer who was very talented with sales. His name was Alexander Michailov. We called him Sascha. Sascha had been deputy-head of the Police Academy in Pushkin. He was my Liaison Officer and he was Deputy Chief of the enterprise. Looking at him was like staring back into Soviet history, because he looked exactly like a young Stalin, with black slicked down hair and a huge black mustache. He was a natural salesman: outgoing, a great listener who was interested in the people to whom he spoke. But best of all, he was a closer. As a policeman, he's the guy you brought in when you wanted to clear the case—when you want the perpetrator to confess and all the ends tied up. And he'd do the same thing for me. He'd go out; go to the most remote places and bring back sales, contracts, and orders. He was really good at it.

We—more specifically I—had not yet discovered exactly where I should be concentrating our efforts. But Sascha instinctively knew, and led me toward the areas producing oil and gas in the Tyumen province, which lies roughly 1,800 miles northeast of Leningrad and a thousand from Moscow, the Karelian and Komi republics to the north, and Ekatarinenburg 1,700 miles to the east, where they log timber, mine rare earth elements, and just about every type of metal-based export from zinc to copper.

We also needed translators for German and English so I could get my paperwork done. I checked with the German and American consulates. They recommended people who I hired. And I began work on bringing Kamenny Ostrov up to speed. My budget for the initial renovation work was DM 700,000 which came out to be approximately $350,000. I thought it was a solid investment.

By mid-summer, the SWAT and the police cars had been built and all the tactical equipment for the Volzhskiy police department arrived in Munich. I called Deputy Mayor Kuzmin and chief Aparin and told them to send their people to Leningrad in ten days to pick up their order. Then I took a second Leningrad police delegation as well as representatives from the Ministry of the Interior—their OMON people and also members of the fire brigade, which in Russia comes under the Interior Ministry—and brought them all to Munich so they could play with the goodies I was about to deliver to Volzhskiy.

I took the GUVD and OMON guys to the Bavarian State Federal Bureau of Investigations, where I showed them capabilities from the automatic fingerprinting database to the ultramodern pathology lab. And I made sure to connect them politically to the German Ministry of Interior. That way, we established a rapport, a relationship, with Bavaria – the state of Bavaria and the city of Leningrad. Everyone was happy. And then the Russians got to drive the SWAT and police cars, imported from the U.S. and outfitted in my Munich work shop. I'd designed the vehicles with every bell and whistle—literally. Heavy suspensions, big engines, blue lights, sirens, grille flashers—the works. We even designed a unit logo for the Volzhskiy GUVD's cars and uniforms: a running wolf. Unit logos were unknown in the USSR, and ours became immediately popular. There were so many requests that we ended up using the running wolf as my company trademark!

We went to some of Munich's advanced law enforcement facilities as well. I took the Russians for a session on the police shooting range and gave them a specialized course in defensive driving—something only the most elite of Russian units ever were allowed to do. The Russians never stopped smiling. Of course they didn't: it was the ultimate police playtime. They drove fast, shot lots of free ammunition out of dependable German and Austrian weapons, and afterwards there were vast quantities of good Bavarian beer, white Munich sausage and pretzels, and Bavarian ham hocks.

Believe me, life doesn't get any better for cops.

Except, *mirabile dictu*, it did! Because then we drove the new police cars and SWAT vans with all our goodies from Munich to Travemünde, caught a ferry boat to Helsinki and then drove into Russia. Once we hit the Russian border, I allowed them to turn on the sirens and blue lights. And guess what: they weren't switched off again until the vehicles reached Volgograd—almost 1,200 miles southeast.

Of course we stopped in Leningrad at the Police Academy. I put on an exhibition of the SWAT capabilities, using my trainers. I'd spread the word long before we'd left for Munich, so local officials, including a just-retired

KGB lieutenant colonel named Vladimir Putin, came to watch. So did a number of prospective clients from across the Soviet Union.

And then the police guys from Volzhskiy showed up and my Leningrad contingent sadly gave up their toys, while I put the new owners through a quick familiarization course and a short, but effective, defensive driving class. And then we set off to Moscow and Volgograd.

In those days, the highway to Moscow was only two lanes wide. And Russian roads weren't exactly safe because everyone drove like they were Rambo on steroids. For safety and security, I wanted to keep the convoy — we had 16 vehicles — together. Which meant clearing the road in front of us. So what I did was send a lead car — it was a Ford Explorer with full lights and siren — ahead of the scrum. That vehicle would wave all the other vehicles to the side of the road and we'd hi-diddle-diddle straight down the middle with lights flashing.

The only other major problem was fuel. In 1991, most gas stations were still 'guarded' by elderly women known as babushkas. None of the babushkas ever seemed to want to sell gas. All they wanted to do was guard it. After being turned away and with our gas tanks nearly empty, I had an idea.

I climbed into the lead vehicle — the Ford Explorer. We pulled into the next gas station, lights flashing and siren going. I jumped out with my translator, waving my German passport in her face, and yelling, "Oh my god, please help us. I need gasoline, I have to get to Moscow!"

And, taking pity on the poor foreigner, and seeing the flashing lights, and since it was just one car, the babushka took the key from the chain around her neck and unlocked the pump.

Which is when I pulled out my walkie-talkie and said, "Okay, send them in," and suddenly there was a line of 15 more vehicles. And I looked at the babushka and said, "You, madam, are the greatest person in the world."

The police guys from Volzhskiy slipped her a wad of cash and told her, "Here's a little something for you, sweetie. And by the way, if you let us inside we'll make some tea." And just like that, they took over the gas station and they had tea with her while we topped off. Then we left, with the babushka happy, well compensated, and waving good-bye.

If a ploy works, use it. We probably repeated the same routine half a dozen times before we reached Volzhskiy.

But first there was Moscow.

We pulled into central Moscow at about 3 a.m. Blue lights on, sirens on, they never went out. I'd booked us rooms at the Hotel Ukraine, which turned out to be one of these oversized, ornate old Stalinesque palaces with multiple spires and towers. The Evil Empire Hotel was probably how Ronald Reagan would have described it because it just reeked of Soviet Union overkill.

But I didn't know that as we drove into the city. In point of fact, I didn't know much about the layout of Moscow at all. I'd been here a couple of times for meetings, but certainly couldn't claim familiarity with the place. Plus, nobody knew we were coming—except reception desk at the hotel. Certainly, nobody knew who we were. We'd entered the city from the northwest, and then at some point we'd driven onto what I thought was some sort of ring road that paralleled the Moskva riverbank. Then the convoy turned north.

And drove into Red Square.

Oops.

I was the boss. I made a decision. "Okay, let's try this again."

So we went north around Red Square, and then back west, then south to the river, and turned north.

Back into Red Square.

Double oops.

Now, there were traffic lights all around the perimeter of Red Square, and directly north of the Square on Mokhovaya Street stood the Hotel Nationale (which we'd now passed twice). And, in those days, they had probably twenty or so cops and twenty or so traffic lights on the roads that surrounded Red Square. The cops were traffic cops. And they were able to manipulate the traffic lights individually by hand with special keys. Obviously, that was so they could allow VIPs and official motorcades to move quickly in the Red Square area by switching the lights manually. The first time we'd driven by, I saw a couple of cops saluting with their right hands while turning the light control switch with their left.

Of course they did: we had lights and sirens and the cops thought we were an official motorcade. So they saluted, turned the lights green, and waved us through.

Being cops, they surmised something was wrong the fourth time we came around the square. On that circuit, the cop on Mokhovaya Street in front of the hotel waved his baton at us to flag us down. We stopped in the middle of the street.

The cop shouted, "What's going on, comrades?"

The window of our lead vehicle cracked open. "Hold on." Then the door opened and Misha, one of the Volgograd cops, climbed out. He was wearing his uniform shirt, Adidas sweat pants, and sandals. He ambled up to the cop and said, "Excuse me, comrade, but we were looking for the Hotel Ukraine. Can you help?"

The cop looked at Misha's appearance and freaked. "You fucking idiot! Driving with lights and sirens? And you're looking for a fucking *hotel?*" He was jumping up and down and waving his baton in Misha's face. "You assholes! We thought this was the Putsch!"

Putsch? Putsch? What Putsch? We knew nothing about any putsch. This was crazy. I mean, the traffic cop was like exploding. Finally he calmed down and pointed toward the west. "See that bridge? The Hotel Ukraine is that way you assholes. Just get the fuck out of here."

So we stayed overnight in Moscow. The next morning we met some people from the Interior Ministry—they certainly didn't mention anything about a putsch and we didn't ask—and then we got the hell out of Dodge. In fact, nobody mentioned the word putsch again. Little did we know....

❖

Within five, six hours of leaving Moscow, we got stopped at a checkpoint. A big checkpoint. A checkpoint that had its own police station attached. We thought the officers would just go through our papers and wave us on our way. But no: these cops wanted to take the cars and equipment away from the Volgograd cops. It turned into a Mexican standoff pretty quickly. There were the guys from Volgograd; there was Stanley Olchovik, the Special Forces colonel; there were a bunch of western police trainers, and there was me. And some of the Volgograd guys had drawn their weapons because they weren't about to give anything up. But at this particular checkpoint there weren't the normal just two or three traffic cops, but somewhere close to forty. It was like a GUVD raid, and they were looking for some way to hijack us.

They began checking documents. But all the Americans and all the Volgograd cops' papers were in order. In fact, everyone's papers were in order. Except mine.

I had totally forgotten to get myself a *marshrut* stamped into my visa document. In those days, if foreigners were going to travel within the Soviet Union, they needed a special stamp with a specific travel route on their visa document, which in my case should have stated that I had the permission of the Interior Ministry travel to Volgograd by road. So, here I was—an illegal. Subject to arrest and detention.

Luckily, the Volgograd cops knew what to do. They pushed their way into the police station and went up to the radio room. And from there, they called the KGB station in Volgograd, and got the Volgograd KGB station chief on the line, and the station chief called Deputy Mayor Kuzmin, who vouched for me and after three or so hours the whole thing was sorted out and we got back on the road.

Later that night, we hit the river Volga. Which meant we were entering the last leg of our Odyssey. It was time, the Volgograd cops decided, for a celebration. So, we pulled the convoy over and the Russians built a huge campfire and we broke out all the food we'd brought from Germany and Finland. We opened cans of sausages and bottles of vodka and we sat and we told stories and it was like one big happy family of cops, Americans, and Russians.

The fire finally burnt down to coals. Stanley was drinking vodka from a half-liter bottle. He got up to get himself a pickled cucumber, then tried to sit cross-legged but lost his balance and fell right into the fire. But Stanley was…Stanley. He held the vodka so that nothing spilled (or burst into flames), and we pulled him out quickly.

I thought he'd be scarred for life. But when we brushed him off, all he had was a tiny burn above his left eyebrow. His clothes weren't singed and he'd even held onto the damn cucumber.

Stanley plopped himself down, swigged the vodka, chewed on the cucumber and said, "Boy, that was close."

The next morning we drove toward Volgograd from where we'd cross the river to Volzhskiy. But first we stopped so we could wash the vehicles. Stanley and I walked down to the bank of the Volga.

"The fucking Volga." He peered across the wide expanse of water. "The longest river in all of Europe. Remember, Franz, I told you how I've always had this dream to swim the Volga?"

"Sure." In fact he'd mentioned it to me when I'd first told him about the Volzhskiy deal.

Stanley squinted. "I wonder how wide it is." He shook his head in awe. "Gotta be more than a mile. Maybe close to two."

"Could be."

"What an incredible swim that would be, huh?" He walked down the riverbank, knelt, and dipped his hand into the water. It may have been July, but the water was freezing. "Whoa," Stanley said. "That's cold."

"Franz?" He swiveled toward me, his face serious. "What a dumb fucking dream that was."

We walked back to where the Russians were working on the vehicles. They were taking their time, making sure that everything looked 'just right'. It was a Russian thing. Russians like to give a good presentation, so the Volzhskiy cops didn't want to drive into their jurisdiction in dirty vehicles.

That particular aspect of the Russian character was something I hadn't thought much about before, but it made sense: I remembered the photographs of the Americans when they left Vietnam. It was chaos: the people fighting to get on the helicopters taking off from the embassy compound roofs. When the Russians left Afghanistan, when they rolled over the bridge to the Soviet border, it was an orderly withdrawal, and the last individual to cross was the commanding general.

So, they finished drying and polishing the vehicles, and we drove into the city in a tight formation—lights flashing, sirens wailing. They wanted to make a good impression.

In fact, when we arrived in Volzhskiy, the only damage to any of the cars was a single broken headlight lamp. We presented the vehicles and the equipment to Chief Aparin and Deputy Mayor Kuzmin, and he presented me and the Americans with a huge jar of fresh locally produced black caviar.

Chief Aparin looked at me and said, "No major problems, right?"

I shook my head. "Nope. Just the headlight—and we've got spare parts so it'll be fixed."

The police chief turned to the Deputy Mayor. "See? I told you. I knew from the start nothing would happen."

I looked at the Chief. "How do you mean you knew?"

"Ah," he said, "We have this local cleric, like our local pope. And he likes to get drunk and chase girls. And he got drunk, chased girls, and got into an accident."

"And?"

Chief Aparin smiled a big, happy Russian smile. "So I told him, 'I won't lock you up if you go straight home, and you stay there and do nothing but pray for the safe arrival of my convoy.'"

"And here you are—arrived all safe and sound! *And I—I* knew it all the time!"

CHAPTER 5
Joseph V. Stalin 101

"What's the difference between a Russian and a Ukrainian? If a Russian sees a deserted apple cart, he'll steal all the apples he can. If a Ukrainian sees the same cart, he'll steal all he can, then take a bite out of the rest so nobody else gets any." — Stalin-Era NKVD Joke

I signed a contract establishing Kamenny Ostrov as a joint venture on Wednesday, August 28, 1991. It was a rushed, two-day finish for a process that had taken up the better part of two years of my life.

So why did it finally take just two days?

The answer is the putsch.

What putsch?

The selfsame putsch the Moscow traffic police were talking about in July when my motorcade and I had driven around Red Square four times. It is commonly known as the August Putsch, or the August Coup Attempt. It ran from 19 to 21 August, 1991 and ended not with a bang, but a fizzle.

It had been in the air. A friend of mine, a deputy of the Supreme Soviet (the USSR parliament) had warned me in the spring of 1991. He said, "They are all clapping again," referring to the *homo sovieticus* eagerly displaying their loyalty to the Communist Party hardliners. Those actions demonstrated preemptive obedience in its most obscene form. And, although it was inconceivable at the time, the world would see similar behavioral obscenities again—but not until Putin took over.

In a nutshell, the plotters were Soviet hardliners, including KGB chairman Vladimir Kryuchkov, Defense Minister Dmitry Yazov, Internal Affairs minister Boris Pugo and the premier, Valentin Pavlov. They believed Soviet President Mikhail Gorbachev and Russian President Boris Yeltsin were dangerously liberal and that the very existence of classic Marxist-Leninist values was in jeopardy. The plotting had begun as far back as December of 1990. Their goal: to bring back the old Soviet state.

They struck on August 19, while President Gorbachev was on vacation at his dacha in the Crimea. They cut Gorbachev's communications lines. Then, backed up by army units and elements of the KGB and Ministry of the Interior, they declared a state of emergency. Within hours, tanks rumbled into Red Square. Meanwhile, pro-democracy barriers to keep the tanks at bay were hurriedly erected outside the Russian Parliament building on the Moskva River known as the White House.

But the plotters made fatal early mistakes. They failed to detain President Yeltsin, who had returned from a trip to Kazakhstan on the 17th. From his dacha outside Moscow, Yeltsin declared any putsch attempt to be illegal. On the 19th he went to the Parliament Building, where he told the crowd an anti-constitutional coup had been attempted and he called for a general strike. Then Yeltsin clambered onto one of the tanks surrounding the building and spoke to the demonstrators, telling them that he, not the plotters, was legally head of the Russian State.

His impassioned remarks from atop the tank headlined television newscasts across the globe and turned the tide against the hardliners. The plotters also lacked the universal support of both the military and the country's internal security apparatus. In fact, there were numerous progressives in the Red Army, the KGB, and in GUVD police units all across the Soviet Union.

The bottom line is that the putsch that was launched early on Monday, August 19, was kaput, and the coup leaders detained by about 8 p.m. on the 21st. The only casualties were three civilians killed and several more wounded in a clash with military forces near the White House.

And guess what: I missed the whole damn thing.

I was back in the United States—in St. Louis to be precise—taking some down time after the delivery of the vehicles and equipment to the Volzhskiy GUVD, and dealing with the business affairs of my American corporation. When I saw what was happening on CNN, my instinctive reaction was: what's going to happen to my friends? Most of the people I dealt with were progressives, and the first tranche of news emphasized that the plotters were arresting progressives. My second thought was to call someone. Maybe Kolbasov: he was close to the KGB. Or Venjamin Fabritzky—he'd know what was going on. But there was no way to contact either one because I couldn't get through. You actually had to schedule phone calls because of the lack of lines on the Russian side, and there was something like a three-day waiting period in those early hours.

And of course, I was thinking about the joint venture. We'd been negotiating the contract for months. It was almost signable. If the hardliners won and Gorbachev was replaced by some Marxist ideolog, there'd be no place for a Westerner in that totalitarian system and the last two years work would have all been for nothing.

I dropped everything and headed back to Mother Russia.

By the time I arrived in Leningrad, it was all over, thank God. Gorbachev and Yeltsin were back in power and the coup leaders had been arrested.

I went straight to the Big House—GUVD headquarters, where they were serving drinks and watermelon. And I learned what had happened.

In Leningrad, the hardliners had made plans to arrest Anatoly Sobchak as he arrived at the airport from Moscow on the 19th. The liberal, pro-democratic former law school professor was a close associate of Boris Yeltsin's in the Congress of People's Deputies in Moscow and a deputy of the Leningrad City Council. The hardliners thought he'd be an easy target because the Leningrad KGB station largely supported the plotters.

Vladimir Putin, who now worked for Sobchak even though he was still a serving KGB line officer, discovered the KGB plan to take Sobchak into custody. But by this time, Sobchak's political views as well as the mayor's personal ambitions had rubbed off on Putin, who now believed Sobchak to be his sole and most important mission in life. Looking back at it now it was obvious: there was no way the ambitious Putin would surrender his seat on the Sobchak gravy train—the coziest job he'd ever held—for those sad clowns in Moscow.

The story we were told was that Putin, who'd come out publically against the hardliners, put together an armed anti-putsch militia made up mostly of former Ministry of Interior OMON (riot police) shooters to safeguard his boss, Anatoly Sobchak. They raided the ministry's armory, then at Putin's insistence drove to the airport to intercept Sobchak. When confronted by Putin, the 'official' KGB arrest party backed down. Of course they did: Putin's group had more—and heavier—weapons than the KGB did.

Free and now protected, Sobchak—with Putin at his side—put together a huge anti-putsch rally where he came out in support of Boris Yeltsin. Almost simultaneously, the same thing had happened in Moscow, spurred on by Boris Yeltsin. The Russian people simply did not want the old Soviet Union back. I couldn't have agreed more.

As soon as I could, I met with General Kramarev to ask if the putsch had affected our joint venture contract, and if it had, how.

Kramarev was blunt. He said, "Franz, we're going to sign this thing."

That brought a relieved smile to my face.

And then he said, "And we're going to have it ready tomorrow. We'll sign it tomorrow."

Instinctively, I understood. The earth was shifting—perhaps permanently. Things were in flux. Everything could change in a heartbeat. After all, in June there'd been an election: the democrat and liberal Anatoly Sobchak was the city's new mayor. There'd already been a referendum, too: a majority of voters wanted to change the city's name. In early September, Leningrad would revert to its Czarist name: St. Petersburg.

All these changes—and above all, the attempted putsch—had spurred Kramarev to act. The general wanted to get the Kamenny Ostrov Company officially up and running before anybody changed the laws or wrote new rules and regulations. That way we'd be grandfathered, so I thought.

I was delighted. "Wonderful. You tell me the time, General, and I'll be here."

We concluded the deal the following morning. I signed as the sole Foreign Stockholder. General Kramarev signed as one of the two Soviet stockholders. I'd always assumed Colonel Frolov would be the second. But he was nowhere to be found.

Frolov, it turned out, had sided with the putschists. So he was gone. And in his stead was a Ukrainian GUVD colonel named Leonid Pinchuk.

This was not the best of news.

I'd known Pinchuk in passing over the previous two years. A veteran of the Afghan invasion, he was the Deputy Chief in charge of procurement and supplies—the department they called HAZO, which had already tried to muscle into my agreement with GUVD. Even so, I'd developed a working relationship with him, although not especially close.

Not especially close because, instinctively, I held Pinchuk at arm's length. Everything about him told me he was a man of the new generation, in that he recognized that his rank, his position, and his influence existed solely so that he could help himself to material things. To Pinchuk and his new generation of Russian *nachalniki*, the terms 'privatization' and 'entrepreneurship' were simply synonyms for 'stealing'.

Short and slight of build, with a pinched, weasel-like face, round eyeglasses, and nervous gestures, he was one of those men who always look as if they're wearing their father's clothing. Nothing fit him. There's more. Leonid Pinchuk was perpetually…fidgeting. He never stopped moving. In his office he fiddled with his papers, and his pen, and his desk chair, and the phones. In restaurants he fiddled with the silverware, and the napkin, and the menu, and the glassware. When he walked he was constantly rubbing his fingers together and adjusting his watch, and his tie, and his shirt cuffs, and hitching his trousers and checking his pockets. It was maddening.

I'd taken Pinchuk to Munich in July as part of the delegation to see the vehicles and equipment we'd assembled for Volgograd. Guess what: not only did he never stop fidgeting, he also never stopped bitching. He demanded special food at restaurants. Not because he didn't like what I'd pre-ordered for the group, but because as *nachalnik*, he felt he was entitled to something special. He blew off meetings at German ministries so he could go shopping for a cheap shower cabin. He changed the schedule of our drive from Munich to Travemünde—and remember, this was a convoy of sixteen vehicles—because a friend of his, a fellow Afghanistan vet now stationed at the Red Army headquarters in Berlin, had bought him a video recorder and he wanted to take it back in the convoy to save any duty fees.

So when Pinchuk, not Frolov, showed up to sign the GUVD contract, his presence gave me pause.

But I'd worked things out with Frolov. I'd do the same with Pinchuk.

With the contract signed, I created a complete inventory of everything on Kamenny Ostrov. I did this for two reasons. First, the contract specified that everything within the compound belonged to the company, so I wanted to know exactly what was there, from the physical plant items, the office equipment, the furniture and décor—curtains and drapes—right down to the dinnerware, glassware, ashtrays, and knickknacks. Second, I'd need to know what *wasn't* in the inventory so I could bring it from Munich. I planned to do a lot of entertaining, and we'd need more stemware, glasses, beer steins and plates than were on hand.

The inventory complete, I returned to Munich. We packed up the showroom, all the office equipment I'd need, the police and fire gear, outfitted new vehicles—police cars and SWAT and medical vans—and then, in October, I returned to St. Petersburg to set up shop.

Except: half of the stuff I'd inventoried before I left was now missing. All the china was gone. So was most of the crystal, as well as some furniture and paintings. Even the cutlery had disappeared.

I called over to the Big House and checked in with GUVD.

And was told, "Don't worry, Franz, everything's cool. Col. Pinchuk just needed a few things from Kamenny Ostrov and sent a truck to collect them."

That wasn't the way I do business, and I told them so.

Except, as they explained to me, that was the way the system had always worked. Under the Soviet system, all objects had a formal lifetime after which they would be replaced, so that the factories that made all these objects were kept constantly busy and the Soviet System could check the box that read: 100% employment. So, let's say for the sake of argument, a dinner plate's lifetime was two years. After that, the plate got replaced. So, every two years you could steal all the dinner plates because you knew they'd be replaced.

And who got to steal all those dinner plates? The *nachalniki*, of course. They'd just come through and take what they wanted. No one was going to say a word. Of course no one would: they were *nachalniki* and they could do no wrong.

But I'd been in the 'Wild, Wild East' long enough now to be able to make a distinction between *nachalniki*. And the way Pinchuk played the role gave me very negative vibes. Here's the difference between the Frolov style of *nachalnik* and the Pinchuk style: Frolov took the Zippos right in front of me. Didn't give a damn what I thought. In fact, he was proud to do it—just the way President Vladimir Putin took Robert Kraft's Super Bowl Ring right in front of Fox boss Rupert Murdoch and Citicorp's Sandy Weil. Putin gave them a smile, a hearty 'fuck you' wave, stuck the ring in his pocket, and walked off, proud of what he'd done.

Pinchuk? He was the sneaky *nachalnik*. He'd send a flunky to do his dirty work because he wasn't man enough to just take what was his. And if, by any chance, he was found out by someone up the food chain, he'd throw his subordinate under the proverbial bus.

Okay. This behavior was nothing new. A few months previously, the GUVD's chief bookkeeper had shown up at Kamenny Ostrov. He'd handed me a draft lease he'd written, demanding $30,000 a week rent for the chalet, and asked me to sign it. And guess what: there were extra charges for using the sauna, or taking the row boat out on the little lake. I stayed polite. I didn't tell him to stick the frigging lease where the sun don't shine. I politely suggested that he take his lease and show it to General Kramarev, and if the general approved, I'd consider talking about it. Otherwise, he could just leave.

Of course he left. And I never heard about the matter again. Except here's what: that bookkeeper wasn't operating on his own. He didn't have the juice.

No: Pinchuk had sent him. And if I'd been fool enough to sign, Pinchuk would have pocketed all the money. The incident taught me a lesson.

And the lesson was to keep an eye on GUVD. Especially on one particularly fidgety Ukrainian GUVD colonel.

I went to Munich for new inventory and brought in a crew to start the renovations. And on November 1, with Stanley Olchovik in tow (he was visiting), he and I signed the official document accepting the transfer of Kamenny Ostrov to me and my company. On it, the Russians misspelled our names. I kind of enjoyed becoming a *Zedelmayer*.

By the beginning of November we were ready to operate, and on Thursday, November 21, I put on our first Beer Call. The concept wasn't mine. Military Liaison Officers at U.S. embassies all over the world have regular beer-call events as a way of networking with locals and putting them together with their colleagues from the embassy. So they'd get together, usually on embassy grounds, and drink beer and eat finger food. I'd been to dozens of beer calls. They were both fun and valuable because you always met contacts.

Additionally, that sort of socializing was unknown in Russia. And so the Kamenny Ostrov Beer Call became one of the best business social events in Leningrad/St. Petersburg. They took place without fail on the third Thursday of every month. I'd send a couple of hundred RSVPs out—and most would come back positive. The party started at 6 p.m. I served only beer—good Bavarian beer, although many of the Russian police who showed up brought their own vodka. And of course we served German and Russian finger food—sausages, pretzels, chips—appetizers you could eat off a plate. And the gimmick was that there were no chairs. You had to mingle. You had to make conversation. Make new friends. Network. The idea was to get everybody mixing and connecting.

Ultimately, Beer Call @ Kamenny Ostrov would prove very, very successful. It became an event not just for businessmen like me who were looking for contacts in Customs, Security, the Police, or Tax Inspection. We had people from the City Office, people from the Russian government, and people from the various diplomatic missions. Some nights we probably had American spies, Cuban spies, and KGB officers in the same room. Imagine.

Expats new to the crowd had to watch it, though. The Russians, especially my friends from the Big House, loved to get foreigners drunk on vodka. The comrades always made sure to share a toast with the expats, then pass them off to the next, thus politely forcing them to down two dozen or more shots before the night was over. Most expats learned quickly. But some never picked up on it and were consistently much the worse for wear the next few days. I knew people had a good time when guests would return the next morning because they'd mistakenly taken the wrong fur cap.

On a good night I'd entertain somewhere between a 100 to a 150 guests. On a bad night, perhaps 80. Either way, I held the event in our banquet hall, which was separate from the Chalet building and had its own kitchen. One reason: security. I didn't want spies or potential competitors prowling around my office.

❖

Indeed, I still had some fine-tuning to do about the personnel. Pinchuk's Lady GUVD Commander was nominally in charge of the staff—the staff that did nothing. And she reported on our every move. No good. So I took her aside and said, "No more reporting, please."

She looked at me incredulously.

"I'm serious. If you do it again I'll fire you."

Next morning, she picked up the phone and started talking. I hung it up for her and told her to get out, and take the staff as well. The only people I kept were the GUVD guards, and the techs who staffed the boilers.

By December, we'd started renovating. I made sure that the basement was dry. I had the roof repaired. I put in a new heating system. I redid all the pipes. By the time I finished, the cost of the renovations totaled about $890,000, including late-model electric heating systems that I'd flown in from the U.S.

By January, 1992, we were totally operational. Everything had been redone—top to bottom. Kamenny Ostrov was a real showcase. We had thousands of gallons of gasoline and diesel stored because gas was sometimes hard to come by in St. Petersburg. The stainless steel barrels we used were empty Löwenbräu kegs supplied to us by the chief bartender from the Karelia Hotel. I'd imported state of the art vehicles; we had a warehouse full of the most modern police and special operations equipment available; we had up-to-date communications equipment.

And then, once everything was on-site, when everything was complete and we had an inventory of goodies worth millions of dollars, that's when I started experiencing problems with Leonid Pinchuk. Of course I did. He thought I was ripe for the plucking, and he was the *nachalnik* motherplucker who'd do it.

❖

His first gambit was a clumsy attempt to insinuate his own people into the company's management and get rid of the individuals I'd hired. For example, I'd hired a liaison officer and Deputy Director at GUVD's request, bby the name of Alexander Michailov. Sasha was the Deputy Chief of the Police Academy in Pushkin. I found Sasha, unlike so many of his peers, both dependable and reliable, qualities that would ultimately make him unpopular with some Big House denizens. Indeed, by early January, the GUVD bureaucracy—that would be Pinchuk—started to demand daily reports from me. I wasn't in the habit of doing business that way, so I asked Sasha to handle them.

And he did. Which got me a visit from Pinchuk.

It was the second week in January, 1992. Pinchuk called. He was abrupt to the point of rudeness: "I want to talk to you. We have serious problems. I'll be right over."

Half an hour later, he strode into my office, which was on the first floor of the Chalet, accompanied by three sleazy individuals who looked like TV versions of used-car salesmen. I took them over to my conference table. It was a big table—over six feet wide and thirteen feet long, and I'd brought it from Munich to impress: it was made of clear, very thick Plexiglas.

I invited them to sit and took my position at the head of the table. "What's the problem, Leonid?"

Pinchuk fiddled with his glasses. He wiped them with a handkerchief, then adjusted them back on his face. "I've been watching you."

"Yes?"

His fingers drummed on my table, leaving prints on the Plexiglas. "And all this, this activity that's going on here, I don't think it's productive."

I said nothing.

"I don't think anything you're doing will help us. And Michailov? He's completely incompetent."

Again, I said nothing.

"So, as you see, I brought in new management." His hand swept backwards, indicating the three sleazeballs. "They will start today."

I shook my head. "No, they won't. I don't think you understand how this thing works, Leonid. I'm the president of the company. I determine who I hire; I determine who I fire. You? You're a partner and because you are, I'm happy to inform you of what I choose to do. But I run the business. I—not you. Now, it is in my interest to make a profit for myself—and for you, as one of the stockholders. But I am not in business to make a profit for you, Leonid, as an individual, as a *person*. I'm in business to make a profit for you as the GUVD stockholder."

I looked across at him with as Teutonic a war-face as I could muster. "This is the end of the discussion. If you think you're testing me, make no mistake: I will not have my authority challenged. Will. Not. So, we're finished here."

Pinchuk went white. He blinked rapidly. And then he pushed his chair back, stood up, swiveled awkwardly, and lurched out of the conference room trailed by the three stooges. He uttered not a word. Not a syllable.

I was outraged. The contract was specific about these sorts of actions. I wasted no time: I wrote a formal letter to Arkady Kramarev to tell him what was going on right under his nose, and to start creating a paper trail about Pinchuk's activities.

There was no response. But the following week, Kramarev came to our Beer Call with Pinchuk in tow.

I took the chief aside. "Arkady, what about Pinchuk?"

Kramarev was dismissive. "It's nothing." He saw my dubious expression. "Look, Franz, this can all be worked out over a couple of shots of vodka." He turned and scanned the room, found his target and waved. "Leonid—Pinchuk—come!" The Chief turned to me. "We'll have some vodka and we'll all be friends."

I knew Pinchuk and I would never be friends. And I now saw what my friend, Dr. Andreev, the Chief Pathologist of St. Petersburg, had meant when he told me just after Kramarev had been appointed Chief to succeed

Voshinin: "Franz, Arkady's a very good investigator, but he's a very bad *nachalnik*."

Arkady was a remote, hands-off boss. Moreover, he was weak. Obviously, he didn't have it in him to fire people.

So, when the following week and right into the spring I started receiving a flood of letters bearing Arkady Kramarev's name, but with Pinchuk's signature in his capacity as deputy chief, I understood that Arkady not only hadn't written them, he probably didn't even know about them. They were Pinchuk's work. They had to be: they bore the musty scent of the bureaucrat.

> "...You have not informed us in adequate detail about the activity of the Company in the past week. Moreover, the information that is provided us by your liaison, Michailov, is neither satisfactory nor accurate in our opinion..."

After two or three of these letter bombs I wrote back, explaining point by point how the contract worked and how a successful business was run. But I knew my response wouldn't do any good. Pinchuk was building a case against me—against the company—so he could take it over and gut it.

To do this, he'd need inside information. Intelligence. And in this, I had the advantage: I controlled all the information inside the company. We had one photocopy machine, which was situated next to my office so I'd be aware of anyone copying documents. Our telex, phone system, and computer server were centrally-located so nobody could get to them without my being aware. And when I was out of the office, all of those areas were secured and locked.

In February, Pinchuk sent a Revision Commission to Kamenny Ostrov. These commissions were GUVD's investigatory boards, comprised of a lawyer, an accountant, and a logistical officer. They presented me with a completed, damning report and stipulated that I sign it immediately.

Of course I refused, because it was fiction. "Tell Mr. Pinchuk that this—" I shook the report in their direction—"is baloney. So take it back to him with my regards, but not my signature."

The situation couldn't go on as it was, but Kramarev kept kicking the can down the road. If I wanted to fix things, it was imperative to understand why Kramarev was so ineffective in reining Pinchuk in. There had to be some logical explanation—and a way to get around it. So, I invited the general to dinner at Kamenny Ostrov. He accepted graciously. Arkady spoke, by the way, very good English, and so we'd never needed an interpreter. It was just the two of us. Mano a mano. We smoked cigarettes and drank vodka and talked about our lives, and how we'd both ended up in this beautiful, but messed-up city at the mouth of the Neva River. It turned out Arkady was not only the GUVD chief, but also was the acting *ataman* (commander) of the Cossacks, who years later under President Putin would take on a vital role in internal security and also augment Russia's military in the campaigns in Ukraine and Georgia.

And after the cigarettes and the vodkas, and the food, I looked over at him and I said, "Arkady, there's something you don't understand. Pinchuk is acting alone. He's using his position in GUVD and taking advantage of your confidence in him to make himself rich. But he's a thief. He takes money from businesses—shakes them down. And now he wants to siphon off what I've built here. He wants to take it all; sell off my inventory and put the money in his own pocket. That is wrong, Arkady—and I won't let it happen."

Kramarev's neutral expression never changed. Not a hint. Not a flicker. He sucked on his cigarette, raised his eyes, and exhaled the pungent smoke.

He was opaque—totally unreadable.

I really—*really*—wanted to get through to him. "Look, Arkady, I neither want nor need this fight with GUVD. It can only be bad for business. And if the business fails, then it's you—GUVD—who fails as well as me. So, why not just move Pinchuk aside? Let him run his games somewhere else. Replace him as the Russian stockholder with Michailov or even Kolbasov. Because what's going on now is bullshit, and neither you nor I need it."

The police chief stared at me, his eyes watery from the vodka and the smoke. His expression was empathetic. Then, he sighed. It was a long, despondent sigh; so melancholy it reminded me of the way the characters sigh in the third act of a Chekhov play. "Franz, I won't remove Pinchuk because I cannot." He read my face. "That's right: *I* cannot remove Pinchuk. That decision must come from the Minister of Interior."

And then I understood.

I understood that even though there was no more Soviet Union, the chain of command system that had been established back in the days of Stalin, Malenkov, Khrushchev, Brezhnev, and Andropov was still in effect.

It was the iron-fisted Joseph Stalin; Stalin who'd run the USSR for 30-plus years, who'd introduced a system to keep himself in power. All across the USSR, he ensured that every major position in every single city was filled not by locals, but by strangers. They'd all be brought in. Appointed. Appointed by him—*Stalin*, so that their loyalty was not to their peers and colleagues, not to their friends, or family, or clan, but to the brutal *nachalnik* in Moscow who'd given them their good job.

Arkady couldn't bestow Pinchuk with *kruglak*—all the freebies you got as a part of the ruling class—only Moscow could bestow *kruglak*. I thought about it. In the St. Petersburg GUVD, Pinchuk was from Kiev, Kramarev was from Volgograd, Michalkov, Kolbasov—none of the deputy chiefs and department heads were St. Petersburg natives. All came from elsewhere.

The USSR was dead. But Uncle Joe Stalin's divide-and-conquer system was still in place. So, even though he was a proud Cossack, which in literal translation means "free warrior", Kramarev's hands were tied. He could, in, point of fact, do nothing about Pinchuk.

And me?

Me? I was screwed.

Part Two

At War with GUVD

CHAPTER 6
Russia's Scorched Earth Policy
"You don't want to be the one-legged man in an ass-kicking contest." — Col. Stanley Olchovik, USA

Speaking of getting screwed, on November 6, 1991, Russian president Boris Yeltsin issued Decree No. 169, which banned the Communist Party. The decree also nationalized all the party's property, declaring it "property of the state".

Screw you, Commies. Screw you big time.

Yeltsin's decree had advantages and disadvantages, so far as I was concerned. The big disadvantage was that the people with whom I did business on a national level were, all of a sudden, not around anymore, because their offices or departments had been abolished. There was no more USSR, but a Russian Federation made up of separate republics.

What became even more significant in the long run was that when Yeltsin seized all the Communist Party assets, he took over UsPRF, the Office of Affairs of the Communist Party. UsPRF was the Soviet organization that held and controlled all the Party's property. What Yeltsin did was redirect everything so that whatever had once belonged to the USSR now became the property of the President of Russian Federation. UsPRF became known as the *Upravlenie delami Prezidenta RF*, or UdPRF, which translates as the Office of Affairs of the President of the Russian Federation. UdPRF essentially served Yeltsin (and later Medvedev and Putin) as a blunt political instrument to take over whatever assets, money, or land the president desired. Whether the property was public or private didn't matter: all it took was a presidential decree. Incredibly, UdPRF, which is sometimes referred to as *Upravlenie*, has operated from Yeltsin's time until the present, largely unnoticed by Western governments and even more incredibly, by Russians.

Because of UdPRF, Boris Yeltsin became the most powerful individual in Russia, because he—the occupier of the Office of the President—now owned everything the Communist Party had once owned. All the property occupied by Russia's embassies and trade missons. All the property housing the federal government's agencies and printing houses, its mass media holdings, hospitals, and medical service providers; its manufacturing and construction companies, transport services, hotels, and food companies—all of it belonged to him.

UdPRF owned the USSR's complete overseas assets, and, in time, even the property of Russia's parliament—the Duma—would be owned by the President of the Russian Federation. Every bit of state property that wasn't controlled by the central government, the military, or the Ministry of Interior belonged to Yeltsin. And what about natural resources—oil wells and coal mines? What about strategic minerals?

Yeltsin now controlled those, too. He could sell them, lease them, or give them away through rigged public auctions. And he did all three: to his friends…or the highest bidder. And later, both Putin and Medvedev would follow in his footsteps. In fact, Vladimir Putin's first job in Moscow would be at *Upravlenie*.

Overnight, Boris Yeltsin had crowned himself the King of *kruglak*; the Emperor of graft. Yeltsin could give. And he could take away. He was the Peter the Great of *nachalniki* because not since the days of the czars had so much property belonged to one individual. Not to Lenin, not to Stalin. No one.

The power of controlling UdPRF is almost unfathomable to anyone from the West. Literally, every Russian judge, every politician, every high ranking bureaucrat is financed by the UdPRF. This means their family housing and dacha, their medical services, their car and driver, elite schools, choice vacation locations, and other perks are all supplied directly by the office of the president. It is vertical hierarchy in its most effective—and oppressive—form. Oppressive, because any official viewed by the president as disloyal, useless, or an obstacle can be denied *kruglak* at a moment's notice.

In fact, Vladimir Putin's first 'political kill' as the newly appointed head of the FSB in 1999 was UdPRF-inspired. Yuri Skuratov was the Russian Prosecutor General. His 'crime': going after President Boris Yeltsin and his family and UdPRF director Pavel Borodin. Skuratov initiated a graft investigation known as the Mabetex scandal, which directly implicated the Yeltsin family and Borodin for taking tens of millions of dollars in kickbacks from Mabetex, a Swiss-Albanian contractor hired to do restorative work on the Kremlin on behalf of UdPRF.

In March, Russian television aired video of what looked like the prosecutor general frolicking in bed with two prostitutes. According to a Los Angeles Times report on April 3, 1999, "Vladimir V. Putin, who heads the Federal Security Service (FSB), the main successor to the KGB, said Skuratov's 'party' with the prostitutes was paid for by people involved in criminal cases." The result: Skuratov was removed from office and ultimately resigned, and the criminal case against the Yeltsins and UdPRF evaporated. The Swiss authorities, however, continued their own investigation and eventually arrested and convicted UdPRF's director Pavel Borodin for money laundering.

The Yeltsins remain unscathed until today. As does UdPRF.

In fact, today, *Upravlenie*, whose budget is comprised largely of black funds, is probably President Vladimir Putin's main instrument for *kompro-*

mat, the sort of compromising blackmail material used against prosecutor Skuratov, or the unsubstantiated files about presidential candidate Donald Trump that were leaked to former MI6 officer Christopher Steele by a KGB contact who was, incredibly, murdered shortly after he'd provided Steele with raw, unconfirmed intelligence that was so intensely, perfectly, damaging to Trump that it had to be too good to be true.

UdPRF's black funds are also used to finance *dezinformatsiya*, the disinformation 'active measures' campaigns used by both Soviet and Russian intelligence to plant false information in the West through the use of agents of influence, the financing of Russian and international media, and nowadays internet trolls, hackers, and what is known as "The Fifth Column," Western extremist political movements and parties that hammer away at democratic institutions.

Indeed, the Western press—as well as Western governments and their intelligence agencies—often get it wrong. It's not the SVR or the FSB or the KGB that's doing the mischief, but *Upravlenie* and its almost unlimited access to black funds.

Another result of the Yeltsin family's corruption was that a lot of money and a lot of property disappeared into what in the new Russia became known as 'Dark Channels:' the Party officials, KGB officers, members of the Komsomol (the youth organization of the Communist Party), as well as criminal organizations and that new class of Russian entrepreneurs known as oligarchs, who became millionaires and billionaires almost overnight." The bottom line is that from the President of Russia down to *nachalniki* like Leonid Pinchuk, Russians of a certain rank or class took the opportunity to lay their hands on as much money, and "privatize"—steal or take over as many businesses and industries as they could get they hands on. And that included not just the former state-owned properties and endeavors, but businesses started under Gorbachev's *perestroika* by Westerners like me. Point of fact. What ultimately killed business for me and many other Western entrepreneurs like me was an unpleasant reality of post-Soviet Russian culture: when some particular individuals saw that you were making serious money, they became jealous. They wanted what you'd achieved, but they didn't want to work as hard as you had to achieve it. And if they couldn't do it by taking over your business, they would do their utmost to destroy your business and you with it.

In Russia, the rules suddenly become simple and brutal: what Russians could take, they'd take; what they couldn't, they'd destroy. Or try their damnedest.

All of which made the first half of 1992 an... interesting time. On the plus side, my business was expanding. My contacts were expanding, too: because of Yeltsin's Decree No. 169, I couldn't sell to centralized Soviet organizations anymore but was forced to build new relationships in the now autonomous Republics. So, I traveled East—to Kazakhstan, Kyrgyzstan, Uzbekistan—as well as the Baltics—Estonia, Latvia, and Lithuania, building new customer bases.

And on the minus side, there was Pinchuk. Unsuccessful at placing his pals at Stone Island, he decided to kill me with paperwork. It was the bureaucratic equivalent of World War I trench warfare. You dig in. You lob artillery at the enemy and you wear him down. Then, after he's cold and wet and demoralized because he's been living in mud and filth for weeks or for months, you fix bayonets and go over the top and kill the sorry sons of bitches who'd lost the will to fight. That was the campaign Pinchuk mapped out for me and the Stone Island Company.

In most countries, if you get into a dispute with a business partner or organized crime makes a move on your enterprise, you have somewhere you can go to—the police, the prosecutor, or the newspapers. You've got possibilities. In Russia, not so much. The police wouldn't help me. In point of fact, it was the police who were trying to steal my company.

So, it became trench warfare. Or, as Stanley Olchovik described it, "a pissing contest." (Whenever I'd bitch to him about Pinchuk, Stanley used to tell me, "Franz, the one thing you don't want to be is the one-legged man in an ass-kicking contest.") He also warned me, "And by the way, you don't bring a knife to a gunfight," which was particularly appropriate when it came to doing business in Russia. Because if you're not prepared to fight to the death, to attack when provoked, to engage in constant conflict, and to kick ass with legs, fists, and teeth, then don't go to Russia.

And if you do go, you not only have to plan for conflict, but also for contingencies. There was another relevant Special Forces mantra by which Stanley had lived his own life: "If you fail to prepare, then you prepare to fail." Those words would ultimately become the watchwords of my particular branch of entrepreneurial faith when I took on not just GUVD but the entire Russian Federation.

So the pressure is constant. And if you give in—even once—then comes the deluge, because you've been marked as a target, a sucker, a loser.

It is, as Stanley told me more than once, like operating behind enemy lines. As long as you're on the ground, you're exposed. And while there are ways to mitigate exposure, the exposure itself will never go away because the threat is constant, the situation's in permanent flux, and the rules are changing minute to minute, sometimes second to second.

I'd seen it happen. A new business would open in St. Petersburg. The owner would renovate a building or a store. They'd put in brand new shelving. And, a couple of days later, a couple of firemen from the local Fire Brigade would pay them a visit.

One of the firemen would say, "We've been told you built new shelves. We're here to inspect them and certify they're fire resistant."

The owner would say, "*A?*" which is "Huh?" in Russian.

"To certify the shelves, *idyot*," the fireman would say pedantically. "Without a certificate from us you can't operate your store legally."

Then they'd look at the shelves and tell him, "We're sorry, but your shelving doesn't meet code. To get it up to grade you'll need to purchase special anti-inflammatory wood preservative from us. The cost will be $5,000 and we'll deliver it to you tomorrow. Otherwise, we'll come and shut you down and confiscate the shelving." Of course the poor guy would pay—he didn't have a choice.

But the fire brigade wasn't the only vulture circling. Next came the phone company, which demanded money to connect the poor schlemiel's already-connected phone lines and keep them connected. And six weeks after that, the tax police would show up. They'd inspect his books and tell him they were illegitimate. But the helpful tax policeman had a cousin or an uncle who's an accountant, and that individual knew exactly how to keep the store's books legal—for $1,000 a month. So, the businessman paid up. He was operating on a pretty thin profit margin by that time—just under $2,000 a week, but at least he was operating.

Then, a month or so later, a Mafiya hooligan shows up. He explains to the shop owner he's the representative of the neighborhood protection society, and it would be wonderful if the owner would contribute $1,500 a week to the society so thieves don't come into the store and beat the crap out of him, or that he shows up one morning to find his business had burned down overnight. And y'know, it was absolutely amazing that the hooligan asked for $1,500 a week as opposed to any other amount, because $1,500 was exactly the amount the businessman could pay, yet still make enough of a tiny profit so he wouldn't go out of business altogether.

Of course it was: because the Mafiya hooligan had bribed a banker to hand over the shop owner's latest bank statement.

This was how "entrepreneurs" practiced free enterprise in Boris Yeltsin's Russia. And to make things absolutely Kafkaesque, in the midst of all this cosmic-level thievery, Boris Yeltsin actually issued a presidential decree inviting more foreign investment in Russia.

The decree announced that Russia was open to free enterprise. Foreign investors, said the law,

> *"Shall have the right to invest in the territory of the [Russian Federation] by way of acquiring ownership interests in enterprises established jointly with legal entities or citizens of the [Russian Federation];...establishing enterprises wholly owned by foreign investors, as well as affiliates of foreign legal entities...[acquiring] enterprises, properties, buildings, structures...as well as other assets..."*

It went on for a goodly number of pages. It was all a lie.

And yet, there were companies dumb enough to believe Yeltsin without realizing that the Russian definition of 'free enterprise' was not the same as theirs.

Like Subway. The American sandwich chain. Which thought that opening in Russia was the entrepreneurial chance of a lifetime. And it might have been: a virgin market; a population with an appetite for things Western; an abundance of good prospective locations.

The first Subway franchisee was an American who'd bought from Subway a franchise that gave him access to various regions in Russia to build and operate Subway sandwich stores. The businessman linked up, as foreigners did, with a Russian partner named Vadim Bordug, who controlled a building directly on one of St. Petersburg's most popular streets, *Nevski Prospect*. Once they'd founded the joint venture, Subway sent in all the equipment and they opened their flagship store to great fanfare.

The Western partner was delighted. Let's say it had cost him half a million dollars of his own money for the franchise and the seed money—but the store was doing well. Everything was, as they say, hunky dory.

Except it wasn't. Unbeknownst to the American, Bordug, the Russian partner, was a lieutenant in the Tambov criminal gang. Which meant he lived by the Russian definition of free enterprise and privatization—steal, steal, steal while investing nothing. Meanwhile, the American had not only outfitted the sandwich shop, but also supplied all its daily requirements: meat, cheese, bread, vegetables, toppings, beverages, cups, even wrapping paper.

But the poor guy never saw a penny. Instead, he discovered that his Russian partner had skimmed all the joint venture's profits and deposited all the proceeds into an Irish bank account. When confronted about this, the Russian and his Mafiya goons from the Tambov gang beat the living daylights out of the American. Then they warned him: "It's time for you to go home. We'll take it from here."

Within hours, all the Subway signs had been taken down, and new ones that read "MINUTKA SANDWICHES" were up.

The American businessman lost every penny of his investment. So, he sought arbitration in Stockholm. But even though he dropped a huge fee on an expensive lawyer, paid all the arbitration fees, won the arbitration, and got the award domesticated in Russia, he never recovered his money.

Of course he didn't: the award was Swedish, his debtor was a local mobster, and the bailiff—the individual responsible for actually enforcing the award—was Russian and in on the joke. Subway became one of a long, long line of Western companies to be "privatized". And every one of those who sought arbitration and won, ended up like Subway: the Russians paid not a penny. Not one penny. Ever.

I know this story because I actually spent time with Bordug after all of this took place. He was brought to my office in 1994 by Albert Stepanov, a shady bureaucrat who was the head of St. Petersburg's municipal registration department. Bordug told me straight out he'd skimmed the money and where he'd put it. His problem, he said, was he couldn't figure out why his American partner had gotten so upset. Didn't he understand how business was done in Russia?

❖

So yes, I was expanding my business. And I was successful in keeping my nose clean: no bribes, no handouts, no cash under the table, no payoffs and: no kickbacks. But there was still Pinchuk, waging trench warfare. And in some ways, thinking back on it, I underestimated him because he turned out to have a lot more 'juice' than I'd given him credit for.

For example, at one point I'd set up a meeting in Moscow with a general named Gerchikov, who was responsible for international connections of the Ministry of the Interior, and a major named Ryzkhov, who was the ministry's Chief of Protocol. The Interior Ministry had access to police units all over Russia, and if we could supply them with equipment, it would be a hell of a deal for me — and for my GUVD partners.

The night before the meeting, the Russians housed us in a secret hotel right next to Red Square. It was fascinating. On the ground floor was a fire station with ladder trucks and pumpers parked with the big doors open and firemen milling around. But when we walked around the back and went up a flight of outside stairs, there, behind an anonymous-looking door, was a luxury hotel for dignitaries.

It was run like a top-secret installation: no one working in the hotel was allowed to exchange a word with us. There was absolutely no conversation — none. If I addressed a bellman or one of the waiters, or even one of the room maids, they'd listen and nod. If I needed something, I'd ask and they'd bring it — in total silence.

It was surreal.

We met with the general and the major and everything seemed to be moving along nicely. They even supplied us with a limousine and a driver to get us around Moscow in style. I was on track.

The following morning, I walked into our meeting with the head of HAZO—the logistics and supply arm of the Interior Ministry—feeling pretty confident. He was a general, and judging from the number of phones on his desk, he was a pretty important guy.

But I'd no sooner sat down than he gave me a funny look. The corners of his mouth turned down. And then he said, "I just received a call from my colleague in St. Petersburg, and he has nothing good to say about you. Nothing at all."

It was Pinchuk, of course. Sabotaging my business in Moscow.

And why did he do that when he had to know it was a self-inflicted wound. By killing my deal, he was damaging GUVD's interests?

He did it because in Russia the rules were scorched-earth simple: what Russians could take, they'd take; what they could not take they'd destroy. Pinchuk was just demonstrating his... Russianness.

In early March, I learned that Pinchuk was going to take Kamenny Ostrov from me by force: an assault using GUVD personnel. I learned of his plans from a KGB colonel named Alex Sibarov, who'd started coming to our Beer Call receptions with my architect friend Venjamin Fabritsky early on and with whom I'd gotten close enough so that he'd just show up at Kamenny Ostrov unannounced and we'd sit over coffee or beer and chat.

On that particular day, he seemed preoccupied. I noted a concerned look on his face. "What's up, Alex?"

"If I were you I'd be worried about Pinchuk."

"Why, Alex?"

"He's planning an assault on Kamenny Ostrov."

"Right—using paper as a bulldozer?"

Sibarov waved his hand. "No-no-no, Franz. He's planning an assault. A real one. And you shouldn't make a joke of it because Leonid is a very vindictive person. You threw him out, remember?"

"He brought gangsters with him. As if I'd—"

Sibarov cut me off. "Ukrainians."

Except he didn't say "Ukrainians." He said "*Khokhly*".

It was a derogatory term for Ukrainians, borrowed from the historical look of the Ukrainian Cossacks, who traditionally shaved their heads but grew little pigtails of hair at the napes of their necks.

"Franz, listen to me. Leonid is *nachalnik*, and you made him look bad in front of his inferiors. That alone makes him dangerous when it comes to you. He's got *Khokhly* friends—and his fellow Afghanistan veterans. Some are GUVD now, some are Mafiya. They're ruthless. And some are even completely crazy. Leonid's part of all that. He's not just some pencil-pusher. Look at his friends. Like Gorbachevski."

I knew Gorbachevski. He was a deputy chief who headed GUVD's Investigative Division, which dealt with Organized Crime. Of course the Investigative Division didn't stop Organized Crime—they just 'controlled' it. Another example of Russian "free enterprise" in action. I'd seen Gorbachevski at the Chaika, a 'beer, women, and song' dive bar, where expats, cops, and hookers hung out. The owner came from Hamburg's red light district, which kind of said it all. But it was neutral turf. It didn't matter whether you were KGB, GUVD, or Mafiya, you got decent German pilsner, occasionally decent German food, and proposals from the Russian hookers, which one could accept or turn down.

Gorbachevski seldom turned the hookers down.

"I can handle it, Alex."

"How?"

"I'll—I'll" Truth was, I didn't have a plan. I'd known the day would come when I'd have to deal with Pinchuk—and deal with him decisively. That was a certainty. I also knew Pinchuk had stacked the deck in his favor. For example, the compound was guarded by OMON personnel—the riot police of the Interior Ministry. I'd hired them after I'd fired the do-nothing cops who'd originally been a part of the Kamenny Ostrov staff. And OMON was good: young, alert, responsive, and appreciative of augmenting their meager salaries with hard currency *valuta*.

But when push came to shove—which it most certainly would—the chain of command was that OMON reported to GUVD. And with the head of GUVD, who was my cigarette-smoking, 'drink a few shots of vodka and we'll all be pals' General Arkady Kramarev, unwilling or unable to do anything about Pinchuk, OMON wouldn't be a neutral player. If Pinchuk put enough pressure on them, they'd cave. They'd leave their posts. Or worse, turn against us. And Kamenny Ostrov would be unprotected.

Alex interrupted my train of thought. "Can I make a suggestion?"

"Sure."

"Forget OMON."

"OMON?" How the hell did he know what I'd been thinking?

He lit a cigarette and inhaled deeply. "What if the guards at Kamenny Ostrov were my guys? I've got a personnel problem these days: Moscow's not paying my people on a regular basis. If I don't come up with supplemental funding, they're going to leave the service. But they're smart and they're capable, and if they work for you they'll make a living wage and stay with KGB."

"Alex, that's a great idea." Tactically, it made perfect sense. Even though they shared the same headquarters building, there was little love lost between the two organizations. First of all, their cultures were totally different. There was even a KGB joke about GUVD that said it all:

A new guy goes to work in GUVD's Traffic Police division. A couple of months later, his boss calls him in to headquarters. "Igor," the *nachalnik* says, "how come you don't come in and pick up your paycheck every week?"

And the traffic cop says, "What? You're giving me money, too?" Because GUVD traffic cops made their money by harassing motorists.

The KGB was the big dog. It was responsible for state security; it was tasked with counterintelligence, dignitary protection, and foreign threats. GUVD handled everyday crime and traffic. And because the KGB's mission included rooting out corruption, and because the vast majority of GUVD cops had their own profitable sidelines of shaking down people or businesses, it fell to the KGB to police the policemen.

KGB had investigated and cleaned house at GUVD on several occasions. In fact, one of the people who initially worked for me as head of in-house security was a KGB general named Evgeny Ratkovsky. Ratkovsky had once been assigned to GUVD to head internal affairs in order to root out graft and corruption.

And he'd been successful: he was credited with several hundred convictions. In fact, I'd made Pinchuk nervous just by employing Evgeny Ratkovsky because the general knew where all Pinchuk's skeletons were buried. He most certainly knew, for example, that Leonid Pinchuk and his fellow GUVD officer Albert Vorontsov, commander of the city's central district, had been shaking down hotels, restaurants, and the markets in the central district of Leningrad back in the pre-putsch days.

I'd been in Russia long enough to know that KGB recruited better people than GUVD; and hands down, it had better resources and a lot more 'juice' than its little sisters in the police.

By the time Alex left, we had a handshake deal. He'd provide the people and I'd provide the equipment and pay them a living wage.

❖

Fast forward. By the time Pinchuk staged his assault in late April, we were not only prepared, we had an after-action plan waiting to go. First, I sat down with my management people and my lawyer. We had everyone who witnessed Pinchuk's assault write a report on what they saw. Then my lawyer took the reports and filed them with the Prosecutor's Office for the District of Petrogradskaya. The reports and my lawyer's statement provided enough evidence so that the prosecutor, whose name was Filinenko, issued a restraining order within twenty-four hours. It forbade Pinchuk from launching any more direct assaults on Kamenny Ostrov.

The restraining order really rocked Pinchuk because he'd never considered the possibility that anyone would be able to obtain a restraining order against GUVD. I would have given just about anything to have seen the look on his face when the prosecutor's office served him with *that* piece of paper.

Pinchuk immediately wrote a memo of protest to the prosecutor. But it did no good. The restraining order held firm.

Once I had the restraining order in hand, I made sure both the German Consulate and the U. S. Consulate got copies. I also had them circulated at the St. Petersburg City Hall. My goal was to make sure as wide an audience as possible knew what Pinchuk had attempted wasn't just an everyday business dispute, but a serious violation of Russian law.

I wanted to squash Pinchuk like a bug.

CHAPTER 7
Telephone Justice

"Question: What do an impartial judge and a flying dragon have in common? Answer: They're both fictional characters." —1990s Russian courthouse joke

The Law of Foreign Investment 1991-1992
Chapter Six

Acquisition by foreign investors and enterprises with foreign investments of land, use, rights, and other property rights.

Article 38:
The right to use land and other national resources.

Provision of rights to use land including and leasing rights and rights to use other natural resources shall be regulated by the RSFSR Land Code and other Legislation effective in the RSFSR Territory meaning the Territory of the Russian Federation.

In principle, Article 38 was the basis for all foreign investment in Russia, including mine. And another critical basis for investment—at least we in the West expect this—is that we, as foreign investors, feel secure that no one will take our property away from us and that we can freely transfer the dividends from our enterprise to the outside.

But in reality, Article 38 was simply Russian window dressing. It meant nothing. Because, if something went wrong with your investment in Russia, your first point of contact was one of the local courts. But in Russia, the local courts were generally known to decide in favor of the government or whichever corrupt bureaucrat you were suing. And it wasn't done subtly, either. Usually some high-ranking official, or *nachalnik*, made a phone call to a judge and that would be that—the foreigner got screwed. The practice was so common in the court system the Russians even had a term for it: "Telephone Justice". The bottom line was that even though Prosecutor Filinenko had sent GUVD a restraining order, I, as a typical foreign investor, didn't stand much of a chance against them. Pinchuk and his goons would be back.

But then again, I wasn't your typical foreign investor. I was a hugely outraged Bavarian investor who'd put almost $900,000 cash into a company, because, I believed—perhaps naively, but I did—that a contract is a contract and that your word is your bond, two honorable principles that I now knew were antithetical to doing business in post-Gorbachev Russia. So, I was both pleased and surprised to receive support from an unexpected angle. I'd shown Prosecutor Filinenko's restraining order to Stewart Swanson, the Political/Economics counselor at the U.S. Consulate, hoping he'd have some ideas about what to do.

He read through it and said, "Holy shit. C'mon—let's show this to the Consul General."

That surprised me. I'd already been in contact with the German consulate on the Pinchuk matter. In fact, I was pretty close to both the German Consul General and his wife. Close enough, so that Mrs. Consul General routinely came by Stone Island to fill her car with diesel fuel, which was hard to come by in the city. Even so, the people at the consulate took a typically German bureaucrat's approach to my problem: a 'let's wait and see' attitude. Indeed, even if German nationals were shot, killed, abducted, or thrown in prison, you weren't going to get much of a helpful or supportive reaction from a German embassy or consulate. At best, they'd visit you in jail, hand you a list of local attorneys, and tell you there wasn't much they could do.

But the Americans turned out to be different. And the reason was because of Jack Gosnell, the U. S. Consul General in St. Petersburg.

The first time I'd met Jack Gosnell was late in 1991, when he'd initiated a Business Association in Leningrad for anyone who owned U.S.-based corporations. We met for the first time at one of the few privately owned restaurants in St. Petersburg. The place was called Pirosmani, and it was run by a Georgian who made wonderful Georgian food, and especially Georgian lamb soup. Jack, the newly arrived American Consul General, made a first-rate speech and basically created what would become the American Business Association of Saint Petersburg. I was a founding member, and our headquarters on Stone Island became the first home for ABA's monthly luncheons.

I liked Gosnell immediately. He was an atypical American diplomat in that he actually had language skills: he spoke fluent Russian and excellent French, as well as some German. I'd known a few American diplomats in my time, and very few of them had the language skills to, for example, do a newspaper or television interview in the language of the country to which they'd been assigned. Jack was able to handle himself very well in St. Petersburg that way. I'd find out later that he'd also had mastered Mandarin and Korean — that in fact his area of specialty was North Korea.

He seemed to be always on the go, always busy, always traveling, always talking, and always visiting. He became good friends with such locals as Anatoly Chubais, the dissident economist and reformer who'd become the deputy to Anatoly Sobchak when Sobchak was elected chairman of the Leningrad City Council in 1990. In 1991, Chubais moved up the ladder. He went to Moscow to become the minister for privatization in

Boris Yeltsin's cabinet.

Jack also had a somewhat roguish attitude toward the folks at Foggy Bottom, which is how he referred to his bosses at the State Department back in Washington D.C. After I got to know him better, he told me, "When I want to get something done, I tell them what I'm going to do, and I always add, 'If you don't want me to do that, please advise.' And y'know what? They never advise. So, I do what I want to do."

And he wasn't afraid to get involved. There'd been an incident in 1991 in which sixteen border guards got ambushed and shot on the border between Russia and Estonia. He personally made it a point to go down there to see what was going on and investigate the incident. In fact, he rubbed some Russian officials the wrong way because he was deeply involved with human rights issues and wasn't afraid of bringing the issue up face to face.

Jack was an effective speaker—people hung on his every word—and unlike the previous consul general, he wasn't out of the State Department's political or intelligence cone. He was a science and technology analyst. His wife and three daughters had accompanied him to St. Petersburg, where he'd arrived in the latter part of 1991, and they'd occasionally go with him to receptions, which was a very American thing to do. Russian officials went to receptions solo. For example, in all the time I knew and was in contact with Vladimir Putin—from 1992 to 1996—I never saw him at a single reception, dinner, or business function with his wife. It just wasn't done. In Russia, family is family and business is business.

Stew ushered me into the Consul General's office and showed him Filinenko's restraining order. Jack took it, looked up at us, and said, "This may take a while. Why don't the two of you grab a seat."

We did. He perused the document, then peered over at me. "So?"

"Mr. Consul General, I hope I'm not stepping on anybody's toes by coming to you, but since my company's based in Missouri, I thought you might be able to help with this matter." I paused. He was looking at me with a very earnest expression. "And to be honest, I'm actually over my head with this…situation." I pointed at the paper on his desk.

He nodded knowingly, then smiled encouragingly. "Mr. Sedelmayer, don't worry."

"But you have to know I'm a German national, even though it's an American company, and—"

"Mr. Sedelmayer," he cut me off, "Who cares what you are. I certainly don't." He paused and tapped the restraining order with his finger. "Most of the people who own or are employed by American companies here aren't U.S. citizens. We've got Germans, we've got Dutch, we've got Swedes—even Afrikaans working here for U.S. corporations. Bottom line is that we are here to support American business—it doesn't matter who's running it."

He looked straight at me. "Here's how it works. You explain your problem to me, Mr. Sedelmayer, I'll tell you how we're going to fix it."

It didn't take me more than 10 or 15 minutes to take the Consul General through the events of the past seven months. He listened intently, taking an occasional note. When I finished, he made a steeple of his fingers and sat quietly for about half a minute.

Then he looked at me. "Mr. Sedelmayer, the way we're going to handle this is by being direct. Very direct. Under normal circumstances, I'd play the diplomatic game. I'd go and talk to somebody in the Mayor's Office. Then I'd go behind closed doors and talk with whoever it is here in St. Petersburg that has influence with the Ministry of Foreign Affairs, and I'd talk to them, diplomat to diplomat in diplomatic language, to the effect that perhaps it's not in their long-term interests to screw foreign businessmen, blah-blah-blah, and we're entering a world of global economy, blah-blah-blah. And they'd agree with me and tell me they'd look into the matter, and we'd all go away happy. And then I'd write a lovely cable to Washington telling them I'd just had two successful meetings on behalf of an American business enterprise and recount what I'd said and what they'd said and send copies to the Russian Desk and the German Desk with cc's to a few DASes (N.B. a DAS is a deputy assistant secretary). And of course, nothing would happen."

He caught the disappointed look on my face. Then he continued. "But with the Russians, Mr. Sedelmayer, things are different. You can't practice old-fashioned diplomacy with the Russians. With them, you need *this*." He took two business cards from his desk drawer and laid them edge to edge on his desk. Then he pushed them together until they flew into the air and fluttered to the floor.

"You know what you just saw, Mr. Sedelmayer?"

I shook my head. "No, sir."

He said, "That was *confrontation,* Mr. Sedelmayer. And I like confrontation."

Then he started talking about what the German Consul General could do. "I'll bring them in of course—we'll do it together. A pincer attack. That'll knock GUVD back on their heels."

He looked at Stew Swanson. "Stew, call your counterpart at the German Consulate so we can coordinate diplomatic letters of protest."

Now his eyes were bright. He grinned at me. "Your man from the German consulate and my man will meet and they'll draw up dovetailed letters of our diplomatic notes. Then we'll file a formal protest. And once we've done that? *That's* when I'll report to the State Department with a simultaneous copy to the Ambassador in Moscow." He grinned at me as

I started to open my mouth. "That's right—when it's too late to tell me, 'No.'"

"That way we'll already have everything on file—on the record—so there won't be any misunderstandings." He gave me an aggressive look. "Because as you already probably know, Mr. Sedelmayer, the Russians are very good at being misunderstood. And we don't want that, do we?"

I was blown away. All I could say was "No, sir. Thank you, Mr. Consul General."

Then, Stew took me back to his office, and while I was there he called his German counterpart to set up an appointment so they could sit down that very same evening and agree on language for the letters of protest.

Stew hung up the phone. "And I have one more idea," he said.

That was when he told me about Vladimir Putin, and how close Putin was to Mayor Sobchak. "Putin might be the perfect target for you," Stew said. "He's KGB, which means he has good contacts and he's probably prejudiced against GUVD. And the story's that he saved Sobchak's ass during the putsch last year. That has to count for something. And the last thing is that Putin doesn't take bribes—at least so far as we can determine."

I knew Putin's name of course, and I'd heard much the same story about what he'd done during the putsch. "Do you know him?"

Stew shook his head. "No, not personally. But I think he'd see you."

"Why?"

"He loves Germans and Germany. He served in East Germany in the KGB. I'm told he's nostalgic about his days there. So he'd probably be more open to meeting with a German national than some American embassy guy like me who he probably thinks is a spy."

"Okay..."

"And here's the other thing," Stew said, "he's very close to Sobchak." Stew rubbed his two index fingers together. "Very, very close. And from our prospective, what we've learned about Sobchak is that he's not the sort of guy who volunteers to take action if he, A), doesn't have to, or B), if there isn't something in it for him, if you catch my drift."

I caught his drift loud and clear. Sobchak may have been a reformer; a legal scholar; a devoted democrat. But in matters that concerned business he was a cash-on-the-barrelhead kind of guy. And, I wasn't about to trade one crook for another. Been there, done that.

"But Putin?"

"If you can get to him, he'll be straight with you."

I did get to Putin within a couple of days. That first meeting, as I described earlier, didn't go all that well. Still, Putin had been cordial, if detached. At the end, he'd shaken my hand and dismissed me in a manner that indicated he didn't expect to see me anymore.

And I'd told him, "Mr. Deputy Mayor, you will soon realize the city needs the Stone Island Company and the people who run it. We are true friends of St. Petersburg. Don't worry—I'll be back in touch soon."

Putin's reaction had been to stare at me in total disbelief. He thought Pinchuk had gotten the best of me. That I'd pack up and leave because a fight with GUVD, which had more than 10,000 employees and the ability to arrest its enemies, was a losing battle.

And Putin might have been right. Except that Leonid Pinchuk had already unwittingly come to my rescue.

Because, while I was meeting with Jack Gosnell at the consulate, Leonid Pinchuk, being Leonid Pinchuk, did me a huge favor: he sicced a reporter on me.

And not just any reporter: he made a call to the Russian equivalent of Geraldo Rivera.

❖

Between 1987 and 1993, the most popular TV show in Leningrad—and ultimately beyond—was a rabble-rousing news show called *600 Seconds*. It did a mix of investigative reporting and shock TV. There might be topless bathers in one segment, and an expose about prying gold teeth from corpses in the local crematory in the next. It was hosted by a larger-than-life anchorman named Alexander G. Nevzorov, who the *New York Times* Moscow Bureau Chief Bill Keller had called a "swashbuckling 31 year-old" in a 1989 article about *600 Seconds* headlined, "Hip, Hot and Hyper: Soviet TV Cuts Loose."

"This is television for the gut," Keller wrote. "Six days a week, *600 Seconds* is like a jolt from a cattle prod following the usually soporific evening news..."

You get the idea.

GUVD—no doubt Pinchuk himself—had called *600 Seconds* and told them about how they'd been ripped off by a sleazy German businessman, and didn't the show want to send Alexander Nevzorov and a camera crew to this guy's place of business and get some great ambush journalism?

So, by the time I got back to Kamenny Ostrov from my visit to the consulate, I arrived to find Nevzorov already filming in my offices. My employees had just let him and his crew in. Of course they had: he was the most popular guy on TV in Leningrad and his show was seen all over Russia.

I was reticent, but one of my people waved me over. "C'mon, Franz—do this. It'll be great."

I was dubious until Nevzorov himself came over to me and after a bit of verbal jousting said something to the effect of, "You've got a lot of really cool shit around here," and asked how some of the SWAT gear worked. So I showed him. And while at first he'd been prosecutorial and aggressive, he was now attentive and almost friendly.

And while he could have been dissembling, it didn't seem that way. I could see it in his face and his body language. Maybe he had come intending to do a hit piece on us. But now, it seemed as if he was veering toward more neutral coverage—the 'we report, you decide' kind of stuff.

Finally, he took me outside for the all-important on-camera interview, which he set up in front of our impressive three-story log chalet. And one thing I knew instinctively: I couldn't give him the opportunity to edit my comments out of context. If I gave him short answers—mini-sound bites, he could make hamburger out of them and I'd look like an idiot.

So, when he asked, "Who's doing this to you?", instead of saying something to the effect of, "It was some corrupt people at GUVD," I started naming names.

"Colonel Leonid Pinchuk is the primary instigator, Alex. But he wasn't acting on his own. He brought his stooge Nefiodov of course," and then I named half a dozen other GUVD officers who were involved, and described in as fine detail as I could what Pinchuk and his raiders had done to my employees, and the damage they were doing to a successful business that had, after all, been established as a joint venture. If I made money, I told Nevzorov, so did GUVD. But obviously, I added, Pinchuk didn't want to make honest money: he wanted to steal my company.

The anchorman absorbed what I'd just told him. And then, his face grim but the soft ball pitched slowly from his hand so I could hit it out of the park, Nevzorov paused dramatically.

And then he said, "So exactly *what*, Mr. Sedelmayer, do you think has to be done?"

Smaaack!!! I can say with pride that I hit that particular ball over the center-field wall. "First of all Mr. Nevzorov, I believe that all those corrupt individuals who invaded this company—a company established legally and whose papers were co-signed by me and the commander of GUVD, have to be fired and replaced by loyal servants of the state; individuals who are incorruptible. After all, Mr. Nevzorov, this matter is not about a simple business dispute, this matter is about corruption—deep, institutional *corruption*, that is bringing shame to GUVD. I'm outraged, Mr. Nevzorov, outraged! Because I'm here to stay; I'm going to fight this bullshit and I'm going to bury their asses, full stop and end of story."

Within a couple of days, the *600 Seconds* report ran nationally. The gist of Alexander Nevzorov's narration basically went, "This is a stupid conflict. Anyone can see that this is a wonderful company with a wonderful product, and yet, out of the blue, some greedy individual appears and screws it all up. Why would some stupid idiot do that when the company is making money? Who needs this? We have other problems to deal with." And over that audio was a close-up of me, looking defiant and calling out all the GUVD's names. Nevzorov bleeped me, of course. But, as the first President Bush once said, "Read my lips."

Between the *600 Seconds* report and the diplomatic notes from the U.S. and German Consuls, the message became clear: The Kamenny Ostrov-GUVD incident was a commercial dispute that should have never resulted in an armed assault by the police. Pinchuk, of course, was his usual self. He gave an interview to the government TV station and every newspaper that would talk to him. And when the articles and segments came out showing him in a negative light he sent a letter to the prosecutor, charging that I was the provocateur and he was the innocent victim. The blatant lies in his letter and the negative coverage he'd gotten as a result of the *600 Seconds* piece and his own interviews resulted in the KGB initiating an investigation of what GUVD had done to me.

Shortly after that, I was invited to a reception at the U.S. Consulate. Jack Gosnell took me aside with his Regional Security Officer James Wellman and another individual to whom he never introduced me, leading me to believe that he was one of the CIA case officers working at the consulate.

Then, Jack—with whom I was on a first name basis by then, said, "Franz, I want you to give the names of the people who were involved with this raid to this gentlemen, because we're going to deny them entrance into the United States by putting them on the 'no visa' list." Pinchuk, Nefiodov, and the rest of them would be blackballed from ever visiting the United States.

❖

Even so, the two questions that nagged me all spring and into the summer were, first, why was Pinchuk doing what he was doing—aside, of course, from his personal motivation to steal stuff, and second—and perhaps even more troubling—why was no one at GUVD taking my side?

I got my answer—and the administrative and emotional deluge that commenced thereafter fittingly enough on Bastille Day, 1992, when I received a letter from an entity that called itself The Property Fund. It was, so it seemed, an office or branch of the Duma (the Russian Parliament).

It was jointly addressed to the Chief of GUVD, Major General Kramarev, A.G., and Director General, JSC "Kamenny Ostrov" Mr. Zedelmayer, F., and it read:

> According to the State Privatization Programme of state and municipal enterprises on the Russian Federation for 1992 that was authorised by the Resolution of the Supreme Soviet of the Russian Federation No. 2980-1 of 11-06-91992 (p.5.1), the exclusive right to the assignee to founders and partners (share holders, stockholders,) of enterprises that have been founded earlier by government bodies, is entitled to respective property fund.
>
> According to resolutions 13 and 14 from St. Petersburg City Council's sessions, the property Fund in St. Petersburg should get all shares (stocks, equities) in corporations and joint ventures owned by local bodies in St. Petersburg.

> Since the Property Fund in St. Petersburg has got the rights of a territorial department within Russian Fund for Federal Property, all shares, stocks and equities of administrative bodies in corporations, associations and joint ventures should be handed over to Property Fund independently of property level.
>
> In view of the above I would ask you to provide for the assignment concerning the rights to contribution share in the JV "Kamenny Ostrov" to the Property Fund before July 20, 1992.
>
>   Deputy Chairman of the Fund   Pejbo A.B

By the third reading, both my nagging questions had been answered. The Property Fund of the Duma wanted GUVD to give up its 50 percent share in the Kamenny Ostrov Joint Venture and turn its stock over to the Duma's property fund. Pinchuk had probably known the property laws would be changed. He'd probably realized that GUVD was not going to be able to remain a partner in Kamenny Ostrov—that its half would have to be handed over to the State. But he also had to know that if he could take my company over, dispose of all its assets, and hide the money he got, that when the Property Fund finally sent its letter asking GUVD to hand over its assets from Kamenny Ostrov, Kramarev, Pinchuk, Nefiodov and the rest of them could say, "Assets? What assets? Kamenny Ostrov went out of business months ago."

The only thing they hadn't figured on was my fighting back.

And then I realized something even more ominous: Leonid Pinchuk was no fool. And he had highly placed friends in Moscow, no doubt about that. He'd have to have known that the property laws were going to change as early as the previous summer right after the abortive August putsch when Kramarev pushed me to sign the joint venture agreement. That made GUVD's perfidy even worse. Because they'd set me up—all of them. The whole joint venture scheme had been a bait-and-switch from the get-go. And I'd put almost a million dollars of my own cash into it.

Now, I really did want to kick their asses.

But I had other problems to solve. If I'd read the letter correctly, there were now two competing organizations looking to take GUVD's 50-percent share. The Property Fund was controlled by the Duma. That's who'd sent the letter signed by Mr. Pejbo. But there was another organization, the State Property Committee, or GKI, which had local outlets called KUGI. GKI was run by the central government; it came under President's office and it was also looking to partner with foreign business joint ventures that had originally gone into business with police and other local municipal authorities.

I knew the St. Petersburg representatives of both. The Property Fund's guy was named Titov, a nice, soft-spoken, friendly gentleman and a true democrat. GKI's man was Sergei Belyaev. Belyaev was known for being something of a wishy-washy bureaucrat *cum* opportunist. We had met for the first time at Stone Island when he appeared at our front gate looking, incredibly, for former president Richard Nixon, who during his visit to St. Petersburg stayed on Kamenny Ostrov, but at a different residence. Belyaev would in fact later become the head of GKI in Moscow. But Belyaev had more 'juice' than Titov because he worked with a friend of Putin's named Vladim Glazkov, who was, like Putin, former KGB. And it was Putin who suggested to me that since I had to partner up somewhere, KUGI, the property committee that was part of the government overseen by the president's office, would be a better bet in the long run than anything run by the Duma.

KUGI was fine by me. But as was the usual case in Russia, the preliminary negotiations dragged on for several months. That was the way Russia worked in the early 1990s. It was all about finding the best route: who knows who? Who is a friend of whom? Who can I talk to so I can push the right buttons? Who can slip me through the back door so I won't be in a three-month-long line to get one form approved? It was labyrinthine and convoluted and very, very...Russian.

I knew the players. Putin, Belyaev, Glazkov, they were all were *nachalniki*. But even when you're working with *nachalniki*, you have to find a practical mechanism—a way of making things actually work. And that took time.

Also, my sense of Russia during those months was that it was still a traumatized country. You could almost smell it—it was that palpable. It was what the British call a "dark cloud." If you were a foreign businessman in Russia in the 1990s the problems never stopped. The corruption and the organized crime were bad enough. But overriding it all was a legal system that was rigged top to bottom. Sure, Telephone Justice was a huge problem. But that was just the tip of the iceberg.

Most nations, when they change the law, modify it in the light of previous rulings. Things are grandfathered. Not in Russia. In Russia what is legal on Monday can become illegal on Tuesday, and off you go to jail.

So, by the time I received my Bastille Day 'gift' letter from Moscow, I was ready for it mentally. By mid 1992, I understood that I wouldn't be in Russia for the next 20 years. I'd keep the company alive for as long as I could, expand where I could, shrink where I had to, and remain flexible. If the Stone Island Company lasted ten years, great. If it was only going to be five, so be it.

It was time, I realized, to start thinking like a Russian.

So, when I finally walked into Putin's office in November, I was mentally prepared. By November I'd gotten to know Putin a little bit. We actually quite enjoyed one another's company. He was smart but understated. He drove an inconspicuous Japanese sedan. His German was excellent, and he'd also obviously gone through the KGB's 'knife and fork school', because his manners were punctilious. He was not a drinker; in fact he'd have one beer or maybe two at the most. He was always controlled—more

KGB training, I guessed. His favorite beverage was Bavarian beer, which, of course, I kept at Kamenny Ostrov. And in the months after we'd first met he warmed up to me gradually, to the point, early in 1993, where he'd occasionally drop by Kamenny Ostrov and we'd have a beer and talk one on one. He'd also show up at our beer calls.

Socially, Putin was at his best in small groups. I'd occasionally see him at a reception. He'd never be in the center of a large gaggle but always one-on-one, or one-on-two or three. He was curious, and, of course, observant—all that KGB training again. And he was always…in control, both of himself and of the situation. My overwhelming impression of Putin in those days was that he was a 'people person', someone who could relate to you. Not a spymaster so much as a spy recruiter—a talent-spotter. One reason for that was that, when I observed him at social gatherings, he'd project himself differently to different people. He was chameleon-like. He'd give them back a mirror image of what he thought they'd like to see. He was also good at eliciting information from people, but reserved about talking about others.

Except when it came to corruption. I mentioned someone who worked for him in passing during one of our conversations. Putin looked at me and said, "Don't deal with him."

"Why?" I asked.

"Because he's an idiot, because he's dishonest, and because I don't like him."

He was not a person who opened up to people. There's a word in German: *Mentalität*—mentality. The term has nothing to do with intellect; it has to do with how you relate to others. Putin's *Mentalität* was to keep his private life private. He wasn't someone who would talk about his family to you just because you were friends or drinking buddies. The opposite was true. He continually kept a wall between people he knew and his family. Putin might have learned this because of Gorbachev. Mikhail Gorbachev took his wife Raisa everywhere—and he was resented for it. In the USSR you didn't bring your wife to official functions. Or, it might just have been Putin's KGB training. An intelligence officer's life is compartmentalized; you don't mix business and family.

Whichever it was, Putin never talked about his parents; he never talked about his wife. I think he mentioned his daughters once or twice, but only to praise their language capabilities. When I think about it now, I can't remember a single occasion where I had the feeling he was telling me anything revealing about his personal past. He would not talk about his problems. You could be his best friend and he'd never mention that he had a problem. He might ask a favor—like installing a blue light and a siren on his car because he needed to get through traffic when he came back Monday mornings from his dacha. Stuff like that he was willing to share. But he'd never tell you his grandmother was lying on her deathbed in the hospital.

Nor would he talk about his role as Sobchak's fixer, although we talked quite a lot about Sobchak. Putin was counting on the fact that Sobchak would someday become either prime minister or even president of Russia, and was probably hoping to accompany him to Moscow. We also never spoke about his days in East Germany. Never. Why? Because it was work; and work was behind the *Mentalität* wall. It wasn't to be discussed. Even when I'd see him in a restaurant, there was none of the waving and 'hail, fellow well-met' stuff. I'd catch his eye and sooner or later he'd come over to the table and say hello.

The other thing about Putin was that he instilled confidence. Not in the larger-than-life manner of a Sobchak or a Yeltsin, but in a competent, reliable, efficient bureaucratty sort of way, and I mean that in the most positive of respects. He exuded quiet, understated competence. There was—surprisingly, now that I think back on it—no evidence whatsoever of the cold-blooded manipulator, the socio-political cutthroat, the swaggering, macho, Napoleonic *Nachalnik* who is now president of Russia.

❖

On this particular November morning in 1992, the situation was perfect for him. He knew all the players and he could be in total control. I entered the Mayor's suite, and was waved into Putin's office by Igor Sechin. The others were already there. Putin glanced up and gave me a quick smile. "Morning, Franz," he said in German, "Ready to go?"

"Absolutely, Mr. Deputy Mayor."

He was all business. "Then let's get to it."

The agenda was straightforward. There were two choices. Either I could work with the Property Fund, which was the Duma and in which case there was no need for this meeting, or I could work with the Property Committee, which was the office of the president.

I looked at Putin, Belyaev, and Glazkov and told them the truth: "Look, I don't make the choices here. You guys are the government, and you've got to decide. Me? I'd be comfortable with either arrangement. My priority is getting rid of GUVD by applying Russian law."

Putin said, "Franz, as we discussed earlier, if it were up to me, I'd go with KUGI."

"Then KUGI. Absolutely." And with that we got down to business. Glazkov had done a short description of my company, which he presented orally to Putin and Belyaev.

"It sounds good," Belyaev said, "But I'll need specifics for Moscow. How much is the Stone Island Company worth? Exactly what does it do? How does it expand its market? Moscow needs all these things so it can make an assessment."

"Then let's get this thing off the ground." Putin tapped a pen on his desktop. "We have a lawyer here in City Hall. Krinsky." He turned toward me and said in German, "Krinsky's a good man—he'll make it work." Then he resumed in Russian. "We'll have him do the forensics. Look over the spreadsheets, evaluate, and then prepare a new contract. It shouldn't take too long."

Putin looked at me. "Franz?"

"My files are ready to go. Anything Krinsky needs he gets."

Putin pushed back from his desk and stood up. "Then it's settled." He shot his cuffs and adjusted his tie. "Good work. Meeting adjourned."

CHAPTER 8

The Discovery of Flight

"Why does GUVD always patrol in threes? Because it takes one to read, one to write, and the last to keep an eye on the two intellectuals." —St. Petersburg KGB Joke

Looking back at it now, I realize that the unruly galaxy that comprised my existence in Russia changed for the better in the year after Leonid Pinchuk's bungled attack on Kamenny Ostrov. Black clouds cleared. The quality of my life improved. The business expanded. My relationship with Vladimir Putin sprouted, developed, and finally flourished.

In truth, some of that change took place because of the supportive press coverage that had ridiculed GUVD's actions and depicted me as a David standing up to the corrupt GUVD Goliath. That's because there were very few individuals in Russia in those days willing to take on GUVD, which was universally known not only for its corruption—the bribes, the skimming, and the shake-downs—but also because GUVD was notorious for throwing people into jail for crimes they hadn't committed. Wrongful convictions were yet another throwback to the box-checking "from each according to his ability, to each according to his need" Soviet era. It was all about quotas. Steel plants, wood processors, state-owned farms, tractor factories, they all had monthly quotas. Whether the tractors worked or the vegetables were rotten was someone else's problem. All anyone cared about was whether the number of tractors or the crates of carrots matched the number on the quota document.

It was the same with law enforcement. GUVD had quotas to fulfill because in the USSR's Utopian worker's paradise there could be—by government edict—no such thing as an unsolved crime. If someone was murdered, someone had to be convicted of that murder. The fact that many of those convicted were innocent didn't matter. The box had been checked. It was yet another reason for ordinary Russians to resent GUVD and for them to instinctively feel good about someone—in this case *moi*—who'd caused the hated GUVD to look stupid and incompetent. And since the consistency of their stupidity hasn't changed, today's St. Petersburg GUVD still has arrest quotas!

My new found celebrity didn't go unnoticed by Smolny, which was how the locals referred to St. Petersburg's City Hall. Indeed, all at once I'd become a 'known quantity', the German guy who GUVD couldn't take over. And things changed. Sure, my first meeting with Putin hadn't gone well at all. But after my appearance on *600 Seconds* I started hearing that the mayor's office was happy with how I'd handled the situation. And not long after that I received a visit from a chap named Mr. Slava Butin, a friend and KGB colleague of Mr. Putin's, who told me straight out that Mr. Putin and his other colleagues in the mayor's office were delighted at the way things had turned out.

"Thanks to you we're all laughing at GUVD," Slava Butin said. "You made Pinchuk look like the ass he is. Smolny couldn't be happier."

Shortly after that my friend from the KGB, Colonel Alex Sibarov—he's the one who'd first warned me about Pinchuk's impending attack—came by Stone Island for a visit. We sat over coffee and laughed about the fact that GUVD was now being investigated and on the defensive.

"Franz," Alex said, "You should start dropping by the KGB offices. I know you still have one or two friends at GUVD, but frankly, there's not much you can do over there anymore. KGB's different—there are possibilities. I've got a couple of colleagues you should meet. Like the guy who runs our counterterrorism stuff—I think you two would get along. And some others as well. Think about it. It'd expand your horizon." And I did think about it, and Sibarov's suggestion did indeed expand my horizon. The only caveat was that I insisted meetings with KGB officials, just like with any other potential customer, should take place on Stone Island. I was independent—and vowed to stay that way.

But there was another post-GUVD major event that improved my quality of life even more than getting to know the KGB: at the end of December, 1992, I'd gotten married to a beautiful Russian woman named Vlada.

I'd known Vlada since shortly after I'd arrived in Leningrad. She'd been recommended to me as a translator by an export manager of Siemens, the German electrical conglomerate. I actually hadn't hired her; a colleague did because she was an outstanding translator. She didn't speak perfect German yet, but her English was super, her appearance was very professional, and she had a talent that far too few interpreters have: she not only got the words right, she also was able to read the cultural context of what was being said. So, she provided me with not just a literal word-for-word translation, but she was also able to tell me exactly what whoever I was speaking to actually *meant*. In business, that's invaluable. And in a short period of time, Vlada became an irreplaceable employee.

Which was tough, because she'd agreed to work for me, but only temporarily. "I'll work for you three months," she'd said, after which it was her plan to move to Europe. To Germany, in fact. But she overstayed those three months more than once.

It all came to a head-at-the-end of 1991, when it became imperative to go and visit some clients in Volgograd.

I sent my sidekick and GUVD liaison Sasha Michailov (in time he'd become my best salesman) to get us on a flight. I said to Vlada, "Please tell Sasha I need three tickets." It was Sasha's responsibility to provide all infrastructure services, including travel, for the joint venture.

An hour later he came back empty-handed. "Can't do it boss. Nothing's available."

I wasn't about to take no for an answer. "Whadda mean nothing's available? There are always tickets available—and if you can't find'em then buy us a goddam airplane. We're due in Volgograd day after tomorrow."

After all, this was Russia. In Russia there were always tickets. You just had to come up with the right price.

Michailov was back half an hour later.

"I got one, boss."

"One what? One ticket? We need three."

"Not tickets—an airplane. You said buy an airplane."

I had not known this previously, but the time it takes for the word "bankruptcy" to detonate inside your brain once you've heard the phrase "buy an airplane" can be measured in milliseconds.

Vlada told me later I'd kept a totally stoic expression on my face.

That may have been. But the truth was, when Michailov told me what he'd done the top of my head almost exploded.

And then Michailov added (and Vlada simultaneously translated), "But I'm sorry, Franz, I couldn't buy the plane. I could only rent it. I hope that's okay."

It was very okay.

Very, very, very okay. He'd probably found something like a twin-engine Beechcraft, or whatever the Russian equivalent thereof might be. Renting was doable.

"What did you rent?"

"Multi-engine jet, Franz. A forty-seater."

The bankruptcy thing exploded in my brain again. Vlada says the noise I made sounded like an idling lawnmower "But-but-but-but-but-but-but..."

Michailov's and Vlada's lips were moving but I couldn't hear either one. At that point the company—me—had about $30,000 cash left in the safe. That amount wouldn't even cover the flight time. I finally managed to blurt out, "Oh my God—I'm bust."

"It's two hundred and fifty dollars." Michailov shook me by the shoulders. "Franz, Franz—two hundred and fifty dollars!"

"I don't give a shit how much the fuel costs, Sasha. That's peanuts. I'm talking about the plane. A 40-seater? Are you out of your fucking mind?"

"For the plane, Franz, and the fuel. And landing fees—everything. Two hundred fifty. Dollars. Cash."

Geezus H. Only in Russia. And only with *valuta*. Cash was indeed king here.

Time to regroup. I paused, gave him a mock-stern look, and said. "Why so expensive?"

It was ten minutes before he stopped laughing.

The result of Sacha's serendipitous action had huge consequences for my company. The incredibly low cost of aircraft rental in Russia, if you had dollars, resulted in a giant leap forward for our marketing and transport logistics. We had instantly and by sheer happenstance discovered the most economic method to travel anywhere in the former Soviet Union. Cheap rented jets allowed us to reach the most remote cities all across Russia's vast landmass and its newly independent republics to the East, and put on equipment, vehicle, and equipment demonstrations. At one point we visited three Siberian cities in a week! We could load two Jeep Cherokees with equipment and a sales/demo team of eight people onto one cargo plane. When we fulfilled customer orders, the shipments were flown directly to the oil and metal producing regions a couple of months later. We flew everything from boots and batons to light trucks and long custom trailers containing mobile crime labs. We even provided VIP charters for Western clients to include a protective detail, supplies, and vehicles. Best of all, we ran circles around potential competitors.

And it was all because I'd told Sacha to buy a plane.

When Michailov left, I said to Vlada, "See, there's always a way to do things around here."

And she said, "Do I have to come with you on this charter airplane?"

It would be the first time she'd be traveling with me. "Of course you have to come. How else can I do business? I can't—not without you." I looked at the confused expression on her face. "Vlada, don't you want to come?"

She looked at me closely. "I don't know, I don't know. I'll have to ask my dad."

The next morning I was working at my desk when a stranger walked into my office unannounced. I looked up at him, startled. My compound was guarded by KGB with instructions to admit no one who didn't have an appointment. My staff on the ground floor knew that nobody was allowed in without my permission—and certainly no one was permitted to come upstairs uninvited. But there he was. A Russian guy, silver haired, athletic and very much looking like a movie actor. Average height, wearing jeans and a sweater and a leather jacket. Probably in his late 40s.

He looked at me for some seconds, then smiled and said, "Hello." Then he turned and left, closing the door behind him.

I followed him, almost catching up as he hit the bottom of the staircase. "Hey—you!"

He never looked back. He walked straight up to Vlada, spoke to her quickly in Russian, and slipped out the front door.

I said, "Vlada?"

"That was my dad, Dima. He told me 'He's okay, you can fly with him.'"

Did Dima know something I didn't? Maybe. Because the beginning of our romance was on that trip to Volgograd, and it's gone on unabated for the last quarter century. And by the way, I still don't know how Dima made it to my office!

❖

We dated all of 1992 and decided to marry in the winter, in Germany. But when I checked, the German authorities told us we had to post Vlada's name on the courthouse wall for a year, just in case she'd been married to someone else before.

In some ways, Germans are stupidly bureaucratic.

So we tried to marry in Russia. But we learned that in Russia, my name would have to be posted for two years, and the paperwork might take longer than that.

I told Vlada, "See, this is a sign from God. He doesn't need us to get married because we're in love anyway."

The look I got from her left no need for translation.

One evening, I happened to mention our problem to Consul General Jack Gosnell over a beer.

He said, "Franz, don't tell anyone you got this from me, but the easiest place in the world to get married is the United States. All you have to do is fly in, go to the Courthouse, show your IDs, pick up a marriage license, and that's it."

So, that's what we did. I had business in St. Louis. My old friends and compadres Jack Gaffigan and Don Strate, both Stone Island trainers and seasoned St. Louis police officers, helped plan and organize the visit of a

Russian police delegation coming in late December. Vlada and I went a week early, flew in a bunch of friends, and had a ceremony in Creve Coeur, Missouri. It was a truly multi-faith and multi-ethnic wedding ceremony. Sigi Herbst, our Lutheran priest, was a German emigrant who'd become an American citizen. As compensation for holding the ceremony Sigi asked for and got a case of Beck's beer! The church was Presbyterian. Vlada did not want to choose between being Jewish or Russian Orthodox. I'm Catholic. Col. Stanley Olchovik, an Agnostic, recited a poem from Sergei Yesenin in Russian in front of an audience made up of Americans, Germans, Russians, Italians, and Swiss. It was a very moving ceremony, followed by a very liquid reception in a Ukrainian restaurant close by.

We even had time to do pre-nups. We had two lawyers: one representing Vlada, one representing me. And the magic question they both asked was: How much money do you owe? I said, "I have no debts." And Vlada said, "I have no debts." And one of the lawyers said, "You guys are the only couple I've ever done this with who have no debts."

So, 1993 had indeed begun well. Vlada was a beautiful bride. My contacts at the KGB were expanding; GUVD was for the most part out of the picture at Kamenny Ostrov, and the business was growing. St. Petersburg was to be the site of the 1994 Goodwill Games, which were conceived by Ted Turner, the brash, loud-talking American entrepreneur who owned CNN Cable News. Turner thought the Goodwill Games could improve U.S.-USSR relations during the Cold War after the U.S. boycotted the 1980 Olympics in Moscow over the Soviet invasion of Afghanistan. Turner's initial Goodwill Games had been held in Moscow in 1986. St. Petersburg would be the venue for his 1994 Games.

For me, they presented a number of opportunities. Foreign business was already expanding in St Petersburg, but security wasn't. There were robberies, there were murders, and foreign enterprises were often the targets. In fact, St. Petersburg, with its magnificent architecture, its treasure-laden Hermitage, and its reputation as a hub of Russian literature also had the reputation, deserved or not, as being the crime capital of Russia. I'd already received numerous inquiries from western companies in St. Petersburg that were looking for someone to help them with their security concerns. And James Wellman, the Regional Security Officer at the U.S. Consulate General; told me he was looking for a private security company to guard Consulate perimeter.

He asked me, "Could you supply us with the right personnel?"

Of course I could. Wellman's query cemented it for me: a private security company that worked with individuals, corporations, consulates, and events would do well. So I started one—and it took off.

At the same time, I realized the Games would also put additional pressure on the KGB, because while GUVD was responsible for certain aspects of local security, the police did not do dignitary protection or counterterrorism. And the more I interacted with KGB the more I realized that its counterterrorist and hostage rescue capabilities were next to zero. They had elements of special operations units—they called them their *Teams Special*. But to be honest, the KGB unit was no more *Special* than GUVD's OMON riot police. Their equipment was inappropriate for the job. They didn't even have the proper vehicles: *Team Special* traveled in old military trucks with a top speed of 40 km an hour—that's 24 mph.

What the St. Petersburg KGB office needed was a western-style SWAT team, trained and equipped no different from any American police SWAT unit in such cities as New York, Los Angeles, Miami, or St. Louis. I'd already spoken to one of the honchos at KGB, Colonel Kuznetsov, about the idea and he was very interested in the possibilities I was offering.

So, I discovered, was Vladimir Putin.

Putin and I had our first one-on-one dinner at Stone Island early in 1993. We'd seen one another at various functions over the past year, and of course I'd been at his office for meetings, especially after I started dealing with the Property Committee and KUGI. We'd actually became friendly, almost collegial. Between Putin's German 'thing'—the language, the culture, the gestalt—and our similar take on the local political situation, I thought we'd developed a pretty simpatico relationship.

So, shortly after Vlada and I got back from the States, I called him. Sechin put me through immediately. We spoke in German. "Herr Putin, it's Franz Sedelmayer. Why don't you come over to Kamenny Ostrov for dinner tomorrow night? I'll do a Bavarian pork roast for you, and some fresh Bavarian beer. There's a lot to talk about."

He said, "Let's do that. Sure."

He got to Kamenny Ostrov about five thirty. I poured him a beer straight from the keg. He congratulated Vlada and me on our marriage and asked how the U.S. had been.

"Everything's great. We really showed the Russian contingent some interesting stuff. I brought some of it back and I'm having the rest shipped over. You'd like it."

"Can I take a look?"

"Sure." We walked through the display area. He picked up one of the samples I'd unpacked, a two-foot Monadnock polycarbonate baton with a side handle. He played with it. He was a martial arts guy—actually a pretty good martial arts guy—and he knew instinctively how to use the weapon, jabbing, parrying, poking, and striking with it.

He put it down, not even breathing hard. "Nice piece of kit."

"They're super. Cutting edge." I watched as he fingered a pair of hinged handcuffs. He shook them at me. "Wish we'd had some of these during the putsch."

I showed him a set of new plastic flex-i-cuffs and demonstrated how easy they were to put on, watching his reaction. "But these would have been a lot easier to carry!"

"Yes they would," he laughed. He looked at a German police riot shield. It, like the baton, was made of polycarbonate. On its interior side it had a shock-absorbing pad that ran vertically beneath the grip.

"Pick it up, Vladimir."

He did. "Great weight. Much lighter than I thought." He moved it around as if he were being jostled. "Well balanced." He hefted it, swung it aggressively, then swiftly pulled it up in front of his face. "Nice."

"Hold it right there for a sec." I grabbed a three and a half foot long, glass fiber reinforced riot baton and swung it at the shield as forcefully as I could. "Feel anything?"

He lowered the shield just enough so he could see me. "Not a thing. Wow!"

"Okay—here I come. No mercy!" As he raised the shield I came down hard, then changed grip and held the baton like a baseball bat, swinging as fiercely as I could.

Behind the shield I heard Putin laughing. He was having a hell of a good time.

"You're having too much fun. I was too easy on you!" I swung even harder. *Bam!-Bam!-Bam!-Bam!-Bam!*

I finally dropped the baton. It clattered to the floor. I'd beaten the shit out of the shield but it showed no evidence of the blows.

Putin lowered the shield, swung it around, and examined the rubber coated polycarbonate shock absorbing plate built beneath the handles. It had completely neutralized the strikes' impact. "It's crazy—I didn't feel a thing." He began laughing. "I thought you were going to give me the beating of my life, but..." He put the shield back on the demo table. "That's incredible."

"I've got two more toys you gotta see." I showed him a full size replica of a Heckler & Koch MP5 submachine gun. It was made of red polycarbonate and weighed exactly the same as a real MP5 with loaded magazine. It had the three-point HK sling with a front handle integrated weapon white light/laser designator combo on it. Perfect for basic SWAT training.

And I'd saved the best for last: an assortment of automotive running lights. I had bar lights that go on the roofs of police cars, and also the ones that go behind the grille. I turned them all on for him. He was most impressed with the multi-tone electronic siren and the public address system, allowing the driver to communicate without rolling down the windows.

He was blown away. Sure he was: they had nothing like this anywhere in Russia. "Y'know what? You need a set of these for your car."

He laughed. "I'd never be late for a meeting."

Putin walked back across the display area and picked up his beer. He looked at me in a way he'd never done before. It was, thinking back, a look of respect. I think perhaps that was the point when he realized I wasn't just another businessman trying to make a buck, but a professional—someone who not only knew how to sell equipment, but who knew how to use it and could therefore understand his clients' needs.

He tilted his mug in my direction. "*Prost,* Franz. Thanks for the demo. And for the suggestion about the light for my car."

"*Prost.*" I raised my mug toward his. "Just let me know and I'll get it done."

Our conversation grew serious over dinner. Putin wasn't one of those empty-headed 'hail fellow well-met' guys. He wasn't given to small talk. So, pretty soon the subject turned to my new relationship with the Property Committee. I was still in negotiation with them, although we'd handed over a huge pile of paperwork to the lawyer Krinsky, and I'd even brought over my company accountant Mike Johnson from Little Rock, so we could provide whatever information the lawyer needed about our books and finances.

I put my fork down. "Volodya, you know that I can't make this new arrangement work without your involvement, and of course Mayor Sobchak's, too."

"Understood, Franz."

Of course he did. "So what do I need to do to make this work?"

"Hmm." Putin chewed on a forkful of pork. "My guess would be," he said slowly, "that to make this arrangement work—we're talking KUGI, the transfer of shares and everything else—that you, and I'm talking about the Stone Island company here, that you would have to show in some concrete fashion how loyal you are to St. Petersburg, and in doing so demonstrate how you've become an integral part of the city's life and its bloodstream."

It was a much friendlier version of what Putin had asked me at our first meeting. Back then he'd put it bluntly: "What have *you* ever done for the city?"

This evening, it was, "So, what are you willing to do for us now?"

Of course, I knew that *he* knew that I'd had a meeting with the KGB's Colonel Kuznetsov and discussed the possibility of a SWAT team for the local office. And knowing Putin, he'd probably talked to Kuznetsov shortly after I'd invited him to dinner. So, I asked if he had.

"I did, Franz, and I think it's a great idea. It's something I can sell to the Mayor; it's something we can work on together. It's something that will do the City a lot of good, especially with the Goodwill Games coming next year."

He put his fork down. "What kind of budget were you thinking of?"

I'd given the funding some thought. "I'm working with a rough concept of a 25-man team. So, between training—bringing trainers from the States, equipment, vehicles, uniforms, weapons, etcetera, the whole package will come in somewhere around a million dollars."

"That's big money for you, Franz."

And it was, too. The St. Petersburg City Police's budget for one year was only slightly less than a million dollars. But if that was what it would take to cement my roots in Russia and not have to worry about any more 'privatization', it would be worth every penny.

"So," he said, how do you want to do this?"

I put my fork down. "I'll create a legal entity for the SWAT team, and I trust that you'll make all the necessary arrangements, so I can transfer SWAT to the government and take the half of Kamenny Ostrov that GUVD held and transfer them to KUGI, which means I'm tied to Moscow, not the local government anymore. Meanwhile, you'll have to trust me to bring in everything we need, get the personnel trained, and get the unit up and running. If all goes well, you'll have a SWAT team by the fall—almost a year ahead of the Goodwill Games."

"Sounds good to me." Putin looked at me. "Can we shake on it?"

"Absolutely."

It was that easy. And Putin and I could seal the deal with a handshake because Putin was a man of his word and so was I. Unlike so many Russians who lied out of habit, if Putin said he was going to do something, it got done. Putin had a reputation for getting things done. In fact, the one thing I have to emphasize about Vladimir Putin, despite all the nasty stuff that happened later, is that Vladimir Putin was always a man of his word. Whatever he said he would do, he would do it. And if he couldn't get it done, or it was politically impossible to do, he would say so up front.

It was a positive aspect of his character that I found very...German.

And so from that viewpoint I can say accurately that Putin and I had a good working relationship. We weren't the best of friends in the sense that we would go to the sauna together or hang out on weekends watching sports. Nor would I be invited to his house.

But for me it was perfect. I didn't need to spend my weekends with him. We both, I think, had much the same attitude: that a certain amount of distance was healthy. And when we met, neither one of us ever had the feeling that the other guy was trying to rip him off or take advantage.

So, I always looked at our relationship as an amicable professional one—a courteous, symbiotic business friendship in which you don't mind spending time with someone because you share common interests and enjoy a mutually respectful, intellectually challenging connection. Those sorts of business relationships are common in the West. But they were largely unknown in Russia simply because in Russia, business relationships—the practice of free enterprise—was normally all about thievery, stealing, and lying.

But it wasn't that way with Putin. In St. Petersburg in the early 1990s, when people had problems, they went to Putin and he'd actually help. Maybe it was his KGB training, or the 'brotherhood' of the security services, but he was fair with me and he consistently helped his colleagues get post-KGB work, and he moved his close friends along as he himself rose. Igor Sechin is one prime example, of course. But there were a lot of others, most of whom never made it to Moscow when Putin went in 1996. And he never, so far as I knew, ever took money from any of the people he helped. Never took a cut or a kickback, which was all too common in those days.

One example about six months later would be a KGB officer named Alexander Sipchenko. Sasha was an Afghanistan vet who had served with Igor Sechin in Mozambique. He, like Sechin, was fluent in Portuguese, and they were both close to Putin. When Sasha retired from the KGB, Putin sent him to me. And as it happened, I knew about a certain job opening and I found him employment as the Security Chief of the Credit Lyonnais Bank in St. Petersburg, where my company held a security contract.

Unlike someone like Pinchuk, Vladimir Putin never thought of asking Sasha Sipchenko for a finder's fee or a piece of his Credit Lyonnaise salary.

And Putin knew the same about me.

Because we were men of our word.

Now, Putin stood up from the table and reached across it.

We shook hands. I said, "To the SWAT Team. And the KUGI transfer. It's a done deal. They'll happen."

"Yes they will." Putin's eyes twinkled. "Perhaps we should seal the deal with a beer."

CHAPTER 9

Love, Death, and Security in Russia
"Love to faults is always blind…"—William Blake

Early in the spring of 1993, in the midst of the seemingly endless negotiations to transfer GUVD's shares in the Stone Island Company to KUGI, which represented the Property Committee associated with the Russian President's office, UdPRF, I got a call from James Wellman, who was the Regional Security Officer at the American Consulate General in St. Petersburg. RSOs are the principal security attachés and advisors to chiefs of mission at U.S. embassies and consulates. They interact with local law enforcement and the local intelligence services on matters of embassy or consulate security and from time to time they advise local branches of U.S. companies on matters of security.

They also oversee the locals who guard the perimeter of the consulate as well as the Marines who provide internal security. In the old USSR, the St. Petersburg mission had no private perimeter security guards. In their stead were KGB operatives dressed in GUVD uniforms. Their job wasn't protecting the consulate but monitoring who went in and came out of the building, 24/7/365. They could also, within seconds, close the street down and stop all access if, for example, a political activist, a *refusenik*, or even a diplomat carrying documents on which they wanted to lay their hands sought to enter the consulate.

One interesting point: KGB control of the space surrounding diplomatic missions has not changed since my arrival in Leningrad in 1989, and more importantly the U.S. has in all those years not managed to 'up its own game' to deal with the Russians forcefully, even as the KGB has grown brasher and more aggressive under Vladimir Putin's presidency. As recently as June of 2016, according to the *New York Times*, KGB personnel stationed outside the U.S. Embassy compound in Moscow "attacked and beat up a U.S. diplomat who was trying to enter the compound, according to four U.S. officials who were briefed on the incident."

❖

I picked up the phone. "Franz, it's James Wellman. "Got a question for you. Do you provide physical security?"

"Nope. Do not."

"Why not?"

"Because I don't think there's money in it."

There was a pause on the line. "Oh, really?"

"Well yes, James, as far as I'm concerned. I don't see any money in providing physical security. You're basically paying minimum wage for people to stand around and do nothing. I started with two people. Currently I've got eight guys on three shifts here at Kamenny Ostrov guarding the compound, driving my family, and watching over anyone I bring to town. Yes, they cost me, but it's not a major expense."

"Well, I have to come up with a budget for physical security here at the consulate, Franz—and believe me it'll be considerable. So I think you should reconsider."

"Okay. For you I'll take another look." But it didn't make sense to me to build a security company from the ground up. First of all I'd developed quite a client list. We were selling police equipment to GUVD and KGB units from Estonia to Kazakhstan. We were equipping the Russian Presidential Guard Service and the KGB and its successor agencies. I'd branched into security planning for such projects as the American Hospital of St. Petersburg and setting up a transport service that ran from Finland to the Russian Federation and the new CIS—the 15-member Commonwealth of Independent States that made up a significant part of the old Soviet Union. My contracts ran into the millions of dollars, but the company was lean—I took people on only as I needed them. Security work can be labor-intensive. I wasn't convinced it would make good business sense, all of which I laid out for the RSO.

And, despite which, James said "I believe you should reconsider."

"Still doesn't sound right to me."

There was a pause on the line. Then he said, "Okay—if that's how you feel. I think you're wrong. But whatever the case, can you at least help me out just this once?"

"For you, sure. What's the story?"

"There's a guy who's the office manager at Ernst & Young. He has a problem in the St. Petersburg office. It's security related and I'd like you to talk to him."

"Henk? Henk Vankempen?"

"That's him."

I knew Henk Vankempen. He was a Dutch national. I knew him because he showed up at the monthly luncheons of the American Business Association I hosted at Stone Island and was a regular at our Beer Calls. He was in his late thirties, tall, blond, blue eyes and athletic. He always dressed impeccably. Because he was the local head of the accounting practice, he was usually followed around by a good looking young assistant in a tight dress. It appeared that her job was to carry his first-generation cell phone, which was the size and weight of a brick.

"I know the guy, James. I'll give him a call and take care of it."

And I would. Ernst & Young was a Big Fish. Headquartered in London, it was one of the Big Four accounting firms with roughly 125,000 employees scattered all over the globe. I made the call.

Henk's problem turned out to be typically Russian in that it was probably organized crime and/or gang related. It turned out he was being blackmailed. They were trying to extort him for $30,000.

I met with Henk and asked him to spell out exactly what had happened.

He told me it started when he'd had an auto accident. He'd been driving along when the car in front of him had stopped suddenly. Probably, Henk admitted, he hadn't been paying enough attention and so he'd rear-ended it.

Then, one of the passengers claimed they'd been injured, and the people involved were demanding $30,000 from him or they'd make trouble with the authorities and Ernst & Young. They were being very insistent, and one of the Russians had made a veiled threat of violence.

Henk said, "Could you please help me, Franz?" He obviously was very nervous, because he didn't know what was happening to him and felt powerless to deal with it.

"Of course I will."

Henk was a nice individual and very good at his job. But he was naive. He'd been the victim of a panic stop scam. That's what it's called and it's one of the oldest automotive scams around. A car full of people pulls in front of you. One of the passengers keeps an eye on you and the second you take your eyes off the road they slam on the brakes and you to smash into them. But Henk had no idea he'd been scammed. Nor had he any awareness of how bad some of the locals could be; how manipulative and how ruthless. Still, I wanted to make sure that he was on the level. So, I called his boss at Ernst & Young, a U.S. national, and asked what the guy knew about Henk's situation.

Oh, he's on the level," his boss said. "But my guess is that his young girlfriend—her name's Oxana something-or-other—is somehow involved with this mess."

That was noteworthy. Henk had never mentioned a girlfriend to me. I asked the boss what he knew about her.

"Only that she's Russian, not from around here, and Henk is head over heels smitten with her."

"Do you know her?"

"Not really—just in passing. But the few times I've met her, there's always been something...not right. I think she's a gold digger."

"It could be true love," I told him. "But let me look into the possibility that your instincts are accurate."

The first thing I did was take Henk out of the equation by making him inaccessible to the people trying to extort him. I took three of my KGB people, got him out of his apartment at three in the morning and moved him into a safe location—a foreign-owned hotel where I had connections. We went in the back way, out of sight of the security cameras and directly up to a room I'd rented for him under an alias.

So far, so good.

But Henk was relatively new to the Russian game and totally infatuated with Oxana. And, against my advice, he insisted on calling her on his cell. "Just one call," he promised.

It didn't take long until she started calling him. She wasn't in St. Petersburg—she was somewhere near Moscow. She called him repeatedly, raising the emotional stakes with each call, telling him she was in trouble because of him.

That was bad enough. Worse was that Oxana was trying her best to find out exactly where he was. She was eliciting. That was a trigger so far as I was concerned. He'd told her he was in a safe location and she didn't have to worry, but all she wanted to know was where he was—street address and room number.

Then the emotional stuff began to ratchet up. Oxana started telling Henk people were looking for her; that she was in physical danger. Her calls got more and more panic-stricken.

Henk let me listen in, holding the big cell phone between us. I had to agree: her voice was pretty damn hysterical.

For his part, Henk was now totally frantic. After three or four more calls he got hold of me. "You have to rescue Oxana, Franz."

"What's the problem now?"

"Now she thinks her father is going to kill her. She says he's got a shotgun. She says he's been threatening her."

It was nuts—there was no motive for Oxana's father to act that way. In fact, only a couple of days previously Oxana had confided to Henk how her father was protecting her from the people involved in the auto accident. The more Henk talked, the more the whole thing sounded like a setup to me. But the only way to prove it was to go get his girlfriend, put her on ice, and start dealing with her story, either substantiating it, or unpeeling it layer by layer.

That, however, wasn't what I told Henk. I told him I agreed: Oxana needed help and I'd immediately send my people to extract her safely. Which is what I did. I dispatched a pair of my KGB guys in a car. They picked Oxana up in her hometown, a village near Moscow, and brought her back to St. Petersburg with no problem.

But not to Henk's hotel. I made sure she didn't have a phone, then my people took her to the sauna house on Kamenny Ostrov. It was comfortable, it was warm, and it was guarded.

I told her, "This is for your protection." And it was. But it was also of course for Henk's protection.

And then we spent the next three or so days debriefing her.

She started out frightened. But after about 48 hours she became obstinate and defensive. All she wanted, she told me, was out.

I responded curtly. "That'd be a really bad idea. Ernst and Young's worried something could happen to you. But you are free to leave!"

She said, "They don't have to worry, everything will be cool just so long as they pay."

That response was precisely what I'd been waiting for. It opened the door for me to ask how she knew what she knew.

"Why don't they have to worry? Why will everything be cool?" I bore down on her. I'm physically not the biggest guy in the world. I'm just under six feet tall, but I can be intimidating when I want to be. And at that point I wanted to be just a little bit intimidating.

It worked. It didn't take long after that to unravel her story. Oxana may have been cunning but she wasn't smart. And before long she provided me with information that allowed us to establish a link between her and the gangsters who were trying to extort money from Henk. In fact, she finally admitted that she'd been in on it from the get-go and that she was going to get a cut of the money.

"But I still do care for him," she whined through her tears. "I do. It isn't just about the money."

I called Henk's boss. "You were spot on. It was a classic honey trap. They targeted Henk because they thought Ernst & Young wouldn't give a second thought about paying extortion money if he asked you to."

"But that's not our policy, and Henk knows it."

"Yeah, but the bad guys didn't, and neither did the girl. What they *did* understand was exactly how to push Henk's buttons. And they'll probably come after him when they don't get paid."

"I can deal with that—we'll transfer him back to the Netherlands so he'll be out of harm's way."

It made perfect sense. The company couldn't afford to have a vulnerable individual working in St. Petersburg—or anywhere else in Russia. But that was a minor matter. What was important was that the extortion plan had been foiled and Henk was going to be safe.

We moved Henk to a second safe house. I told him it was all over—that it had been a setup by Oxana and her Russian pals. I showed him the evidence.

He told me he didn't care.

I was flabbergasted. What no one, especially me, had counted on was the fact that Henk had totally fallen for Oxana. He didn't give a damn that she'd played him for a sucker. She was a great love of his life and he was going to stick by her, no matter what. And he did.

The denouement of this story does not turn out well. Henk refused to be transferred out of Russia. I got a call from his boss who said the Dutchman had just told him something to the effect of, "I'm not leaving the country; I'm not leaving my girlfriend. I'm staying here. I'll quit. That way nobody can extort me because I won't have access to any money."

When I heard what he was planning I immediately rushed over to Henk's apartment. I sat him down. "Henk, do me a favor: don't quit. Take some time off. Clear your head. Or if you feel so strongly about Oxana, then take her with you to Holland and go back to work. Just don't ruin your life over this."

But he didn't listen. He quit Ernst & Young. He stayed in St. Petersburg. And he married Oxana.

The extortionists didn't come after him. But about a year later he was found dead. He'd hanged himself in Oxana's apartment.

When I heard the news I called my old friend, Dr. Andreev, the chief pathologist of St. Petersburg and asked how Henk had died. Was it self-inflicted or was there something suspicious?

Andreev said he didn't know, and wouldn't: Oxana had insisted that no post-mortem examination take place.

The widow Oxana collected his life insurance, hung around St. Petersburg for a little while cruising the local bars, and then she disappeared.

So, was Henk's death suicide? Maybe. Was it murder? Certainly murder wasn't out of the question.

Was it sad and unnecessary? Yes. Undeniably.

Love and death in Russia.

Not long after the Ernst & Young episode, I was hosting a luncheon of the American Business Association at Kamenny Ostrov when a nicely dressed Frenchman introduced himself to me. His name was Jean-Luc Julien, and he said he was the deputy-general manager of Banque Credit Lyonnais Russie headquartered in our town. He had a very Mediterranean look, not tall, slightly overweight and a broad, friendly smile. He smoked cigarillos.

He and I, as well as his wife Marlene, a German emigrant from Los Angeles who also worked for the bank, became close friends.

"I wonder," Jean-Luc asked, "if you'd be interested in taking a security contract from us."

Enquiries like this do not come out of the blue. I looked at the Frenchman and asked, "So, how did you know to ask me that question?"

"I asked because I know Jimmy Falls at the American Consulate and he suggested I speak with you."

"Really? What did he say?"

"Jimmy said 'Franz is the only guy in that line of work who doesn't take shit from anybody and he's loyal to the bone.' So if that's the case, you're our guy."

I was flattered. Jimmy Falls (his name is an alias) was the CIA base chief. I walked Jean-Luc over to a corner of the room where we could speak in private and I asked him for his story.

It turned out the Frenchman had an interesting background. He was *un Français* of course, originally from Montpellier. But as a youngster he'd emigrated to the United States where he'd joined the Army. Ultimately, the Army posted him to Germany and after he left service he'd stayed in Europe. Because he was multi-lingual, he was hired by Paris-based Credit Lyonnais, France's largest bank, as part of its Export Enterprise Division.

Recently, under the patronage of Mayor Anatoly Sobchak, Credit Lyonnais had secured the very first license allowing a foreign bank to open in St. Petersburg (the second had gone to Dresdner Bank with the help of Vladimir Putin). Credit Lyonnais had appointed Jean-Luc as deputy-general manager which also put him in charge of security.

His problem was theft. Credit Lyonnais had obtained an impressive property on the Nevsky Prospekt, a very prominent Belle Époque building that they were in the process of renovating. The bank branch would be on the ground floor. A separate entrance would lead to the second floor, which would hold a private VIP banking area and a full-service gourmet restaurant with stairs that led to a huge wine cellar right next to the vault in the basement. The upper floors would hold offices as well as apartments for the resident managers and staff and their families.

But the renovation was in limbo. The problem, Jean-Luc explained, was that all the materials, from the concrete to the wiring, flooring, trim, fuses, all the fixtures, right down to the circuit boxes to the closed-circuit TV cameras and bullet-proof glass for windows—all of it had to be imported. Some components came from Finland; others from Italy, or Germany. The exquisite antique furniture, the paintings, sculptures, crystal, and the china all came directly from Paris. Everything was shipped in containers and brought to the construction site. But currently, security was lacking. And so the Russian workers had started stealing.

As Jean-Luc put it, "Monsieur Sedelmayer, it is as if they consider our storage containers their private hardware store."

The Russian workers would, he said, make off with power tools and supplies—whatever they needed—then go away for the weekend and use the stolen items to fix up their dachas or *kommunalkas*. None of the tools or supplies would, of course, ever be returned.

It was, he said, like a permanent slow leak. "At least it isn't as if they were stealing whole containers."

And then he thought about what he'd just said and slapped his forehead like a typical Frenchman. "Oh, my God they *did*."

"Did what?"

"They stole the entire contents out of a 10-meter container—every one of the light fixtures we were going to use for the bank. Every single one. The damn container was completely emptied out overnight. And nobody saw a thing."

But that, Jean-Luc said, was not the pattern. Normally, it was small stuff: wood trim, boxes of screws and nails, flooring, tools.

Lately, it had been tiles. "We had a container of tiles shipped in. They're expensive, ornate handmade Italian tiles, *Cotto d'Este*, which we brought for the upstairs bathrooms and kitchens. But the workers steal them to re-do *their* bathrooms."

Because of the pilferage, he explained, the contractors couldn't finish the tiling, and by the time a new container of tiles arrived it would be four to six weeks.

"It is crazy," Jean-Luc said. "Madness. We are way behind schedule. And why?" He gave me a Gallic shrug. "Why? Because we're hemorrhaging." He frowned. "Monsieur Sedelmayer, something has to be done—and soon. We need a comprehensive security plan. And so Jimmy Falls, he suggested you."

Jean-Luc was correct about a comprehensive security plan. Even after the pilferage problem had been solved there was the bank itself. Once it opened, the threat level would be relatively high. It hadn't taken Jean-Luc much time to realize that St. Petersburg was dangerous on any number of levels. The police and much of the government were corrupt; organized crime was everywhere; thievery was commonplace and kickbacks were expected. The bank, simply because it was a bank and had extensive cash operations (this *WAS* Russia, after all), would become a prime target. And he'd need help keeping it safe and its staff and customers secure.

The result of my conversation with Jean-Luc was that within a matter of days, Credit Lyonnais flew the head of its Export Division to St. Petersburg, he and I negotiated a contract and signed it. The Kamenny Ostrov Company was now officially in the bank protection business.

It would not be an insignificant undertaking. The bank itself was of course a natural target for criminals. But its expatriate staff and the staff families were also targets for potential kidnappings or extortion by organized crime. The site would therefore need 'hardening'. The Russian staff was also vulnerable as we feared recruitment by local mobsters to obtain customer data. So, background checks and vigilance became another important aspect. Security protocols would include protecting the bank building, escorting the wives and kids around town—going shopping, to school, and so on, providing security for visiting VIPs, and also providing an armed escort for the bank's couriers to and from the airport. I even added a 10-man quick reaction team armed with automatic weapons, shotguns, and pistols as a second line of defense available 24/7.

It was a huge responsibility that would ultimately require 20 of my people on the job every single day. That meant lots of uniforms—fresh ones on a regular basis, which had to be ordered. It meant vehicles that were easily identifiable and whose appearance told onlookers, "SECURITY—don't mess with us."

And there were other perhaps picayune, but nonetheless important details to consider as well. For example, in the early 1990s, deodorant was not something that could be commonly found in Russia. Lack of deodorant combined with irregular bathing resulted in—to be blunt about it—

smelly security guards. So, I made sure that not only did we have sufficient clean, pressed uniforms so that our people would look sharp every day, but I made sure we brought in plenty of deodorant from Finland.

What I didn't count on was that one of my shift managers would treat the deodorant as if it was gold. He never passed spray cans out to each guard. Instead he'd line them up shirtless, order them to raise their arms as if they were surrendering, then march down the line and spray each one individually. It was typical Russian behavior. Besides, it was fun to watch.

But bank guards, drivers, and a QRF would all come later. For the moment, pilferage and theft from the Credit Lyonnais construction site were the immediate problems. Until they were stopped, the renovation would move at a virtual crawl. It was pretty straightforward. I had construction site guards, and I had shift managers. And the guards, by the end of the first day, had caught a couple of the workers carrying materials and tools off the site. They took the culprits to the management of the construction company, which was French. And the French construction manager, a nice enough guy I guess, wagged his finger at the workers and said something to the effect of, "Guys, c'mon, if you, Ivan, or you, Sergei, need to borrow some tools from the site all you have to do is come to us and ask. Just remember it's not appropriate to take stuff without permission."

And Ivan and Sergei told him, "Sorry, boss, this won't happen again" and they left with the tools.

And guess what? A couple of days later, there was Ivan, leaving the site with a bunch of tools and a roll of electrical wiring. And my guards took Ivan back to the French manager, and Monsieur Manager slapped his wrist and told him, "Don't do it again, Ivan."

Well, a couple of days later they caught Ivan again. And they caught

Sergei, and Kiril, and Pyotr, and Vasily, and Nikolai, and—well, you get the idea. And every time my guards turned one of the thieves in to the manager, the manager repeated the 'don't do it again' mantra and let the guy go.

After a couple of weeks of this my shift chief came to me and complained. "It's the French," he said. "They're nice people but they have no idea how to get anything done. All they do is catch and release. That ain't going to stop the problem, boss."

I looked at him and said, "So?"

"I'm sure we can fix the problem, but I'd like to handle this in my own way."

"You're the on-site shift manager. You do what you think is best."

Ten days later Jean-Luc came to me, a big smile on his face. "Monsieur Sedelmayer, I can report that theft has dropped precipitously," he said, "It's actually declining daily. We're getting close to being back on schedule."

I said, "That's great news, Jean-Luc."

He looked at me. "How on earth did you do it? We've been trying for months."

"Honestly, I don't know. I let my shift managers deal with it, because they're on-site and it's up to them to solve the problems. I'll check."

So I called my guys and asked them to come up to my office. When they arrived I pointed at Jean-Luc and said, "Monsieur Julien is very happy with what you've accomplished about the pilferage and theft."

That brought a smile to their faces. "Thanks, boss."

I pointed at the VP. "Monsieur Julien wants to know how you did it."

My shift manager was named Lyosha. "Boss," he said, "you know how ineffective the French were—sorry, Monsieur Julien, but it's true. Your guys would tell the workers 'don't do it' over and over. But there weren't any consequences. Maybe you didn't realize it, sir, but that kind of approach doesn't work here in Russia."

The Frenchman gave Lyosha a quizzical look. "So how did you handle things?"

"We told Ivan, 'don't steal anymore,'" Lyosha said. "We told him once. And the next time we caught him stealing, well, somehow he fell down the stairs." He paused. "And *that* worked. It worked good. Everybody got the message and now nobody's stealing."

Jean-Luc's eyes went wide. He looked at me, his expression reflecting shock and awe. "I didn't hear that," he said. "*Pas un mot*—not one single word of it."

I said, "Me neither." But I said it with a mile-wide grin on my face. Then I made a big show of pulling a note book out of my pocket, and in letters big enough for Jean-Luc to see I wrote: "REMINDER: MORE SENSITIVITY TRAINING FOR THE GUARDS!!!"

CHAPTER 10

Nelson Mandelas, the Love Boat, and Organized Crime

"One of the biggest lies in the world is that crime doesn't pay. Obviously crime pays—or there'd be no crime."
—G. Gordon Liddy

Between 1993 and 1994 I probably could have found work as a juggler because I had almost a dozen balls in the air simultaneously. I was building up the security company and finding clients, dealing with the renovation and subsequent opening of Banque Credit Lyonnais Russie, and recruiting, outfitting and training a group of young American expats for James Wellman's successor to employ as a perimeter security detail for the U.S. Consulate. I was expanding my police supply business in the Independent Republics; I was in constant negotiation with KUGI in order to effect a satisfactory end to the Stone Island Company joint venture with GUVD, because the Russian government was becoming increasingly centralized around the Office of President Boris Yeltsin; I even had short stint as the Vice President of the St. Petersburg City Security Fund. Did I add that my son Daniel, whom I call Danushka, was also born in that time frame? And as if all of that wasn't enough, I also had to design and implement a training package for the KGB SWAT team I'd promised to Vladimir Putin. My BFF the Deputy Mayor wanted the team ready to go by September and I wasn't about to let him down.

Making the SWAT team not only a reality but an effective tactical unit took a lot more than buying equipment and vehicles. It was finding exactly the right stuff and providing the right instructors for the various training segments we held over a three month period.

To find the instructors, I called Stanley Olchovik and he brought in some of the former operators who'd served in Berlin Detachment "A", the clandestine Special Forces unit Stanley had commanded years earlier. My friend Jack Gaffigan recruited others from the St. Louis Police Department and the Missouri State Highway Patrol. And by chance I ran into a guy by the name of Dennis LaDucer, who was the Deputy Chief of the Orange County California Sheriff's Department. He was visiting St. Petersburg because Orange County ran an informal exchange program with the Russians: Russians would come with their kids to California and subsequently they would invite some of the Deputy Sheriffs to Leningrad. Dennis recruited three of his deputies for me. All in all, I had just under a dozen Americans, all of them with extensive SWAT and special operations experience as my GRAD training cadre.

Finding the right stuff also made for difficult choices because Russian and Western tactics were miles apart. For example, American SWAT teams used shotguns for breaching; Russians didn't. Russians used AKS-74U automatic rifles shooting a 5.45x39mm round for just about everything. In fact, most of the Russian training went something to the effect of "Break in, kill everybody, then leave."

Many Western European and U.S. SWAT teams and special-operations units used short-barreled shotguns for breaching and Heckler & Koch MP5s for entry, Glock, H&K, or Sig-Sauer pistols in 9mm as side arms, and—in the U.S. at least—Remington 700 series bull-barreled rifles in 7.62x51 for precision shooting. I selected Remington 870 pump-action shotguns, Glock 9mm pistols, .357 Magnum revolvers from Smith & Wesson, and Sako rifles—very accurate precision weapons from Finland, which ultimately became the choice of Russia's Presidential Guard Service. I didn't use lasers as I could not get the proper U. S. export licenses issued, but some of the weapons would be equipped with white light. The trainees, some of whom had also worked for us, all came from the KGB's Ninth Directorate which had experience in VIP protection, so they were already trained in some of the basic skills.

Our training regimen was unconventional, too. I didn't want to do one long course, but divided everything into short specialty segments. I wanted to change the way the 25 selectees looked at problem-solving, tactics, and performance. So, we worked on the basics: approach, setup, breaching, and room clearing and how the shotgun was indispensable for breaching. We taught them about speed, stealth, and surprise. We improved their snap shooting, we showed them tactical loading, all done in short, comprehensible building blocks. In other words, as one of the St. Louis Police trainers put it, "We're making this stuff cop-proof."

We also introduced a couple of special operations tactics Russian law enforcement and even KGB's executive protection crews had never done before. We taught them to rappel from rooftops, just the way SAS did when it took down the Iranian Embassy at Princes Gate in London in 1979. And we taught them how to fast-rope out of a helicopter, which is something that elite military units were doing but very few police departments utilized. And at the end of the day—or in our case at the end of just over three months—what we got was a pretty damn good SWAT team.

Both City Hall and the Big House totally loved it. And one of the reasons they did was because the GRAD team was sharp in looks as well as capabilities. The everyday Russian cop was a mess. Officers had no clothing allowance and what meager uniforms and kit was supplied to them was usually in very short supply. Most had only one or two uniforms and they had to supply their own shoes and wet-weather gear as well.

"I haven't been to Russia since the day I left. But I've thought about Russia every day since."

Franz J. Sedelmayer

2015, In Irschenhausen, Germany.

Franz J. Sedelmayer

1988
Photo session in my Munich showroom with an HK MP5 and Emil Palley, CD SEK Southern Bavaria (SWAT).

1991
(Above) In Finland, enroute to the Russian border.

(Above, right) Tactical driving course in the countryside near Munich.

1992
In Tyumen, Russia.

1997
Performing a security assessment with Charlie Bywaters in Cartagena de Indias, Bolivar Region Columbia.

1991
Taking possession of the Stone Island compound on Kamenny Ostrov.

2014
Posing for the Handelsblatt Daily in front of Berlin's City Court.

2008
Making a speech at the University of Cologne's International Investment Law Center. On the right is Karl-Heinz Böckstiegel.

WELCOME TO PUTINGRAD · 163

GRAD SWAT TEAM

1993
Inauguration of the GRAD SWAT Team

(Above) L-R: Col. Shamahov, Russian Customs Service, Vadim Glazkov, KUGI, translator Ben Lehrer, and the author.

1993
(Above) Shaking hands with Gen. Vladimir Schulz of the FSB.

(Left) Gen. Schulz, Vladimir Putin and his aide-de-camp Igor Sechin (today CEO Rosneft).

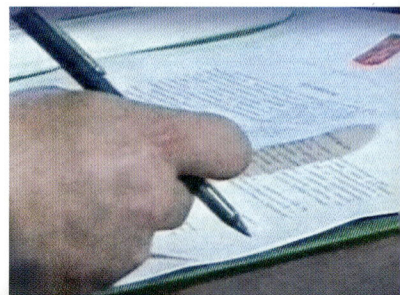

1993
(Above, and left) GRAD Shooters.

(Above middle) Demonstrating a felony arrest.

1993
GRAD Commander,
Sacha Krillov

Vladimir Putin and Vladimir Schulz signing the transfer documents.

WELCOME TO PUTINGRAD · 165

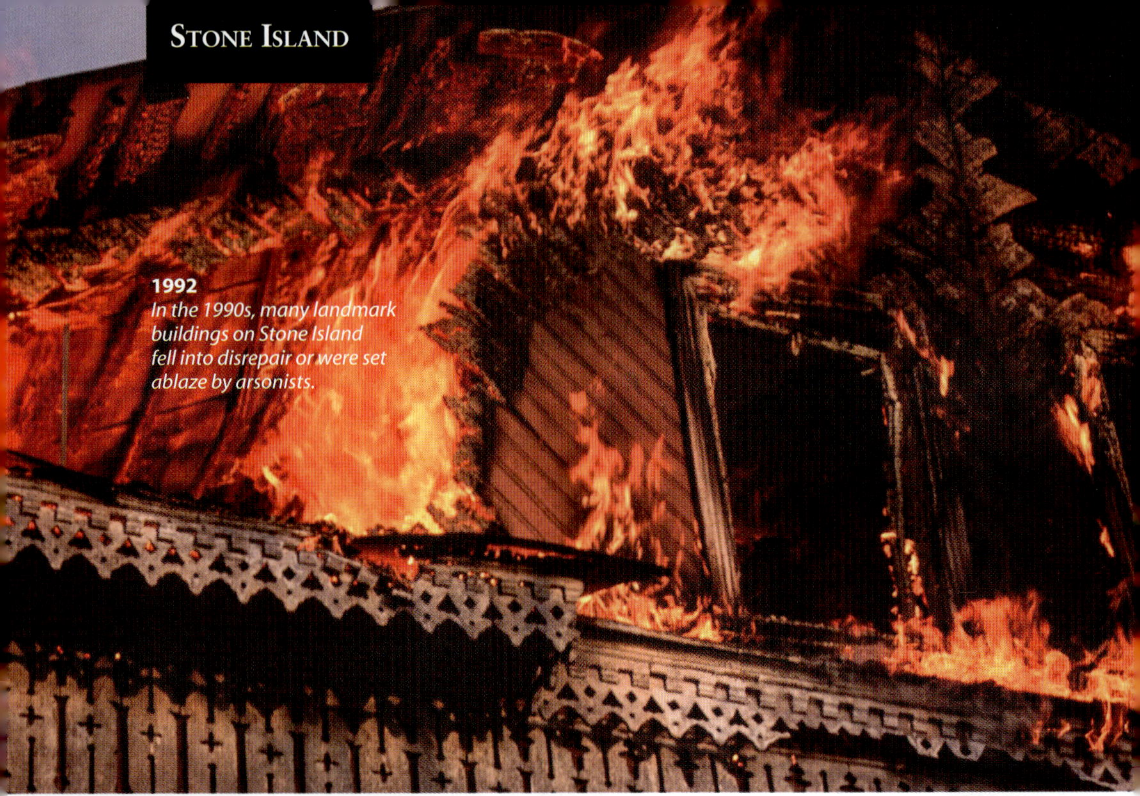

STONE ISLAND

1992
In the 1990s, many landmark buildings on Stone Island fell into disrepair or were set ablaze by arsonists.

1992
(Above) The Gagarin Sauna
(Right) My Stone Island chalet
(Below) Our little lake

TRAVELLING THE WILD, WILD EAST

1992
Loading 2 KOC vehicles onto an Antonov AN-24.

WELCOME TO PUTINGRAD · 167

Travelling the Wild, Wild East

1991
(Right) Col Ludmilla Bystrova, chief of the St. Petersburg Crime Lab (Center), surrounded by staff and police officers from Volgograd.

(Below) Evgeny Trofimov, Minister of the Interior form the Repoblic of Komi surrounded by MVD Komi officers and my sales staff.

1991
At Pulkova airport in St. Petersburg, preparing a flight to different cities in Siberia. Typically, the sales crew consisted of 8 personnel and two vehicles carrying different tactical equipment for demonstration, gasoline and food supplies for a week.

1993
(Above) In Nefteyugansk, Tyumen, Russia. From left to right: Sasha Michailov, Pjotr Denisov, the author and Police Chief Slava Lukin.

1991
(Left and right) Our convoy somewhere behind Moscow enroute to Volzhskiy, Wolgograd, Russia.

1994
KOC Guards training as first responders with a new EMS vehicle.

1991
Don Strate (St. Louis, PD, ret.) and Col. Stanley Olchovik (U.S. Army ret.) speaking to the Leningrad OMON.
(Below) The OMON students.

1993
(Above) L: Examining a load-bearing vest, Middle & R: GRAD and KOC breaching exercises.

(Below) The author demonstrates a felony stop during a tactical driving course in Munich.

1991
Leningrad GUVD officers visiting at Bavarian SWAT Headquarters, Munich with the SEK CO Josef Nefzger.

1993
(Above) GRAD and KOC personnel demonstrating airlift and rappelling techniques.

1993
(Right) GRAD and KOC personnel perform breaching and entry exercises in an abandoned St. Petersburg apartment complex.

1994
TKOC Guards.

PEOPLE

1991 *Galina Chernenka, my friend Venjamin Fabritzki and Julia Andreeva at a Stone Island Beer Call.*

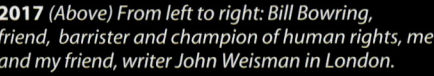

2017 (Above) From left to right: Bill Bowring, friend, barrister and champion of human rights, me and my friend, writer John Weisman in London.

2016 (Above right) From left to right: The author, Mike McCraw, Daniel Sedelmayer and Jack Gaffigan at a local Police Watering Hole in Galway, Ireland on St. Patrick's Day.

1991 (Right) Gennadi Kolbasov and Leonid Pinchuck.

2017 (Below) My friends and favorite human rights activists Irina Hofmann and Marina Litvinenko at the Arri Theater in Munich, Germany.

2001 (Below right) Jack Gaffigan with a Pipe Major in Saint Louis at the Saint Patrick's Day Parade.

172 · WELCOME TO PUTINGRAD

People

1991 Gennadi Kolbasov, head of Leningrad GUVD Intelligence

1993 On the left: My friend Mike Johnson and city officials from KUGI reviewing financial data at the Stone Island company.

2010 My friend Stefan Solotych, a leading expert on Russian and Ukrainian law.

7th SFG's Stilwell Lounge Bell, presented to me by the Olchovik family.

1993 (Right) Stanley Olchovik (l) and Alvin Snaper (r), safely back to Stone Island after being hijacked enroute from Tyumen.

1993 (Second right) Stanley Olchovik in Tyumen, Russia.

1990 My friend Alma Ata Mayor Zamanbek Nurkadilov and his family at a private dinner party in Alma Ata, Kazakhstan.

2006 Charles Kym, a very close friend and old school Swiss-American hotelier and restaurateur, who brought the Stone Island company's wining and dining standards to absolute excellence.

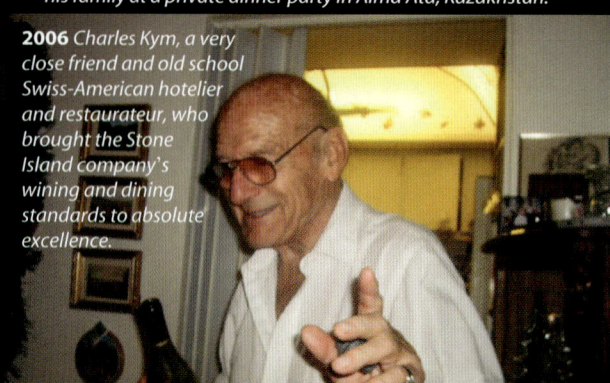

1994 My wife Vlada and I attending the costume ball of the American International Business Association in Saint Petersburg, Russia.

2014 My daughter Corinna in Irschenhausen, Bavaria.

1991 Sergei Ivanov (CD OMON), Sacha Michailov (CD Police Academy), Stanley Olchovik and Albert Vorontsov (CO Central District) in Helsinki, Finnland.

2006 The author and his children on New Year's Eve.

2011 Saying goodbye to Stanley Olchovik in Fayetteville, NC.

1990 (Above) (Big) Sacha from GUVD taking me to a meeting in Leningrad.

1992 (Middle) Vlada in the cockpit of a charter plane in Syktyvkar, Komi Republic.

2016 (Below) At University of Vienna's TTIP Discussion with Nikos Lavranos and August Reinisch.

1990 At Stone Island before setting out to Alma Ata, Kazakhstan.

WELCOME TO PUTINGRAD · 175

EXPROPRIATION

1995
Video documentation of the author negotiating with officials form UdPRF.

1995
(left) Kremlin official with GUVD trooper checking the seals on the Gagarin sauna.

(right) GUVD trooper guarding the same building.

1995
(middle) From right to left: Kremlin official, the author, his translator, U.S. Vice Consul Jeffrey Garrison and an officer from the U.S. Consulate in Saint Petersburg.

1995
GUVD and OMON observing the takeover.

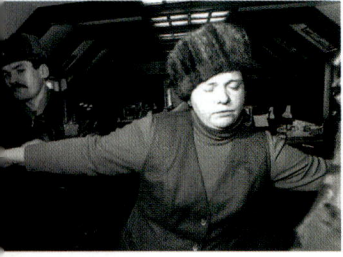

1995
FSB agent Alexander Derugin sealing the Gagarin Sauna.

1996
(Above) Bailiff and GUVD trooper removing KOC staff from a Stone Island company building.

(Above middle and right) Russian Federation Supreme Court Tribunal announcing the takeover of the Stone Island company facilities for the President of the Russian Federation.(right) Our pleadings did not help.

1996
The GUVD officer in charge of the 4 months siege, Gennadi Byzrodny.

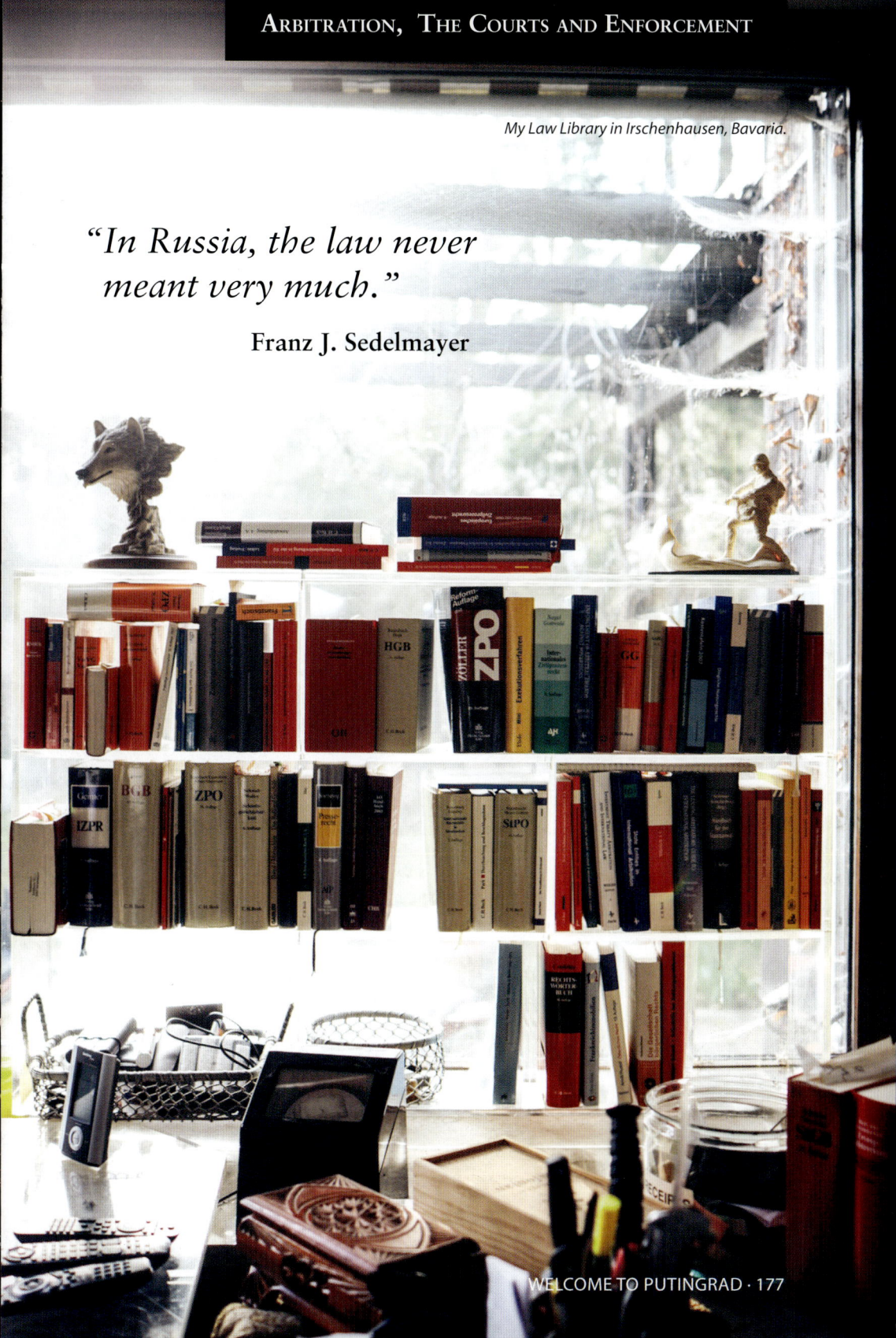

My Law Library in Irschenhausen, Bavaria.

Arbitration, The Courts and Enforcement

2002 Left to right: The author, Rudolph Geiger, Bruno Simma and Vlada Sedelmayer after court hearings in Stockholm, Sweden.

2002 The author and Rudolph Geiger.

2014 From left to right: attorney Jonas Löttiger, author, Anne Kemper -a journalist for Die Zeit- and attorney Hans Forssell in front of the Kronofogden (Bailiff and Enforcement Service) in Sundbyberg near Stockholm, Sweden.

2014
(Left) At the public auction of a Russian Federation Trade Mission building. I watch bidders while a guard watches me. On the left, the two Swedish bailiffs in charge.

(Right) From left to right: Hans Forssell, Jonas Löttiger, the author and Kristian Klasson, former head of Kronofogden and now our consultant.

Stockholm, Sweden

178 · WELCOME TO PUTINGRAD

2014
Showing off my Writ of Execution.

2013
(Above) In front of the Russian Trade Mission Building -in Lidingö near Stockholm- on which we successfully foreclosed.

ARBITRATION, THE COURTS AND ENFORCEMENT

1997
After a day of arbitration hearings onboard a floating hotel in Stockholm, Sweden. From left to right: Our witnesses, Sasha Michailov, Ben Lehrer, Stanely Olchovik, Craig Galle and Michael Melrose.

Appellate and City Court of Cologne

2012
Tribunal of the Cologne Appellate Court entering the court room. Facing the judges: My attorney Wolfgang Heinicke.

2012
Climbing the staircase of the Cologne Palace of Justice, probably for the 100th time!

2012
(Above) In front of the Russia Federation Trade Mission, located in Cologne, which I have successfully auctioned off together with 5 other properties once owned by Russia.

2008
(Above right) UdPRF`s attorney Albrecht Piltz sued me dozens of times since 2003, without ever winning anything crucial. Evgeny Polikarpov a.o. stated, in Germany alone it took $ 17 M to try to stop the enforcement of my $ 2,3 M award.

The author and his attorney Wolfgang Heinicke.

2007
Piltz with UdPRF representatives at the District Court Cologne. Evgeny Polikarpov, the official (far left) was incarcerated, when I concluded most foreclosures. His department was purged.

2006
(l + m) Roscosmos Display at the International Air Show in Berlin.

2006
Russian delegation fleeing the Berlin Airshow to avoid the plane's seizure.

Back in the West

2015
*Franz J. Sedelmayer
In Irschenhausen, Bavaria.*

BACK IN THE WEST

2006 With Gerd and Jenny Beetz in Saint Louis. Gerd was running our U.S. procurement operations.

2015
(Above) Author and his family posing for the Zeit Weekly.

2013 (Right) From left to right: Marina Litvinenko, Alex Goldfarb and my daughter Corinna in Irschenhausen, Bavaria.

2009
(Below) My children, Daniel and Corinna in St. Moritz, Switzerland.

2005 Vlada and I taking time off with the kids in Paris, France.

2006 From left to right: Jack Gaffigan, Mary and Don Strate and the author in Saint Louis, MO.

2014 Enjoying a cigar in Irschenhausen, Germany.

More People

2001 During our "exile" from Russian in the Provence, France.

1990 Attending a traditional barbecue as guests of the President of Kazakhstan, outside Alma Ata. Left to Right: GUVD lawyer Irina Garaburda, Kabil Sümer, a local hostess and Stanley Olchovik.

1991 (Above) GUVD officer Evgeny Guvranov and his assistant checking my Stone Island contributions, just brought in from Germany.

1994 (Above right) attending a vernissage the Nevskij Palace Hotel, Saint Petersburg. From right to left: Larry Bryant our signaling and electronics guru, Vlada Sedelmayer, the author and another guest.

1995 Officials from the Presidential Administration touring the Stone Island compound.

1995 On Nevski Prospect. This photograph was given to me on my 32nd birthday by a friend from the Big House, claiming this to be the very first surveillance picture taken of me in 1989 by the FSB's predecessor, KGB.

WELCOME TO PUTINGRAD · 183

I made sure every GRAD trooper could put on a fresh uniform every day. I got them state of the art winter boots and the latest in load bearing equipment, web gear, and Kevlar armor, so they didn't have to run around in twenty or twenty five kilos of gear. I introduced Kevlar helmets with bulletproof visors too, and even found Kevlar-reinforced full-face black balaclavas. The Russians liked to give nicknames to everything, so they called their balaclavas "Nelson Mandelas", which I thought was funny.

I made sure that GRAD's unit logo was immediately identifiable and did the same with our vehicles—both for the GRAD Team and for my KOC Security Company. Every car, van, and truck had big logo decals on the doors, and all my vehicles had State of Missouri license plates. I kind of liked the fact that whether it was a KGB SWAT car or my private security company vehicle, the plate read "The Show Me State."

In fact, once I got the KOC (for Kamenny Ostrov Security, because "C" is an "S" in Cyrillic) up and running I developed a second SWAT-trained unit that was on call 24/7 in case Banque Credit Lyonnais Russie needed immediate protection for cash deliveries, VIP protection, or hostage rescue. And I made sure that everyone at the bank knew about the team and its capabilities. Why? Because organized crime was everywhere, and even though Credit Lyonnais was good about vetting its employees, I wanted every bank worker to see just what they'd be up against if they ever went over to the "Dark Side." So, on the day the first cash delivery was scheduled, I marched all my armed agents through every single floor of that bank, so every one of the employees could see what they would be up against if they decided to break bad.

And it must have worked, because in all the years of doing security in Russia we never fired a single shot in anger. It was enough for people to see the equipment, see the shotguns, see the vehicles, and see my grey-uniformed guys in their Kevlar and Nelson Mandelas. Nobody, and I mean *no one,* wanted to screw with them.

Actually, that statement isn't quite accurate.

Leonid Pinchuk's GUVD people started screwing with both my KOC security crews and the GRAD SWAT Team almost immediately post deployment. On standing orders from someone high up in the police department, GUVD's traffic cops would pull our vehicles over and hassle the occupants. Of course they did. GUVD was frigging jealous. I'd done most of the training of GRAD in late spring and summer of 1993. The Team's debut and official roll-out came on the second of September with Deputy Mayor Vladimir Putin as the featured guest. My KOC SWAT Team, based at the Stone Island Company compound followed soon after. Both teams had the exact same uniforms, the exact same equipment, and the exact same vehicles with exactly the same lights, sirens, and public address loudspeaker systems.

I did this on purpose. In the spring of 1993, during my negotiations to transfer GUVD's share of the Kamenny Ostrov Company to KUGI, the local branch of the Russian President's Property Fund, the 'little sisters' at GUVD initiated litigation in various courts in the St. Petersburg region to liquidate the Kamenny Ostrov Company entirely. Those frivolous and malevolent suits—which would ultimately fail—were tied up in the system right through the end of the year.

When GUVD lost its liquidation suit, another in a long string of defeats, they took it out on me. Whenever GUVD saw our vehicles on the street they would stop the car and frisk the occupants. Often they would impound our cars. They also pulled us over if we happened to be using our vehicle lights, sirens, and PA systems, all of which we had the proper licenses for.

Then GUVD made a huge mistake. The traffic cops pulled over an Econoline van with Missouri plates, thinking it was one of our KOC crews. Instead it was a GRAD unit heading to an exercise. The KGB SWAT team poured out of the van and confronted the GUVD cops. The situation soon escalated and GUVD called for reinforcements, which resulted in a fight between the two agencies right on the Nevsky Prospekt, St. Petersburg's equivalent of Fifth Avenue, Park Avenue, and Broadway rolled into one. It turned into yet another fight GUVD lost decisively.

After that, word spread quickly at the Big House: don't screw with any of those vehicles from Kamenny Ostrov.

So, GUVD came up with a new tactic. They built a Traffic Police outpost right across from our front gate on Stone Island in the fall of 1993, so they could track as our vehicles left the compound. But a higher power must have been watching: the following week, there was a huge flood on Kamenny Ostrov and not only the police outpost, but a couple of police cars were carried away by the water. Our big wood chalet headquarters stayed high and dry.

My GUVD problem was finally solved not by force but diplomacy. Every time the Traffic Police impounded one of my vehicles, I'd have to go rescue it. To do so I'd meet with the chief of GUVD's International Department, an officer named Garbus. He was a pleasant enough chap and we got along. I'd pay the fine, which wasn't much, and he'd tell me "Don't do that again," and I'd say "You got it, Deputy Chief Garbus," and we'd go our separate ways.

Finally, I'd had enough. I was over at his lot liberating one of my cars and I looked at the Chief and said, "Garbus, let's get real."

He gave me a quizzical look.

"How can we get this thing fixed between you and me?"

"How do you mean?"

"You're costing me time and money. You're costing me the use of my vehicles when they should be utilized by KGB or my security company. Meanwhile, you're tying up your personnel chasing me down when they could be on patrol or actually fighting crime. It's a bad use of both of our resources."

We did some negotiating and what we came up with was that I would loan him, as Chief of the International Department, a fully-equipped Ford Explorer that he would use as his dignitary transport vehicle. I immediately let him borrow one from our inventory and as it happened, within a day or so, he used it to pick up the Minister of Interior, Viktor Yerin, at the airport. When the Minister arrived, there was Garbus in a flashy Explorer, its lights flashing, sitting on the tarmac waiting for him.

Minister Yerin was impressed. "This is a wonderful car," he said. "Where did you get it?"

Garbus said, "It belongs to us!"

The Minister pointed to the decal on the door, which read "KOC," for Kamenny Ostrov Company. "But what unit is that?"

Garbus didn't hesitate. "It stands for Kommandant of the International Department."

"Very enterprising," said the Minister. "Use it in good health. Tell whoever supplied it to you 'Thank you.'"

After that visit, Garbus's people never screwed with us again. The Minister's visit gave him administrative cover because he could tell his bosses at GUVD things were out of his hands: the Minister of Interior had ordered him to make peace with Sedelmayer and what the Minister wanted the Minister got.

To be honest, 1994 was probably the best year I had in Russia business-wise. We achieved a good rapport with the city authorities, we started providing dignitary protection for such VIP visitors as the Pritzker family (owners of the Hyatt Hotel chain), and we handled the visit of Gordon Getty Jr. and roughly 30 of his friends. I also provided security for Vladimir Bogdanov, the head of Surgutneftegaz, a premier oil-producer.

During his visit I introduced Bogdanov to my friend Vadim Glazkov, the former KGB officer from the Mayor's office, and the two of them ultimately founded an oil company called PTK, the St. Petersburg Fuel Company, which ended up worth billions of dollars.

I did not get a piece of their enterprise. Such is life in Russia.

Another ball I had to juggle was dealing with a Banque Credit Lyonnais export manager, a French national I will call Pierre Ustinov (pseudonym). Pierre was the son of a Russian Orthodox priest who'd emigrated to Paris where he doubled as a KGB informant. At some point as a younger man Pierre probably had followed in his father's footsteps—and I don't mean the priesthood. Because he was well accepted in the circles of local power and the intelligence community even before he'd occupied his new position in the bank. Moreover, whenever possible Pierre avoided social and professional interaction with other expats and surrounded himself with a rather exotic local clientele.

He had a real eye for illicit business. If a prospective deal was shady and it concerned banking, you pretty much knew that Pierre would have his finger in the pie. For example, there was in the 1990s an embargo in place against North Korea. So one of the first things Pierre Ustinov did was engineer a deal to handle—perhaps a more precise term would be *launder*—North Korean money.

He also handled Mayor Sobchak's accounts. Anatoly Sobchak banked exclusively with Credit Lyonnais. His particular banking habits made a lot of people nervous: every six, seven, or eight days the Mayor would pull up at the entrance of the bank carrying a suitcase full of cash in various currencies. He'd be greeted by Pierre Ustinov, who'd take him to the bank's private restaurant, where they'd eat French food and drink French wine and then they would count out the money and deposit it. But not into a local account.

Oh, no. Ustinov packed up the cash, put it in envelopes, stashed it in a courier pouch with instructions, and then gave the pouch to whichever of the expat personnel was heading back to Paris that week. Which meant whoever was unlucky enough to be scheduled to take the Paris flight to Credit Lyonnais headquarters had to smuggle the mayor's cash out of the country.

The reason Sobchak operated in that fashion was that in 1992 his wife Lyudmila had been caught by Russian customs trying to fly to Paris with a million dollars in cash. In addition to making headlines in the Russian press, the money had been confiscated and Sobchak had said something to the effect of, "Never again. No more of this shit for me." And so, he obtained a banking license for Credit Lyonnais to open a branch in St. Petersburg, took his cash there, and told Ustinov, "From now on, I bring the money, you get it to Paris."

And since Ustinov was probably taking a taste of Sobchak's cash as a fee, that was just fine with him. If one of the bank's expat staffers had been caught, however, it would have been five years in the Gulag. But then, both Mayor Sobchak and Monsieur Ustinov looked on the expats as disposables—the cost of doing business. Luckily, none were caught. Shortly after we took over the bank's security the practice of using expats came to a halt and Monsieur Ustinov ended up playing courier himself.

1994 was the year of the Goodwill Games. The planning, of course had started the prior year. One of the problems facing the committee putting the Games on was the lack of hotel rooms. The city didn't have enough capacity. But someone had initiative and because St. Petersburg is a port city, a Swedish shipping company that owned several cruise ships was contracted to bring one of its older vessels to St. Petersburg, moor it at the quay, and use it as a floating hotel for the overflow crowds.

The ship was called the *Enchanted Isle*. She'd been launched in 1958 and had at one point sailed for Holland America Lines under the name M/v *Veendam*. The project was conceived as a joint Russian-Swedish venture. The Russians would provide personnel and the local infrastructure; the Swedes would provide the ship, be responsible for all supplies, and overseeing operations on the ship, the hotel, the restaurants, and the casino. All the food, beverages, hotel supplies right down to the sheets, towels, soap, and hair conditioner for the guest rooms—all of that and more would be brought in by the Swedish partner.

The Swedes were represented by a chap named Tony Schoenfelder. And on the Russian side was an individual I will call Igor Borisinsky (pseudonym), who was well-connected to the shipping industry and also to the customs people, which turned out to be…significant.

So, the Swedes brought the ship in and docked it on the quay.

The captain was Swedish. His name was Andersen, just like the author of "The Little Mermaid." But his crew was a real international affair. An Austrian was in charge of the restaurant and the bar; a Swiss ran the hotel part, and they'd hired an American as the chef.

The crew—mostly Russians—was only so-so. As is always the case in the service and hospitality industries, employees are tasked with a lot of work for not a lot of money, with the result that they—the people waiting and busing tables, cooking in the kitchens, cleaning the staterooms and maintaining the exterior of the ship—didn't really put their hearts into what they were doing. But I figured that was normal because I saw the same thing every day in St. Petersburg—the old Soviet '*We pretend to work; they pretend to pay us*' syndrome.

The partners hired a Russian security company by the name of Scorpion to oversee the operation. I checked with my friends at the Big House but nobody pinged on the Scorpion name. I'd never heard of it either but it all became clear to me when I saw the Scorpion crew for the first time on board the *Enchanted Isle*.

They looked like instructors and gym rats at a martial arts sports club—all with the same style haircuts, dressed in matching training suits topped off with gold chains and bracelets. Big military-style watches. Designer running shoes. Trim, buffed out guys with facial hair. I did some checking and word on the street was that Scorpion had made the Swedes a sweet deal and the Swedes, always cost conscious, had accepted its offer without, probably, doing very much, if any, due diligence.

But that would be okay because I was told the Swedes had equipped the ship with state of the art security—it was foolproof. They'd bought an access control system that employed time-stamp cards and magnetic readers. There were sophisticated inventory controls that allowed you to monitor every drink poured and every steak served. There was video surveillance everywhere; there were even magnetometer metal detectors you had to walk through to come aboard.

I gave the system a once-over. It was, I thought, pretty well-conceived. Even the *Dummkopfs* from Scorpion would be hard-pressed to screw things up when they were this well-equipped.

Guess what: before you knew it the guys from Scorpion had broken the video cameras and unplugged the metal detectors. In a matter of a few days nothing was working anymore. It wasn't stupidity either: it was sabotage. And soon after that all the crime families of St. Petersburg and a horde of *gastralyori* (guest criminals) from as far as Moscow descended onto the *Enchanted Isle*.

They came to party with their pals and their girlfriends and no one ever paid a bill. The instant one of the Russian waiters demanded payment, some *pakhan* or *patsani* would smack him in the mouth and tell him

"*Oto'idi a to jebnu!*" ("Getouttahere or I'll kick your ass!") or, "*E'b tvoju mat!*" ("Go fuck yourself.")

It was like a bar scene from the movie "Goodfellas." And next thing you knew there was a huge prostitution ring operating on the ship. The Mafiya had ladies of the night working left and right. It was the Love Boat alright—but rented by the hour.

Scorpion personnel, who were obviously under Mafiya control, operated in three shifts: one was the guard element who ran the now-defunct access control system; the second ran the prostitutes, and the third shift was in the bar, drinking on the house. And as if that weren't bad enough, they also took over the staterooms—and left them looking like the Frat Party scene in "Animal House." Then they started inviting their friends: criminal elements who were working with Columbian drug cartels. In a matter of weeks the *Enchanted Isle* probably saw more drugs change hands than anywhere in Russia.

So, that was the first problem with the *Enchanted Isle* joint venture. It had turned into a purely criminal activity.

The second was that Tony Schoenfelder, the Swedish half of the venture, was getting skinned alive by his Russian partner but didn't realize it.

Think back a few chapters to the Subway Sandwich joint venture fiasco. Remember Bordug, the Russian partner whose definition of 'free enterprise and privatization' was "steal, steal, steal?"

The *Enchanted Isle* was a variation of that theme. Remember I mentioned that Tony Schoenfelder's Russian partner Borisinsky was tight with the customs people? Well, every time a vessel would come from Sweden with the supplies to equip the hotel ship, customs would fine the Russian partner for some minor paperwork violation or non-declaration, seize everything, and auction it off for 5 cents on the dollar.

The buyer, of course, would be Igor Borisinsky, Tony's Russian partner, who then trucked everything over to the *Enchanted Isle* and charged the joint venture top dollar to buy back the auctioned supplies, which Tony had of course already paid for once. Borisinsky's goal—just like Bordug's—was to take over the whole venture, including the ship.

By the time KOC got called in, organized crime was in total control of the ship. Captain Andersen didn't dare leave his cabin anymore: the guards had threatened to cut his throat if he tried to do his job. The American chef's life was also threatened. So were the Swiss hotelier and the Austrian bar and restaurant manager. They were afraid, too—and with good reason. The Scorpion thugs weren't shy about using physical force to intimidate.

I was asked to investigate. And I had the human resources to do it. We had expats and Russian contractors check into the ship's hotel and sent other personnel aboard to patronize the bar and the restaurants. We interviewed the ship's personnel, vendors, and contractors. Within three days we had our evidence on paper as well as audio and video tape, everything we needed to get a police inquiry going. But now we had to get the foreign and Russian personnel under threat off the ship without making waves.

I sent my KOC SWAT team aboard in civilian clothes, armed only with batons and Makarov pistols, in twos and threes so they'd mix easily with the crowd. Once they were all on board the Swiss hotel manager gathered the captain and all expatriate personnel together. Three Tornado guards nervously eyed the group as my men escorted them towards the gangway. But they clearly didn't want to interfere. We led our rescuees off the ship, quickly put them into a black stretch limo that pulled up just as they came onto the quay, and with KOC squad cars escorting, headed straight to Stone Island where a formal debriefing would take place.

First, we interviewed the Westerners: Captain Andersen, the restaurant and hotel managers, and anybody else who had been under immediate threat. Then we debriefed the Russian personnel, who we'd extracted later that same night.

Colonel Vlasov, the head of the Transport Police, came to Stone Island the next morning. As was usual in St. Petersburg, there'd been rumors about what was going on aboard the *Enchanted Isle*, but the police had found excuses not to investigate. Now they were being presented with witnesses who were willing to give explicit evidence about what they'd seen and heard.

Vlasov immediately started a formal investigation. And all the expats we'd extracted left Russia within 24 hours, safe and sound.

❖

A couple of days later some of my KOC people, an ex-FBI guy by the name of Ralph Sturdevant, and Ralph's translator were on board the *Enchanted Isle* meeting with someone. They looked up to see one of Vlasov's Transport Police officers coming toward them.

The cop said "Hey, how are you guys? Good to see you."

Then he looked at Ralph and in English he said, "Ralph, if you don't mind, I'd like to borrow your translator."

Ralph said, "Sure. Why?"

The cop checked his watch and said, "Well, in about 15 minutes or so I'd like him to tell everybody to hit the ground, because that's when we're going to raid the ship."

About five minutes later Ralph and the rest of them watched as a bunch of Mafiya guys scurried down the gangplank and off the ship, running helter-skelter down the quay and scattering into the streets beyond. Obviously somebody'd tipped them off. Because within minutes OMON—the Ministry of Interior's riot unit came thundering down the quay, ran up the gangway like a herd of buffalo and raided the ship. Anybody who resisted or did not follow instructions was beaten black and blue, cuffed, arrested, and thrown into jail.

The raid, as it turned out, was a direct result of our involvement. In point of fact, all we had done was an investigation: we'd found out what was what and who was who. But in doing so we'd made sure that even an idiot could obtain indictment-worthy witness statements once a formal complaint had been filed. And of course we'd been the ones who'd gone aboard the *Enchanted Isle*, extracted the witnesses, and delivered them to the proper authorities.

So, Colonel Vlasov used our actions as an opportunity to get rid of the floating crime problem once and for all. Hence the police raid.

On the one hand, it was a good '*Carpe Diem*' play on Vlasov's part. But it had a potential downside for me and my company because on the other hand, I knew all the bad-guy players and they all knew me and my company. My concern was that if the Mafiya blamed us for the police raid, my company and my employees would become targets.

I happened to be in Helsinki when the police raid took place. The next morning, my office at Kamenny Ostrov started receiving calls from Mafiya figures and crime-connected Russian security companies and all the calls had basically the same message: "Don't worry, Franz, we're all friends here. We don't want to step on anybody's toes and we certainly don't want to get in your way. So relax: everything's cool."

When I thought about it—which I did, a lot—I realized what had happened. Given the timing of our raid to extract the Europeans and the Russian witnesses and the subsequent Transport Police raid, organized crime—from the Mafiya *vori* to the crooked security companies—all believed I had the juice to call in a police raid at will.

Which was something, of course, I didn't. But it gave me and my company the appearance of both power and influence.

Story. A long long time ago, there was an Israeli ambassador to the United States named Simcha Dinitz. Simcha had been one of Golda Meir's political advisors, and later he was very closely involved with bringing more than a million Soviet Jews to Israel in the 1980s.

At a small dinner party one night in Washington, Ambassador Dinitz was asked about a newspaper article concerning a counterterrorist operation in Europe that the press had attributed to Israel's small but effective intelligence agency, Mossad. In point of fact, Mossad had not been involved. But when Ambassador Dinitz was asked by a reporter flat out about whether Mossad was responsible or not, his denial had been ambivalent. Very, very ambivalent.

At the party, which was at the apartment of the Israeli defense attaché— so the ambassador was among friends—he was asked, "Simcha, what kind of answer was that? How come you were so ambivalent?"

He'd had a couple of scotches by then, and so instead of a diplomatic answer, Simcha Dinitz committed truth. "Y'know," he said, "I make it a habit to never deny any story about our capabilities too strongly." He sipped his whiskey. "I like to keep 'em guessing. Because, even if we didn't do it, but people think we might have done it, then we get credit for punching above our weight. And it definitely keeps our enemies off balance."

Good point. When asked about the origin of the Transport Police raid, I never denied our involvement too strongly either. Let people—especially organized crime—believe what they wanted to. It was better for my business, and better for my family's safety.

I, of course, knew that our good fortune in the *Enchanted Isle* incident was the result of the Law of Unintended Consequences.

Even so, one would think that with Stone Island's reputation my immediate family would be safe and the bad guys would stay away from them. After all, when my son went to visit Vlada's parents, he was driven by armed guards. When Vlada went shopping, she was always escorted by my security people. The same went for me when I ventured out from Kamenny Ostrov. So, one would logically assume therefore that the city's criminal element knew my family and I were off limits.

Not so.

One afternoon, I was in conversation with a group of procurement people from GUVD Tyumen, which is an oil producing region northeast of St. Petersburg, when my secretary uncharacteristically interrupted the meeting.

She came into my office, flustered, and said, "Dima just called."

Dima is my father-in-law, Dmitri Shulkin. The only individual to ever get into my office unescorted. I looked up at her and started to say 'Tell him I'll call him back.' But before I could utter a word she blurted, "He asked me to ask you to get him $10,000. In cash. Right now."

Her face was white.

"What's going on?"

"Dima called from some car dealership. He sounded stressed. He said he needed the money but he couldn't come and get it himself right now, so you should send someone with it to him. He gave me the address."

It didn't sound right. I looked at my guests. "Gentlemen, would you excuse me for a few minutes?"

I found Slava, my KOC section manager. "Dima may be in trouble. I need you to go check on him."

"Can do, Boss."

I briefed Slava as he quickly changed into civilian clothes. Then he assembled the stand-by SWAT team, grabbed a radio, and headed for his Lada followed closely by the team in their KOC van.

When Slava reached the dealership, he went inside and asked for Dima Shulkin. He was led to a conference room where he found Dima sitting at a huge table surrounded by more than half a dozen gangsters.

The gangster in charge looked at Dima. "Did you bring the money?"

"I've got it."

"Show me."

Slava said, "It's outside. I wanted to be sure I had the right people." He spoke into his radio. "Bring the money—<u>now</u>!"

Thirty seconds later the SWAT team came charging through the door shouting "Down-down-down! Hands up, arms out, don't move!!"

In their body armor, their Nelson Mandelas, and ballistic headgear, their pump-action shotguns and white-light fitted pistols they were hugely intimidating—exactly what was needed.

The gangsters were caught completely off-guard. Of course they were. They'd been hit by a team of well-armed, well-trained security personnel that looked exactly the same as the KGB's GRAD Team. So when they swooped in, the kidnap gang probably thought they were being taken down by the KGB.

So the kidnappers absolutely froze. And Dima absolutely smiled. And we absolutely took him home without a scratch.

He looked over at me during dinner, a sly smile on his face and said, "So, boychik, what took you so long?"

Another run-in I had with organized crime was my short stint as the Vice President of the St. Petersburg City Security Fund. I was over at Smolny one day and dropped by Vladimir Putin's office to chat.

Igor Sechin waved me through and I walked into Putin's office.

The Deputy Mayor smiled. "Herr Franz Sedelmayer—I was just about to call you."

"And luckily, here I am." We shook hands. Putin indicated a forty-something fellow with a bad comb-over, a cheap wrinkled blue suit and scuffed shoes sitting across from him.

"Franz, this is Sacha Smirnov," Putin said. He caught my reaction. "Yeah—Smirnov. Like the vodka. Sacha works with us here in Smolny coordinating matters between the City and all the Executive Services—the police, customs, etcetera. And he is currently setting up something called the St. Petersburg City Security Fund. I've told him all about you and Kamenny Ostrov, and what we're doing with KUGI, and he thought you might want to get involved with the Fund."

"Well, perhaps I might, Mr. Deputy Mayor. Security is everyone's business these days."

"Exactly," Smirnov said. He extended his hand. "Pleased to meet you, Mr. Sedelmayer."

"And you." I took his hand and received a moist, dead-fish handshake in return.

Putin waved me into one of the other chairs facing his desk.

"So," I asked Smirnov, "what's this security fund all about?"

He fidgeted, buttoned his suit coat over his paunch, and adjusted his tie before speaking. I peered a little closer at him and almost did a double-take: Sacha Smirnov was actually wearing a red Smirnov Vodka promotional tie. He cleared his throat. "Well, Mr. Sedelmayer, we're just in the process of launching. It's a fund made up of business people—banks, insurance companies, large companies, and western joint ventures. The idea is to assist the city in defining the security needs and requirements to deal with crime and corruption as business and entrepreneurism expand in Russia."

"That sounds good to me." And it did. Crime was pervasive; so was graft. It would be constructive— and possibly even profitable—to bring people together and see how we could minimize both. "After all," I said, "security is everybody's problem these days."

"It is indeed," Smirnov said. "And if everyone involved could contribute a little bit toward the Fund's budget, we could I think make a difference here." He looked at me. "Are you interested?"

"Sure. Fine."

"Many thanks, Mr. Sedelmayer."

It didn't take long—probably a couple of weeks—until I got a notice saying that I'd been selected as the First Vice President of the St. Petersburg

City Security Fund. And that we'd have the Founders Meeting on such and such a date.

I called Smirnov. "Got the notice," I told him. "Who's coming?"

He read the list of founding members to me. I was flabbergasted. There were a few genuine businessmen involved, like the head of Sberbank of Russia's Northwest Territory. But far too many of the founding members were Mafiyosi or were running companies controlled by organized crime. This wasn't a security fund; it was a Cosa Nostra infiltration operation.

I said, "Mr. Smirnov, this is not for me."

He started to protest. I hung up. Immediately, I wrote Smirnov demanding the Fund get rid of all the Mafia-connected members and resigning as First Vice President. I sent a copy to Putin and everyone else on the membership list.

The next time I ran into Putin, I told him, "I really would've liked to be a part of the fund Smirnov was helping organize, but you know I can't be associated with anything that has to do with organized crime."

Putin said nothing. But he gave me a knowing look.

Of course he did. I'd never known Putin to take a bribe or ask for a kickback, but those things were around him all the time. Crime was endemic in Russia. It was central to everyone's existence. If you took the train, say to Moscow, you had to understand each train had an official thief who worked under the head of the train, most often the chief conductor. We had a case where a client was robbed on the train. So one of my KGB people who still carried a badge and gun even though he had retired, spoke to the chief conductor about the theft.

The chief conductor explained that he'd make a call to the train's 'official thief'. If the thief said, "Not me," nothing would happen, but if he said "Yes, it was me," the property would be returned. In our case the thief said "yes" and the property was returned.

My own anti-crime and corruption measures both at Stone Island and the security company were pretty straightforward. I controlled access to our facility very tightly—in fact the only individual who ever managed to get into my office without my permission was my father-in-law. There were other measures: I would not talk to anyone who was not a customer; I would not talk to anybody I didn't know; I would not talk to anybody I hadn't first checked out.

Most of the people who worked with me came out of the security services and their bona fides could be—and were—verified. Initially, I hired active or retired police officers, and after we had our falling out with GUVD, I mostly hired from the KGB. My take on hiring was that you were welcome to work for me so long as you had an official position, spoke a language, and carried a badge and a gun. I paid a better-than-living wage and every person who ever worked for me knew—because I told them—that if they tried to skim, ask for kickbacks, or took bribes and/or shortcuts, their butts would be kicked out the door immediately.

There was only one occasion in all my time in St. Petersburg that I was approached directly by a Mafiosi. It was during the period I was first putting together KOC. A Russian friend of mine was contacted, and he believed the approach to be legitimate, so he brought his acquaintance to Kamenny Ostrov without telling me who he was. My hackles were raised immediately because this individual just oozed organized crime. So, yes, we had a sit down. But it was in the banquet hall over a glass of beer. There was no way I was about to allow this creep anywhere near my office.

We sat and I poured beer, and I listened as this…individual made an oblique, almost textbook "Godfather Part I" approach. He couldn't have done it any better if he was Marlon Brando addressing the bosses of the Five Families.

"We're all friends here," he began. "And because we're all friends that's why we would like to participate in, uh…" And then he gestured, his hands spread and moving in parallel circles, "Y'know, *participate* in, uh…"

He was never direct; he never said "We want in; we want to take over your business."

But I got his gist clearly. So I poured him a second beer, and I laughed, and told jokes, and I gave him a good time. But I was always careful to deflect his approaches. And at long last, because his veiled suggestions hadn't worked, he invited me to be his guest of honor at a boxing tournament, "And afterwards, Herr Sedelmayer, we could find some way to agree on some form of *participation*…"

That sealed it. Boxing matches were where you went if you wanted to hang out with Mafiyosi.

So, it was time to be direct. I put my beer down and I said, "First, I'm sorry but I cannot attend because I am so busy I hardly ever leave this compound." I paused. "Second, since we are good friends now, business would be impossible."

He looked at me, confused. "*A?*" (*A* means *huh?* in Russian)

"We're good friends. And good friends don't do business. Didn't you know?"

That was the end of the conversation. I shook his hand and then, as a way of making myself perfectly clear, I had him escorted out of the compound by people armed with shotguns.

But I did it politely.

Manners maketh the man.

CHAPTER 11
Unintended Unintended Consequences

"Question: what do you get when you combine the Law of Unintended Consequences and Murphy's Law? Answer: Boris Yeltsin."—Franz Sedelmayer, 2017

The change wasn't palpable at first. But later, in the aftermath, you could feel it in the air, like latent electricity after a thunderstorm. It was... unmistakable. The stars in my galaxy were being realigned.

It had begun on September 21, 1993, less than three weeks after the debut of the GRAD SWAT team I'd built for Putin, when President Boris Yeltsin declared his intention to disband the Congress of the People's Deputies because the parliament wasn't enacting reforms fast enough for him. The parliament declared Yeltsin's actions unconstitutional and called it an attempted coup d'état. The constitutional court agreed with the parliament and said Yeltsin should be impeached.

Yeltsin's reaction was typically Russian: he called in tanks and shelled the parliament building, known as the White House. By October 4, the Russian Army had stormed the White House, arrested the leaders of the rebellion, and it was, most thought, more or less all over.

Except it wasn't. Because the reverberations of those 10 days are still being felt today. Because what Yeltsin did in its own way was neither progressive nor pro-democratic. It was counterrevolutionary: he concentrated a vast majority of the power of the state in the office of the president. The power of the parliament—which was re-labeled the Duma after 1993—was vastly reduced.

Indeed, today the Duma is little more than a rubber stamp for Vladimir Putin or whoever controls the office of the president and its vast apparatus.

With his strong handling of the October revolt, Yeltsin showed everybody who was boss. All of a sudden, Moscow was the central government again and its nucleus was the president. It was Stalinesque. It changed everything.

There was no more liberal thinking like, 'The Soviet Union is no more; therefore St. Petersburg can decide its own fate.' After October 4,1993, the only real question when making political, economic, or military decisions was, 'What does Moscow say?' And it wasn't just St. Petersburg. It held true for all of Russia's regions. Local initiatives came to a stop. Once again, Russia was back to top-down rule.

Things changed practically overnight. I don't think I'm exaggerating to say that today's Russia—the one man kleptocracy controlled by Vladimir Vladimirovich Putin—had its genesis in Boris Yeltsin's actions back in October of 1993. That's when Yeltsin—the corrupt, alcoholic, iconoclast—bitch-slapped the parliament into obscurity and appropriated all of its assets and all the State-owned assets as well. He transferred everything that wasn't military or diplomatic property into the UdPRF—the office of the President of the Russian Federation—where he allowed the now privatized assets to be sold at fire-sale prices to his pals, the oligarchs.

Oil and gas? Privatized. Media? Privatized. Strategic minerals? Privatized. Whatever hadn't been stolen under Gorbachev was now sold off under Yeltsin. Who took himself a piece out of every transaction.

That's not quite accurate. Since Yeltsin was seldom sober, it was his daughter Tatyana who took it upon herself to manage the presidential graft. In fact, her actions were why the entire Yeltsin family, and not just

Boris, would ultimately receive presidential pardons from Vladimir Putin when Putin became president of the Russian Federation. For the Yeltsins, graft was a family affair. Of course it was: they were *nachalniki*.

In St. Petersburg, the aftermath of the October uprising was a time of celebration. After all, Anatoly Sobchak had been a huge supporter of Yeltsin's. And, although his reaction to the hard line the president took was subdued, he still became one of the main authors of the 1993 constitution that Yeltsin put into force, post-rebellion.

Vladimir Putin, for the most part, remained in the background. In 1991 he'd supported Yeltsin. This time around, he was less active. But in the end he followed Sobchak's lead.

Why? Because he was Sobchak's deputy mayor—and what was good for Anatoly Sobchak was in turn good for Vladimir Putin.

Not everyone agreed. Some of St. Petersburg's more militant liberals supported the parliamentary rebels. Andrei Nevzorov—the Geraldo Rivera-like host of *600 Seconds*, the nightly TV show that had supported me right after the Pinchuk assault on Kamenny Ostrov—actually called for armed volunteers to fight against Yeltsin. His show, despite the fact that it was hugely popular, was immediately taken off the air, another Putin precursor.

For me, life went on more or less unimpeded. My business was expanding; I'd started KOC, the Kamenny Island Security Company, and the GRAD SWAT team was a bright light for the St. Petersburg's KGB office. I finally concluded my seemingly interminable negotiations with KUGI, which meant that the Kamenny Ostrov joint venture could grow unimpeded. I had a piece of paper—an agreement, signed by Deputy Mayor Putin, among others, that consummated the joint venture and registered it with the proper authorities. So, with the exception of an occasional pinprick from the pricks at GUVD, everything was running as smoothly as one could expect in Mother Russia.

Even the GUVD situation looked as if it might improve. The KGB's "Little Sister" was getting a new boss. His name was Loskutov and he just happened to be the brother-in-law of my "old friend" Yuri Yarov, the Governor of the St. Petersburg region. Yarov—the guy who tried to sell me a $300,000 house he didn't own—now was an aide of Yeltsin's and would in time become deputy prime minister, after that the head of the organization of former Soviet States, the CIS (Council of Independent States).

And so, Yarov sent his Korean bag man, Mr. Kim, to give me the good news. Kim showed up at Stone Island and said, "The Governor wants to speak to you in confidence. He has very good news. I will call him?"

Now, under normal circumstances, if my brother-in-law had just been appointed police chief of Munich and I wanted to let a friend or acquaintance know because it might help him out, I'd pick up the phone and call my friend and tell him the good news myself. I wouldn't have had one of my assistants go over with a mobile telephone, call me, then hand the phone to my friend.

But this was Russia. And Yuri sent his bag man over because he wanted me to say "Thank you, Yuri, for letting me know about your brother-in-law's promotion" in Russian style by giving Mr. Kim some money. If there was no Mr. Kim in my office there would be no money for Yuri Yarov.

So I said, "Fine. Yes, call him," and watched as Kim made the call. When it rang, the Korean put the phone on speaker and held it up to my face.

"My old friend Franz Sedelmayer," Yuri thundered. "How are you?"

"I'm fine," I answered. "So what's up, Mr. Governor?"

"Franz, I have good news. My brother-in-law has just been appointed the new police chief in St. Petersburg, and I want you guys to make peace with GUVD."

"Mr. Governor, there's nothing I'd like more."

"You should write him," Yuri said. "Send him a nice letter. Tell him that you're happy about his appointment. Tell him you want a good relationship. I think it will all work out."

"I will absolutely do that," I said. "And I'm grateful for the introduction."

"You're more than welcome. We should get together sometime."

I heard the line go dead. I watched as Kim carefully slipped the phone into his pocket. Then, he looked at me with the eager gaze that bagmen so often exhibit—the one that goes, 'So, now is when you hand me a big wad of money to show how grateful you are.'

Instead, I offered him a grateful handshake and was delighted to see the disappointed look on his face when he shuffled out of my office, cash-deprived.

Still, I wrote the new chief immediately. Basically, I said,

Dear Mr. Loskutov, congratulations on your new post. My name is Franz Sedelmayer. I am a friend of your brother-in-law, Yuri Yarov. We are the Kamenny Ostrov Company and you might have heard on our conflict with GUVD. But that is all in the past. I stretch out my hand to you in friendship, especially as GUVD is no longer our partner in the joint venture because KUGI has replaced it. So, there is no need to continue the old rivalries. I eagerly await your response.

There was no response. Not a word.

Of course not: I hadn't given Mr. Kim any cash. So Yuri'd probably called his brother-in-law and told him I wasn't worth an answer because I wouldn't pay bribes or *pourboires* or whatever they're called in Korean.

At least I'd tried. But there was something else bothersome about Loskutov's silence. It hinted that Russia under Yeltsin was heading in the wrong direction; that in Russia it was still all about pay to play.

❖

There was another worrisome tremor later in the fall. I heard rumors that somebody—no idea who, or from, or where—was trying to convince President Yeltsin to take our compound together with the neighboring tennis club, the kindergarten that adjoined our compound, and the nearby villa that was the official residence of Mayor Anatoly Sobchak (which, incidentally, the mayor rented out so he could collect the money for himself), all for presidential use. I wasn't especially bothered when I heard about it, because there had been many other attempts to take over Kamenny Ostrov and so far everything had failed. And, besides, there was nothing specific. It was just local chatter.

I became a lot more concerned when I ran into one of my neighbors on the Island a week or so later and he excitedly blurted, "Guess who visited us yesterday?"

"Who?"

"President Yeltsin, his wife, and Deputy Mayor Putin."

"You're kidding!"

"No—I'm serious. It was incredible. The president, Mr. Sedelmayer! The president came to visit our house to see if it might be suitable for some presidential functions."

Now I was both interested—and piqued. "And what did he say?"

"You'll love this: almost the whole time he was staring across the lake and admiring your house. He was looking at your whole compound."

"He was?"

"Oh, yes—and he told me, 'That's a nice place over there. It looks as if it has lots of room.' He really, really likes your place!"

"And what did the deputy mayor do?"

"The deputy mayor? Oh, the deputy mayor wasn't doing anything. He was rocking back and forth on his heels, and looking left, and looking right, and he wasn't saying a word."

Looking left, and looking right, and he wasn't saying a word. That's when the warning bells started ringing in my head.

Of course he wasn't saying anything. Because it was Deputy Mayor Vladimir Vladimirovich Putin, whose signature attested to the 25-year lease that gave my company the chalet and the entire corporate compound on Kamenny Ostrov. But Deputy Mayor Putin wasn't about to interrupt the president of the Russian Federation, who'd just exclaimed how nice and desirable my place was and tell him he couldn't have it. No way he'd jump in, shouting 'Sorry, Mr. President, but that place isn't available, because my pal Franz Sedelmayer has a 25-year lease on it and my name is on the lease as representative of the city.'

So, I sat on tenterhooks for a while.

At first I was pissed off at Putin. I thought he should have called me immediately and told me what had taken place. But then I realized: that wasn't his job. His job was to keep things running smoothly and work behind the scenes.

So, I wasn't angry. I even surprised him on his 42nd birthday. One of my U.S. suppliers had sent me a dozen sample mini-microphone transmitters that could be paired with a receiver. My techs played with them and realized they were junk—nothing I'd ever sell professionally. But from the 12 sets, the techs were able to put together four mini-mic units that worked acceptably, and as a joke I sent them, along with a receiver unit and a Dictaphone, over to Smolny as a surprise birthday present for Vladimir.

He was obviously happy with the gift because I got back a note that read, "Thank you, Franz. From one professional to another!"

There was more good news, too: when I finally heard accurate, first-hand news concerning Yeltsin's visit it was positive: the Presidential Guard Service had been tasked to do a physical overview of my compound as well as a security evaluation. And from our sources in the KGB there was good news: the verdict was that Kamenny Ostrov didn't meet either the technical or the security requirements as a presidential residence. The house lay in a flood zone—I knew that already although we'd been spared on the last go-round. And, the Presidential Guard's Security experts decided that it would take a huge number of technological bells and whistles and other goodies to ensure that the presidential family and their guests would be safe. So, despite the fact that the president liked the villa, the Presidential Guard Service was advising against it.

Obviously, they hadn't done a thorough inspection because I'd put hundreds of thousands of dollars into Stone Island. I'd upgraded the chalet and the separate dining facility and sauna buildings. We had a huge, walk-in secure weapons locker, there were new generators and heating, and we were well wired, communications-wise. But the Guard Service's slip-up was just fine with me. I poured myself a good Bavarian beer and thought, 'We're going to get out of this pickle just the way we have so many times before—because of our friends.'

Indeed, I was delighted that I'd had both Deputy Mayor Putin, and Mikhail Manevich, the young, mustachioed Chairman of the Committee for Control of City Property, on my side. In April of 1994, when negotiations with KUGI were dragging, Putin and Manevich had framed a letter to Anatoly Chubais, the Chairman of the State Committee for the Control of the State Property—that's KUGI—in Moscow, basically asking to know why things were taking so long.

> "When Joint Venture Kamenny Ostrov was to be founded GUVD in St. Petersburg and Leningradskaya region did not receive stated authorization....
> Meanwhile, the [Joint Venture] Kamenny Ostrov has made

some expenditures on the reparation of the building and the sum paid was 219 thousand USA dollars and there is confirmation from UGIOP (this was the Municipal Monument Protection Authority) that the expenditures were made....It is to be noted that those expenditures were made out of proceeds of credit without interest, given by the American part. The Joint Venture has to repay the stated credit out of its profit and that is impossible to accomplish if the [Joint Venture] will terminate its activity.

In order to solve the dispute and secure stability for foreign investment in Russia we ask you:

1. To allow KUGI...to be a partner on Kamenny Ostrov as an assignee to GUVD...taking into account that the latter cannot be a participant according to legislation currently in force....

2. To allow KUGI in St. Petersburg to confiscate from GUVD in St. Petersburg...the buildings and constructions on the address: St. Petersburg, Polevya alleya, d.6-8 according to par. 3 Art 5 in the RSFSR Law "On Property in RSFSR."

That letter disappeared into the Russian bureaucratic void. It took more than four months for Putin to receive an answer from Anatoly Chubais and another three-plus months until Manevich was able to confiscate, on behalf of KUGI, the GUVD's shares in Kamenny Ostrov. But at long last, the deed (literally) had been done. Kamenny Ostrov was mine. Finally.

Until, that is, the very end of November. Which is when the proverbial *scheisse* hit the proverbial *ventilateur*.

❖

On November 30, I was informed by KUGI I'd won the fucking lucky contest. Despite the fact that KGB had found my site unsuitable during its survey, the president's office in Moscow had selected Kamenny Ostrov to become the summer residence for President Boris Yeltsin and his Presidential Guard Service.

That's right: my company headquarters was going to become Yeltsin's Mar-a-Lago.

Did anybody have a piece of paper making it official?

The answer was no, not yet. But, since I was about to fly out on a business trip to Yekaterinburg, which lies beyond the Urals roughly 2500 kilometers from St. Petersburg, I made a bunch of quick phone calls to my friends in City Hall and the Big House. I didn't want to be sandbagged so far from home.

But just about everyone to whom I spoke told me "Franz, don't worry."

Mikhail Manevich said, "Franz, this is simply bullshit. It's a mistake — more frigging bureaucracy from Moscow. You know how they're always trying to run things by long distance."

I was finally able to connect with Putin. I told him what Manevich had said. Putin agreed: "Not to worry, Franz. We can get this thing fixed before it's even started."

Putin's response gave me reassurance. But, since this was Russia, where the laws could change in a literal heartbeat, on December 1, wrote a memo to the file covering the subject — just in case.

"Disturbingly, on November 30, 1994, we were informed by KUGI St. Petersburg and the Curator of the Organs of State in St. Petersburg that the President's Office, Moscow, has selected our facility, to provide a summer residence for President Yeltsin [sic]and his presidential guard service.

Even though every official in the city tells us not to worry, we would like to take this opportunity to express our concern. We are confident at this point of time given our good and friendly relations with the city government and several ministries in Moscow, that we can correct the situation before it could develop into another potential conflict. The city officials we have talked to assured us of their good will in helping to preserve this facility and our operations. Reflecting on our past experience, it has cost hundreds of thousands of dollars and three years of valuable time to correct a problem that was mainly handled on a local level. We would therefore certainly want to avoid a similar situation at the federal level."

The memo completed, I flew off to Yekaterinburg, where I toured a group of new facilities that needed access controls and other security enhancements.

On December 9, I got a phone call from Putin on my mobile phone.

"Franz, it's Volodya." Where are you?"

"Yekaterinburg—well, close by."

"Something's come up. When will you be back?"

"A week. Maybe ten days."

"No—you have to come back now. Immediately."

"What's happened, Volodya?"

"It's serious. You have to get back here. We can't be talking about it on the phone."

One of the great things about chartering your own aircraft is that you can change schedules in an instant. So, that very day, we flew back to St. Petersburg. And the next morning I was at Putin's office.

On the morning of December 10, I met with Putin and Manevich and Viktor Ivanov. Ivanov was the St. Petersburg City coordinator for the various security organs of the state—police, KGB, customs, and so forth. He and Putin were very close. Viktor had worked for the KGB for many years suppressing internal dissent. On a personal/personnel level, Victor's stepdaughter Jana worked in my sales department. It was a valuable arrangement: on the most informal of levels, Viktor knew what I knew and vice versa.

So, we gathered in Putin's City Hall office. Manevich, his face grim, looked at me and said, "Franz, I'm going to give it to you straight. The bottom line is you've been expropriated."

I blinked. "Look, we've all heard rumors before. What makes this different?"

Manevich said, "The language. Before, nothing was said that was firm, so we didn't worry too much about it. But now…" His voice trailed off.

Putin looked at me from across the table. "Franz, you have to know this is not my doing; this is not the City's doing."

"I know that Volodya. You've been a great help."

Putin's expression told me he appreciated my remark.

I turned to Manevich. "What's the real story, Mikhail?"

Manevich said, "The message from Moscow is that UdPRF—the property office of the president is going to expropriate the land and use it, quote, 'for its own purposes'."

I frowned. "And that means?"

"They don't exactly specify what they need it for. But in general terms, 'K-4', which is UdPRF's designator for your chalet on Kamenny Ostrov and for the compound's real estate, it's all been allocated as the summer residence of the president."

There are people you fight, and there are people you don't. I knew enough to tell them I wasn't about to pick a fight with the president of the Russian Federation.

I focused on Putin. "Look, guys, I have no wish to resist the president. I'll go quietly. But I also need to be dealt with fairly, which means an adequate substitute property. Preferably, of course, on Kamenny Ostrov."

Putin said, "Franz, finding you a new property won't be a problem," "But," he continued, "you must understand we have limited resources as to how we can help you."

"What do you mean?"

"No one can stop the expropriation of your compound. In point of fact the only thing we can do is offer you an alternative site. It can be anywhere."

"Anywhere?" I interrupted. "Anywhere? Are you sure, Vladimir?"

"Yes, Franz, anywhere. Even on Kamenny Ostrov. You go and select whatever site you need, and I'll make sure you get it." He stopped long enough to smooth his hair back across his forehead. "There's no issue about that. But we cannot pay for your renovations on the new property."

I said, "That's alright."

Putin's expression showed relief. "That's alright?"

"Vladimir, I understand that if I get a new property on Kamenny Ostrov there'll be a lot of work to do. Most of the property on the island needs work. All I need is compensation for the improvements I've already done on this leasehold—the money I invested to make the chalet and the outbuildings habitable."

Putin cocked his head toward me. "Which came to?"

"It's between \$800,000 and \$900,000—I've got the exact figures back in my office."

Putin's eyes crinkled and he gave me a half-smile. "We can give you the land, Franz, but we cannot give you money." He looked around the room. "Everyone here knows we don't have any ourselves—I mean, the city's struggling financially." He paused, then winked. "We all know that, right?"

And then he laughed. I remember that distinctly because Vladimir Putin was not a man who laughed a lot.

Then, his expression grew serious, and he turned toward me. "So," Putin said, his pen tapping a cadence out on the top of his desk, "We need to A), find out how much money we're talking about—and Franz, you should be able to do that quickly—and then B), find out to whom we have to address the matter of compensation. There has to be some responsible individual, and we have to identify them."

And with that the meeting was over.

I felt violated. Damn it—and damn Boris, God-damn Yeltsin and his blankety-blanking UdPRF. One phone call and *poof!*—you're invisible. You don't exist anymore.

I'd been frigging expropriated. I was an unintended consequence of unintended damn consequences.

❖

Two days later we all met again in Putin's office. He said he had good news for me.

"The guy we're dealing with in Moscow," Putin said, "is named Pavel Borodin. He runs the UdPRF. We had real good rapport on the phone. In fact I got on with him brilliantly."

That was good news. I looked at Putin. "Great."

Putin pursed his lips. "He seems like a nice guy and reasonable, and I think—*I think*—we can work with him."

I said, "So, how exactly do we do that? I mean, work with him?"

Putin cocked his head to one side, eyes wide open, lost in scowling thought. For just an instant he looked like one of the double eagles on the Great Seal of the Russian Federation.

Then he turned toward me. "You write him a letter, Franz. A short letter. You tell him you understand about the decision to expropriate Kamenny Ostrov. You spell out what you've already done for the city, for the

KGB, for all of us. You say that you expect to be fairly compensated for money that you've spent improving the property, and that you will also need some form of compensation for the relevant expenses of your move to new headquarters. You spell out what you've done, and what you need. And above all, you keep it short."

"Easy. Can do."

Putin tapped the desk with his pen. "Then do it. Quickly—and then I'll go over it before you transmit it so it contains all the right messages."

❖

I wrote a draft, took it back to Putin's office within hours, and showed it to him.

He was impressed. "That's good—right on target." He made a few minor editorial changes so it would read better to Pavel Borodin and his staff.

I looked them over. It read very well. "So I should send it?"

"Absolutely. Send it off."

The letter went out by registered mail on December 12, 1994, over my signature. It was addressed to Mr. P. Borodin with copies to Putin, Manevich, and Ivanov. It was short and it was friendly.

In part, it read:

> Dear Mr. Borodin,
>
> We were officially informed that his Excellency, President Yeltsin, has made a decision to occupy the residence of Kamenny Ostrov for his own purposes under the strict condition that our company will be compensated fairly, by receiving new facilities and all relevant expenses.
>
> We have met in accordance to your instructions with leading

members of the Mayor's Office of St. Petersburg and have made an agreement that provides an adequate and fair arrangement between the parties, to ensure a correct and timely transition under the terms mutually stipulated....

...Kamenny Ostrov is in good standing and commercially successful. Kamenny Ostrov supports the beautiful city of St. Petersburg and has donated a complete equipment package and training program to the city budget, utilized by the counter-terrorist team "GRAD," valued at over $900,000. Kamenny Ostrov has also been asked by your own presidential guard service to provide special equipment in 1993. Our customer base covers virtually every law enforcement organ from Tax Police to Customs, and that nationwide one of our most valued customers is the President's home town of Ekaterinburg...

...As we expect a smooth transition, we are also prepared to invest an additional funds within 1995, into a security project designed to contribute in its majority to the Russian budget, namely law enforcement and road construction...

...We are convinced that we will conclude the transaction in the most efficient and cooperative method and look forward to receiving your esteemed representative in St. Petersburg. Sincerely,

Franz Sedelmayer
President

In an addendum, I attached the outline of a compensation plan that spelled out what I needed in order to relocate, to redo all my security licenses, to move my considerable inventory out of Kamenny Ostrov, and also receive compensation for the cost of significant improvements—somewhere north of $800,000—that I'd spent on updating, modernizing, and renovating the existing structures. All in all, I thought it was an effective piece of communication.

And just to be thorough, I followed up on the same date with a letter to Mikhail Manevich, with copies to Borodin, Putin, and Ivanov, explaining how pleased I was with the agreement that we had reached, and outlining the interim requirements that I'd need to move out of Kamenny Ostrov and find new space.

That letter ended:

> As agreed to, your office is to assign new facilities on Kamenny Ostrov, for our new joint stock company Kamenny Ostrov. There are several destroyed facilities on the island, which in combination can be utilized for that purpose, provided that SGC International, Inc. rebuilds these facilities in the shortest possible time under the accord reached. All calculations, both for financial details and replacement details are calculated now and are based on our existing facilities, located at Pollevaya Allea 6/8

Much to my surprise, in early January of 1995, I received a quick reply from Moscow.

It was devastating. Pavel Borodin proclaimed that Kamenny Ostrov had been illegally established. And because of that, I was entitled to no compensation whatsoever. I had no rights. None at all. The company was to be liquidated, full stop.

I immediately took Borodin's letter to Smolny. Igor Sechin took one look at my face and waved me through. Putin read it. His face went white. "Franz, you know, this is not my doing."

"I know, I know—but still…" To be honest I was flabbergasted. "Mr. Deputy Mayor, I'm at a loss. We all thought—you, Manevich, Ivanov—"

Putin recovered his composure. He took a breath then exhaled. "Look, to be honest I don't know how to deal with this. I mean, I'll try to find a solution. But, Franz, you have to understand something critical: my hands are tied because *this*"—he waved the letter—"This is coming out of Moscow."

"But—"

"There are no 'buts', Franz. Moscow makes all the rules these days."

He paused, looking at my face, reading my body language. "And there's something else you have to understand: whatever will take place from here on, it's not me. It won't be my doing. I'm your advocate, not your enemy — my name is on your registration papers after all. I know the company's legal."

"I do know, Mr. Deputy Mayor." And I did. Vladimir Putin was the individual who'd registered us, who'd appeared at the courthouse to file our paperwork; who'd worked to help us achieve the high standing we enjoyed in the St. Petersburg community. "And I'm grateful for everything you've done."

Putin's expression reflected his appreciation for my remark. Then his face darkened. "You know I won't do anything behind your back."

"Yes, I do know that."

"That's on the one hand. But Franz, there's the other hand, too. You have to understand that I can't — I won't — risk my career over this matter. I have to tread very carefully here."

"Got it." I did, too. We weren't in Munich, or St Louis. This was Russia. Yeltsin's Russia.

I also understood something else; something that had remained unsaid throughout the meeting. A copy of Borodin's devastating letter to me had to have gone to Putin. And to Manevich. And to Ivanov. They'd all known about Borodin's decision — probably before I did. That's the way things worked in Russia. But because it was the way things worked I wasn't angry. Yes, Putin knew about the letter before I showed up at his office. But that was life in Russia. That was business in Russia, and I was a part of it. There was no reason to be mad at the messenger.

Was I certain? Yeah. For example, Putin never asked me, 'So, when are you going to close down and move out?" And there was good reason for that: Putin knew me pretty well and he knew I wouldn't volunteer to surrender. But he also knew that expropriation was Moscow's endgame, and that he wasn't about to help alter the preordained result.

So, in that sense, everything was clear between us. There was no problem. Still, I wanted him, as well as the rest of them to know—and to pass the message to Moscow—that the matter was not concluded. Not to me at least.

So, I said, "Mr. Deputy Mayor, I think you need to understand something as well. Which is that if I don't get compensation, I'm not moving."

"From your position Franz, that makes sense."

"And I also mean, Mr. Deputy Mayor, that from here on, whatever happens, whatever Moscow decides to do to me, it will all have to be done in public. In fact, I'll make certain to make it happen that way. I won't let this crime—because that's what it is, Vladimir, it's a crime against me—take place behind closed doors, so Moscow can get away with it the way Moscow always does."

Putin's stone-like expression told me all I needed to know.

Which is why, over the next few weeks, I modified my whole modus operandi on any number of levels. For example, I'd always been cautious about dealing with the press. Yes, I'd used the press to great advantage during the Pinchuk takeover fiasco. But ever since I'd kept my head down because in the security business it's better that way. Now, however, I sought the press out, and within the couple of months following Borodin's nasty letter, I'd appeared on multiple TV networks and in several newspapers pleading my case.

It was a perfect television story because television loves victims, and I was a victim. The scenario had the added advantage of being true: Moscow, i.e., the UdPRF, was trying to expropriate a small American company. Worse, the Kremlin was attempting to drive me out of business because

President Yeltsin wanted my property for his summer getaway. And yet, the selfsame Yeltsin had gone on the record about protecting small businessmen like me. He'd issued a significant number of public and well-publicized statements about the necessity of protecting foreign investment in his almost-bankrupt nation, and yet here he was trying to steal all my property and all the fruits of my labor and pay me nothing for it. Zilch. Zero.

And, by the way, that wasn't my take on the situation—it was CNN's. And it made some waves.

German Television's Prime News did a segment that featured Vlada and Danushka. Vlada was introduced as my Russian wife. It was perfect television. She spoke in German while holding the baby: "Thank God Franz is German, because at least he has the consulate to go to. If this happened to somebody like me—an ordinary Russian—I couldn't go to the police or the courts because they always take the government's side. At least Franz has the German Government to stand up for him."

And then NBC News showed up. They taped a segment with me standing in front of my office wall filled with pictures of the SWAT team, and with all the Russian friends I'd made, and I looked straight into the camera and said something to the effect of, "If this expropriation of an American corporation stands and the government uses force to evict me from the property for which I have a signed 25-year lease—a lease signed by the government of the City of St. Petersburg and also an agreement signed by KUGI, which is headquartered in Moscow, then there will be no turning back for Russia, and I'm convinced that you'll see this type of unlawful behavior more and more."

In the light of all that TV exposure even the American ambassador—it was Tom Pickering in those days—got involved. By now, my old friend, the former Consul General Jack Gosnell was back in Washington working at State Department headquarters on the Russian Desk. And even though he and Pickering seldom saw eye to eye (Pickering was an archetypal understated diplomat while Jack was a confrontational maverick), they both worked hard on my behalf and remained optimistic throughout 1995's 'long march.'

As the new U.S. Consul General John Evans put it to me, "Franz, the Czar has many beautiful daughters." It was an old Russian proverb. It means, "We'll find a way."

Well, maybe we would and maybe we wouldn't. But I had to keep trying, had to keep fighting, because I knew that if I caved, if I showed any sign of weakness or vulnerability, the Russians would sweep in, steal everything, and I'd be out on my ear with absolutely no recourse.

After all, who could I go to? The courts? I knew all about telephone justice. I'd have no chance in the courts. And the police? The police had spent a good deal of time and energy trying to steal my company from the get-go. Even my friends at KGB were helpless, because everything was decided in Moscow these days. Pick your image: the deck was stacked; the dice were loaded. Toss a coin? Heads: Moscow wins. Tails: Moscow wins.

And what about my pal, my friend, my compadre the deputy mayor? Indeed: what about Vladimir Vladimirovich Putin?

Putin had told me straight out that he would help where he could, but there was no way he was going to stick his neck out for me; no way he was going to take Moscow on; no way he would go up against Boris Yeltsin.

I couldn't blame him. Putin was a realist. He wasn't playing the odds—he knew precisely how the system worked. If it came down to me or the *upravlenie*—the Office of the President—was going to win, no matter how hard I tried.

Putin knew that. And so did I.

But I'd also vowed to myself that Moscow was not going to win without a huge fight—that I'd do whatever it took to recoup my investment. Even if it took years.

CHAPTER 12
KRYMNASH! (Crimea is Ours)
"Our toilets may not work, but Krymnash!"
—Russian online meme circa 2016

It was on the morning the Columbus Day holiday was celebrated—October 9, 1995—that the Russians invaded Kamenny Ostrov and took us over by force. Of course they did: it was an official U.S. holiday and they figured that, with the consulate closed, all the Americans in St. Petersburg would be celebrating—eating hot dogs and hamburgers and drinking beer.

But the Russians were wrong. As soon as I understood what was happening, I called the consulate's private number to let them know we'd been invaded and the RSO (Regional Security Officer) told me he'd advise the consul and they'd take appropriate action.

The Russians came at about 11 a.m. There was a bailiff, and a court officer, and several other civilians, probably from the UdPRF or the president's office, and a swarm of armed police: OMON riot cops who worked for the Ministry of the Interior.

I had a full complement of people on hand—there were between 40 and 50—because for us it was a normal working day. Vlada, her father Dima, and my son Danushka were upstairs in the living quarters.

Just after 11 a.m. my shift manager, Lyosha, came upstairs to my office. He rapped on my door. "Hey, boss—they're here."

"Who's here?"

"Police—OMON."

How many?"

"Maybe 50 in all."

"Armed?"

"OMON? Oh, yeah. And they have a bailiff and some other assholes."

"I'm on my way."

The invasion was not a complete surprise. Starting in early 1995 we'd even done contingency drills. After all, I held a piece of paper in my hands that came from Pavel Borodin, saying my company and the property it sat on were all illegal. And an armed takeover was a subject Mikhail Manevich, Viktor Ivanov, Vladimir Putin, and I had talked about repeatedly during the previous 10 months. Obviously, some form of action by the UdPRF was going to be inevitable and the Little Sisters of the GUVD would be itching to get their hands on property they believed was rightfully theirs. But I wasn't about to let them do it without a fight.

There was one unsettling anomaly. As I assembled my troops that October morning, I realized that my loyal troika of supporters at Smolny—Mikhail Manevich, Viktor Ivanov, and Vladimir Putin—all must have known what was going to happen, but hadn't bothered to give me a heads up.

The reason I knew they'd been given advance notice was that Jana, Viktor Ivanov's daughter, worked for me. Jana hadn't shown up for the previous two days. And Viktor was basically responsible for the security of the City—he coordinated everything between the various State organs. The police, customs, GUVD, OMON, border patrol, and the fire department all came under his purview. If OMON was going to stage a raid, he'd be informed. If a bailiff was going to serve a UdPRF eviction notice, he'd be informed.

Moreover, Jana had worked for us for a year and a half. She'd showed up every day and on the very few days she'd been sick, she had called me to let us know she wouldn't be coming to work.

Jana hadn't called for two days. She was MIA.

Which told me in bright neon letters her daddy didn't want her anywhere near Kamenny Ostrov…because he knew something nasty was going to happen. And, in that split second, I knew that if Viktor Ivanov knew, then so did Mikhail Manevich as well as Igor Ivanovich Sechin, Vladimir Putin's chief of staff and alter ego.

And, if Igor Ivanovich and Manevich knew, then it was inevitable Deputy Mayor Vladimir Vladimirovich Putin also knew what was about to happen.

In fact, the only high-ranking St. Petersburg official, probably in the dark about my predicament, was the mayor himself—the Honorable Anatoly Sobchak. They seldom told Anatoly anything. They let him collect his suitcases of money, talk his politics, and sign whatever they put in front of him to sign.

Of course they did. It was Russia. That's how things worked.

I wasn't angry with them. Disappointed? Sure. But this was *dikiy dikiy vostok*, the 'Wild Wild East,' where the rules changed on a daily basis, and where, if you were president, there was very little you could not do. As the Putin-era Russian joke goes, "In most other countries, it's the president who gets assassinated. In Russia the president assassinates YOU."

So, I rolled up my sleeves and got to work. We had video cameras on hand. I made sure everything that happened would be captured on tape. I assigned my people their roles. I took my head of security aside. "Keep all the doors to the main house locked. No one gets in. I'll go out and talk to them. On the one hand, we don't want to create the impression that we won't negotiate. But on the other hand, once they get inside it'll be impossible to get them out again without a fight. So: nobody gets in!"

"*Da*, Boss."

I made my way downstairs, opened the front door and went outside, listening to hear as my crew locked the doors behind me. I wasn't alone. My wife Vlada, and my old friend and business associate Tom Church, who was visiting from Chicago to help with the company books, came with me. So did my translator, a handful of KOC guards and my two Stone Island videographers.

The bailiff was standing at the foot of the entrance way. I looked at the two guys holding the cameras. "Get everything—*Everything!*"

"*Budet sdelano*, Boss—Will be done."

I made sure the cameras were rolling. Then I shouted, "Madam Bailiff—"

She looked toward me.

"On whose order are you here?"

She tried to stare me down. It didn't work. Her jowls fluttered nervously. "I am here on behalf of the Kremlin."

"By whose authority?"

She gave me an insulting sneer, straightened the sheet of paper she was carrying so it sat directly in front of her nose, and declaimed loudly: "In the name of the Russian Federation I hereby evict you from Kamenny Ostrov for violation of illegally setting up a private—"

What was this, soap opera? "Madam Bailiff," I interrupted, "You're not going to evict me. Not now. Not ever. You can forget it. You can go home right now."

The bailiff gave me a dirty look and tried to continue. When she did, I interrupted her again, demanding to know on whose authority she was doing this.

And again, she answered even louder. And in doing so, she documented for all time—and on video tape—precisely who was responsible. "I evict you in the name of the President of the Russian Federation!"

And just about that time, the cavalry arrived. Well, better than cavalry. The Americans showed up: the Vice Consul, a few of his Marine Guards, and a handful of consulate employees, one of whom walked over to the bailiff and explained in diplomatic terms that the American presence was to ensure that nothing illegal took place. "The United States does not condone strong-arming," he said.

The very fact that there was an American presence made the invaders nervous, so things cooled down pretty rapidly. It took a while and some tough negotiation, but by about 2 p.m. we ended up in more or less of a Mexican standoff.

I was able to keep the Chalet; the invaders took over the sauna house and the dining facility. I retained control of the weapons locker and some of my equipment. They, unfortunately, took control of my business records, which were stored in the sauna, where Tom Church was staying. I had my people guarding the perimeter of the portion of the compound I controlled; the police had armed officers patrolling their sector. It was like occupied Berlin or the demilitarized zone between North and South Korea. The siege went on that way until late January, 1996.

In retrospect, it was an inconvenient but manageable situation. I'd planned ahead. I'd created a separate off-site facility for my security guard company KOC, and for those of us in the main house, we had a workable, if sometimes uneasy relationship with the occupying force. Given the fact that both my employees—many of whom were KGB and GRAD SWAT personnel—and the OMON police were armed with many of the same weapons, we managed to keep confrontations to a minimum.

Not that the occupation didn't cause problems. We couldn't get spare parts because the occupiers sealed the equipment rooms; we couldn't deliver merchandise to our customers because the products slated for delivery were locked up. Much of the Stone Island Company's traditional activity, therefore, came to a standstill in October of 1995. Still, I'd prepared for an eventuality like this. So, I didn't fire anybody or lay anybody off. Some people quit because they didn't want to be involved in a situation that might end badly. But most stayed.

Even so, I have to admit that for me, that last quarter of 1995 was tough. No: it was extremely tough. More than anything, I felt betrayed: betrayed by the city I'd grown to love; betrayed by the President's office and the goddamn UdPRF; betrayed by a system that encouraged lying, cheating, and stealing.

I'd always taken Vladimir Putin's words at our first meeting to heart.

"What have *you* ever done for the city," is what he'd asked.

My answer then had been "Quite a lot, Mr. Deputy Mayor." And I had. I'd done a lot. Over the past half-decade I'd modernized their policing, both in tactics and equipment. I'd built the KGB's first Western-style SWAT team. I'd fought the Mafiya. I'd added to the St. Petersburg economy by bringing in large amounts of *valuta*—the hard currency that was all too rare except to oligarchs, politicians, and organized crime. The Kamenny Ostrov Company served government agencies; supplied them with law enforcement equipment, specialized vehicles, and training. We'd dealt with fire departments, police departments, the FSB, and the Ministry of Security all across the Russian Federation. We had good working relationships with police and emergency services from Kazakhstan to the Baltic; from the Neva to the Volga. But everything was centered in St. Petersburg—on Kamenny Ostrov.

I'd always considered myself an integral part of the city; a part of its economy, a part of its social life—all those Beer Calls and American Business Association receptions—and an involved citizen. After all, I'd taken on the mob during the Goodwill Games the previous year, and publicly stood up against corruption. And yes, I'd made money. But I'd invested well into the millions of dollars in my businesses, and in the city. I'd assumed—incorrectly as it turned out—that, what I'd done over the past six years, was in a small way important to the future of both St. Petersburg, and in a minor way to Russia itself.

But it was not to be. I'd been expropriated. There were OMON officers roaming my compound. I couldn't get to my supplies. My books had been confiscated. And the situation could go on indefinitely. Months? Possibly. Years? It wasn't inconceivable.

The questions was, what could I do about it? This was, after all, Russia. I knew if I went to court, it would all be over. I'd lose everything. Why? Because Russia was evolving into a kleptocracy and only the kleptos would survive.

Still, there was one possible solution to my problem. It was a long shot, but I'd been mulling it over the past few weeks. It was something I'd come upon by happenstance. It was called arbitration.

Shortly after I opened the Kamenny Ostrov Company, a young friend of mine named Matthias Ebinal, and a Russian lawyer Valery Mitjushkin, wrote a book about business in Russia. "*Das Russlandgeschäft*" ("The Russia Business") was published in 1992, and Matthias inscribed it very nicely to me. I took "*Das Russlandgeschäft*," said, "Thank you very much Matthias," thumbed through it once, put it on my shelf, and never looked at it again.

Fast forward to October, 1995. I remembered that somewhere there was a book about doing business in Russia. I went through the shelves until I found it, blew the dust off, then riffled through the table of contents hoping that I'd find something that would help me fix my current situation. I leafed through the book and—*mirable dictu*—found an entire chapter titled "Investment Protection."

I started to read. My goal at that point was pretty basic: find a way to get compensation for the things I would lose under expropriation. I already knew that Russian courts were out of the question. I knew because I'd already tried. But, whenever I filed a complaint in a Russian Court citing the fact that we'd been expropriated under Presidential Decree by Boris Yeltsin, the court said, "Sorry, we cannot entertain the case."

Why? Because the president and the UdPRF owned the courts in Russia. If I sued, someone in Moscow would make a phone call, the verdict would be predetermined, and I'd be out on my ass. So the courts, which would be the normal way to proceed, wouldn't work for me.

Okay then. No Russian courts. But what about suing UdPRF in a German court? As it turned out, I couldn't file in Germany because in Germany the Government of the Russian Federation has sovereign immunity—kind of like diplomatic immunity on steroids. Further, expropriation, in other words, the taking of property by Presidential Decree for public purpose—this was the case with Kamenny Ostrov—was something that could not be entertained in a Court of Law, especially outside the country where the expropriation had taken place.

It was all hugely disheartening. Demoralizing. My situation was absurdly Kafkaesque. And then, buried in the "*Das Russlandgeschäft*" chapter on Investment Protection, I found a nugget of hope.

In the 1950s, the Germans had come up with a mechanism to protect German investors and entrepreneurs who went into problematic countries—the Middle East, Africa, South America and so on; places where there was a fair chance that a business project would end badly for the investor because of illegitimate government interference, corruption, or expropriation.

What the German government did was create a procedure by which any German national or German-registered company whose investment is unjustly expropriated, has the right to demand fair compensation. If the host state refuses to pay fair compensation in full or in part, the investor can resort to arbitration against that host state. In addition, the compensation has to be—and this was the most important part: "*just, effective, and freely transferable*." In other words, the compensation has to be equal in value to what it was *before* it became known that you or your company would be expropriated, and that same compensation has to be paid out in currency convertible into *valuta* (western currencies such as dollars, euros, or Swiss francs), and finally it has to be freely transferable to a bank account in a country of your choice.

But there was a catch: I couldn't file the case in a German court. In my case I had either to apply to an arbitration tribunal or sue in a local Russian court. I knew all too well I'd never receive a fair deal in the Russian courts. In Russia all the decks were stacked.

But arbitration? Arbitration leveled the playing field.

Once the tribunal took up the case, it would determine what just compensation I'd be entitled to. If I won, they'd hand me an arbitration award, in essence a court judgment that I could collect. That was the up side. The down side was that I'd have to self-fund the process, which could end up costing me millions. Not only that, but arbitration can be lengthy. Some cases last a decade or more. And because it is self-funded, I'd not only have to pay all the legal fees for arbitration, if I won I'd even have to bankroll the enforcement process. That would be a lot of good money spent.

And what if I lost?

If I lost at any point—arbitration or during an attempted enforcement—then everything would go down the drain.

But even with all those potential dangers, arbitration still seemed the best way to proceed. I did more research. I discovered that the way arbitration works is that it's a private affair, which means it exists outside the court system. It's also internationally recognized. Most important, what arbitration did for me was that it opened a way to take my dispute outside Russia.

I decided to initiate arbitration in Sweden, because I, as a German, possessed the right to arbitrate there under a German-Soviet Treaty that had been signed in 1989 and ratified in 1991. The treaty named the

Stockholm Chamber of Commerce as appointing authority for the *ad hoc* tribunal. The Swedes, like the Swiss and the Austrians, have long maintained a neutral status and were known as a center for East-West disputes. And because of this they had the reputation of handling commercial disputes in an even-handed fashion.

I started assembling the paperwork immediately and made arrangements to fly to Sweden after Vlada and I celebrated Christmas and the New Year with friends in Chicago. And so, on January 11th, I met with Ulf Franke, the head of the Stockholm Chamber of Commerce Arbitration Institute, who explained the process to me and outlined what I'd need to proceed. He told me he'd never heard of a case in which Russia's president directly ordered the expropriation of a Western company. That, he said, was a first.

We returned to St. Petersburg on January 13th, and on the 15th, I initiated the arbitration process against the Russian Federation in Sweden.

Three days later I received word that my maternal grandmother was terminally ill. I packed up Vlada and my year-and-a-half old son Daniel, and we rushed back to Munich to be with her.

My absence was all that UdPRF needed: on January 24, the day before we were to fly back to St. Petersburg, OMON broke into the chalet and occupied the entire compound. In that instant, Stone Island was history.

Suddenly, I had nothing to come back to. No business, no property, nothing. I sat in Munich, shattered yes, but as angry as I've ever been.

I understood why they'd done what they'd done: it was all about the leasehold improvements. I'd spent almost a million bucks redoing Kamenny Ostrov. And when I'd been expropriated, Putin, Manevich, and Ivanov told me they'd find me another property on the Island—anything I wanted. But, when I looked at the buildings, I saw buildings with no roofs; burnt out shells or un-renovated, uninsulated, uninhabitable ruins that would have taken as much money to fix as my chalet. And once I'd fixed the property up? UdPRF would no doubt swoop in and confiscate it, too.

That was why I'd insisted on getting my leasehold improvement money back before I'd give up Kamenny Ostrov. But now the whole compound and everything in it had been taken from me. And the hard, cold fact—especially in Russia—is that possession is nine-tenths of the law.

So I was screwed.

I picked up the phone and called Putin's office. He'd know what to do.

The phone rang twice. "Igor Ivanovich." It was Sechin. I could hear Putin's voice in the background.

"Igor Ivanovich, it's Franz Sedelmayer. I'm calling from Munich. I need to speak to Volodya right away."

"Franz, good to hear your voice. I'll get him for you."

There was silence for an instant, and then Putin's voice: "Franz—"

"Volodya, I'm in Munich and I just got word. What are we going to do? I—"

Putin cut me off. "I know, Franz." There was a pause. "Frankly, I don't know what to tell you."

"Isn't there anything we can—"

"Franz, Franz, listen to me. I don't know what to tell you, but they've got it and that's the way it is. I can't change things now that they've taken it all."

I said, "C'mon, Volodya, tell me what do you think I should do. What do you recommend, buddy? You know the system better than anyone. There's got to be a way."

There was dead silence for perhaps ten seconds. And then he said, "What do I recommend, Franz? Sue them. If you don't like what they did to you, sue them."

I blinked. His tone of voice hit me like a slap in the face. When he'd picked up the phone he'd been earnest and concerned. It was the voice of my friend; my drinking buddy, my advisor and counsel. But this voice was none of the above. This voice was cold, sarcastic, mocking. It was not the Putin I'd come to know. But it was without doubt the same Putin who now rules Russia. Was I the first to see this side of him? Not the passionate reformer deputy mayor, but a cold autocrat who'd throw you under the bus without blinking an eye? Looking back on that conversation now, I think perhaps I might have been.

And then Putin repeated himself. "What do I recommend? Sue them, Franz. If you don't like what they did to you, sue them. That's all I can tell you."

We exchanged some small pleasantries. Putin told me not to take what Moscow had done personally, and then we hung up.

It was the last conversation we ever had.

❖

We returned to St. Petersburg on February 8th. My in-laws found us an apartment. I was so numb I don't remember where it was even now, except that it was close to Stone Island. I didn't do much. I conferred with lawyers and went to the American Consulate, and watched as *upravlenie* gobbled up as much of my property as it could find. They had my compound. Now, when they discovered one of my vehicles on the street they'd confiscate it. By the middle of February I was living in a state of permanent flux.

I was fluxed alright. The Russians had fluxed me out of my business, my house, and my livelihood. Oh, yeah: I was totally fluxed up.

My existence reminded me of the anarchist graffiti I used to see spray painted on walls in the late 1970s. It read: "*YOU DON'T HAVE A CHANCE - USE IT.*"

By the end of the month I could read the UdPRF graffiti on the wall loud and clear: I didn't have a chance and there was nothing I could do.

KOC, my guard company, still had contracts to fulfill, and Sacha Sipchenko, the Afghan war vet who'd served with Igor Sechin in Africa—could run it. He'd done well for me at Banque Credit Lyonnais, and he'd excelled coordinating things at KOC.

On March 6th, I decided it was time to go. Why put off the inevitable? I packed a suit bag, took what paperwork I could find, a laptop, and my clothes. I peeled all the KOC decals off my Crown Victoria and drove down to the harbor with my translator to catch the ferry to Travemünde. Sacha Sipchenko drove down too, along with a few other friends. They'd wave me aboard.

I pulled into the customs shed. That was normal procedure. But what happened next wasn't. A customs officer in a bad suit confiscated my car and my laptop. His crew took my suit bag and searched me for documents, confiscating every one they found.

Then Bad Suit Guy looked me up and down, and said in Russian, "You're under arrest."

I looked at him, incredulous. "Oh, that's just fabulous. That's great. For what?"

He laughed. "Don't you worry. They'll figure out something."

I looked back at the knot of friends who'd driven down to see me off. I jerked my thumb in Sacha Sipchenko's direction and told my translator, "Tell him to call the Big House—get hold of both Big House Sachas."

The Big House Sachas were Sacha Krillov, the KGB GRAD Team commander, and Sacha Kusnetsov, the overall head of KGB Counterterrorism in St. Petersburg. Krillov was a baby *nachalnik* so he had some pull. But Kusnetsov? He was a big-time *nachalnik*. He had major juice. And he was my friend. "Tell them what's going on."

I watched as my Sacha made the call.

A couple of minutes later Bad Suit Guy's mobile phone rang. He answered, listened, and then hung up. He looked at me and said, "I'm going to have to let you go."

I gave him a sly smile. "I was expecting that." Actually, I'd been praying for it but I wasn't about to show Mr. Bad Suit anything but a poker face.

But the ordeal still wasn't over. They'd taken all my stuff. I picked up my suit bag and started walking toward the gangway when I was stopped by a border policeman.

I showed him my passport and resumed my trek toward the ferry.

"You can't go this way. Cars only."

I pointed back toward my confiscated Crown Vic. "That's my car. They took it."

"You must have a car. Pedestrians can't come this way."

His idiocy pushed me over the edge. I dropped my suit bag in front of the border cop and walked back to where Mr. Bad Suit was standing, watching. I looked him in the eye and said, "You tell that asshole to let me go on board or I will drop your sorry ass right where you stand."

Mr. Bad Suit looked down at my clenched fists and up at my murderous expression and answered me in perfect English. He said: "One moment, please." Then he went over to the border cop, spoke with him, turned, and came back to where I stood. He looked at me and again in English, said, "I'm really sorry, Franz," then he turned and walked away.

I picked up my bag, marched to the ferry, and went aboard, never looking back.

I haven't been to Russia since that day. But I've thought about Russia every day since.

Part Three

At War with Putingrad

CHAPTER 13
Life in the Abstract

"The strong cannot be called to account for crimes they have committed unless they have violated the rights of someone stronger."
—Article 8, The Russian Mafiya Constitution, 2012

1996 was a seminal year for Anatoly Sobchak and Vladimir Putin as much as it was a seminal year for me. I lost Kamenny Ostrov; Sobchak lost his bid for re-election, and Putin? Putin lost his job as deputy mayor of St. Petersburg. But as I learned later he got a new one. In Moscow. Working for Pavel Borodin, the very same Pavel Borodin who had at Boris Yeltsin's direction expropriated Kamenny Ostrov and hounded me out of Russia.

In retrospect, I should have anticipated it all—the behind-the-scenes maneuvering, the subterfuge, the lies, the invasion, and the inevitable expropriation.

Of course, that's not quite accurate. Yes: the dots were all there. But I wasn't as good at connecting dots then as I am now.

For example, shortly before the October 1995 invasion—the one UdPRF staged on Columbus Day—I received a visit from the KGB. An officer from the Big House dropped by. I don't remember his name, but let's call him Sergei.

"Franz," he said, "So what are you going to do? The Big House wants to know."

"'Do?'" I had no idea what he was talking about. "Do about what, Sergei?"

He spread his arms wide. "About all this. Kamenny Ostrov. Stone Island. Your company. Everything. What happens to you if Yeltsin expropriates it?"

His question made very little sense. Well, what do you think I'd do?"

"I dunno." He scratched his chin. "We think maybe you're going to give up Kamenny Ostrov, and then you're going to keep on working in Russia and put together a new company."

"You mean you think I'm going to stay and start all over again? From scratch? After building all of this—" I pointed in a wide arc around the room—"and having it stolen from me?"

He thought about what I'd said. Then he said, "Well, yes, we do. After all, you still need to make money, don't you?"

He didn't realize it, but in that response he'd epitomized the difference between the Russian mindset and mine. The difference between me and Boris, the poor little guy on skis I saw on the road from Vyborg to Leningrad in the winter of 1989; the peasant who *mush-mush-mushed* and *trudge-trudge-trudged* miles and miles through the snow to his *derevnya* because that's what he'd been doing all his life.

And, if Moscow swooped in and took away his skis, he'd go on trudge-trudge-trudging on foot, because that's what Russians do. They endure. They suck it up. They suffer in silence. They'd done it under the Czars; they did it under Stalin, and now—even though there was no Soviet Union anymore they were doing it under Boris Yeltsin. Sucking it up and suffering. I hadn't heard anybody going nose to nose with a bureaucrat to demand *shratz-i-den'gi*—chow and money—in years. Food shortages? They got in line. No *valuta*? They bartered and traded. Rampant crime and corruption? Just another miserable fact of life that had to be adjusted to.

Well, that wasn't me. I'm not a character out of Dostoevsky. I'm a Bavarian and an entrepreneur and if you take what's mine I won't be sucking it up or adjusting. I'll be fighting back.

So, I told Sergei something he didn't expect to hear. "Yeah—I need to make money," I said. "But I won't be doing it in Russia. Look, pal, I lived very successfully without Russia for more than 25 years and I can do it again. If Kamenny is taken from me I don't have a problem leaving. You guys have the problem, Sergei, not me. Because what I do here helps you—brings you along. Makes you and the city better. And if Moscow decides to take it all away? I'm outta here."

And now, hindsight being 20/20, I understand that the message Sergei carried back to the Big House—and ultimately to Putin, and to Putin's new friend in Moscow, Pavel Borodin—was that if I was expropriated, I'd leave Russia and that would be that. There would be no consequences. Except Sergei got it wrong. Neither he—nor, as it turned out, Putin—understood that I'd stand up for myself and get back what was rightfully mine no matter how long it might take.

And, by the way, it wasn't just the visit from Sergei that foretold the invasion and expropriation. Putin gave me the same message.

On the one hand, as deputy mayor, he didn't need the headache that expropriating a successful foreign company would give him, because of how it would adversely affect all the other foreign joint ventures he'd worked so hard to achieve in St. Petersburg.

But on the other hand, he was afraid that if he protected me he'd end up on the wrong side of history—history being Boris Yeltsin's new Moscow-centric government—and thus demolish his own career.

So, he played both sides against the middle—the middle being *moi*.

He supported me, but he didn't give me all the facts I needed. He tried to find a workable compromise, but when he knew the chips were down, he and his colleagues at Smolny would let UdPRF do its thing.

More than once, Putin told me, "I'm trying to find a peaceful solution here, Franz, and I'd do anything for that. You know me." And he was being honest when he told me that. He DID try to find compromises. But none of them worked.

And more than once he looked me in the eye and said, "Franz, this is not me. This is not coming from me; it is not my choice." And he was being honest when he told me that, too. They weren't his choices, they were Moscow's decisions. I thought they were the wrong decisions and told him so. And he agreed with me. But he wasn't willing to push back. Putin was always frank about his bottom line. "You have to understand, Franz, I cannot go to war with Moscow over this. I cannot risk my career. I will not risk my career."

I was frank as well: "Vladimir, I will not vacate Stone Island unless I'm compensated for what I've spent in refurbishing and improving the property, and also for the loss I'm taking over the 25 year lease that was duly registered with your signature."

So, the lines were clear. Putin stated his case; I stated my case. My bottom line was: no compensation, no moving out. And that's how it went down. UdPRF had to take Stone Island from me by force. Which is exactly what they did—and Putin knew about it in advance and did nothing. Which is exactly what he'd told me he'd do if Moscow forced the issue.

Thinking about it now, I still believe Putin was not happy with how events turned out. Back then, he didn't have a vote. These days of course he's got the only vote that counts.

But back in 1996? Back then he was scrambling for a new job after Sobchak's upset and he found it in Moscow, hired by Pavel Borodin.

And while he was doing that, I was commuting between Munich and Stockholm, about to do something that hadn't been tried in more than half a century. I was about to sue Russia for expropriating my company, thus causing me to lose my long-term investment.

❖

I took the case outside Russia because whenever I'd tried to file a complaint in the Russian Court citing the fact that we'd been expropriated under presidential decree by Boris Yeltsin, the court would tell me, "Sorry, we cannot entertain your case." Now, if they'd obeyed the law they would've had to accept it. But in Russia the law had never meant much, and in Yeltsin's Russia the President's word was the law. Bottom line: I had no chance of winning in Russia.

What about Germany? I checked. The German courts would not entertain my case because it meant taking on a sovereign government. France? *Mais non,* Monsieur Sedelmayer, *pas possible.* Switzerland? Nah. Luxembourg? No way. UK? So sorry, old chap.

It didn't take long to grasp that the only way to go forward was through arbitration in Sweden.

And so, early in 1996, I'd gone to Stockholm, set up an appointment with Ulf Franke, the Secretary General of the Arbitration Institute, and explained my situation to him.

Franke listened to what I had to say, his eyes growing wider with each anecdote. "My God," he said when I'd finished, "This is the strangest story I've ever heard. I mean, it's hard for me to believe they're doing this to you because they urgently need investment in Russia, and if this case hits the newspapers it'll become a huge deterrent for anyone who ever considered investing there."

"So the Institute will take my case?"

"Absolutely."

Franke explained that he needed a $1000 filing fee, after which he'd send out the proper notifications to the parties. Then, the Russians would appoint their arbitrator and I would appoint mine. The two arbitrators would choose a third individual acceptable to them both as the chairman of the tribunal. The two arbitrators would then choose a third party to be chairman of the tribunal. If they could not agree on a choice, that duty would go to Ulf Franke.

In my case the two arbitrators, a German and a Russian, could not agree on who to name the tribunal chairman. So Ulf Franke appointed a retired Swedish Supreme Court Judge named Staffan Magnusson.

I was delighted. Magnusson had a distinguished and long-standing career during which he'd made very controversial decisions with the Constitutional Court. He was a critical and independent thinker and brought a voice of maturity to the process.

Since the tribunal would have to be paid, I'd pay half its fee and the Russians the other half.

But I'd been in Russia long enough to know that Russians don't always pay what they owe. I asked Judge Magnusson, "What if the Russians don't pay?"

"Then the arbitration tribunal can't move forward."

That was a potential problem. I'd researched the subject. The 1989 Treaty between Germany and Russia contained an arbitration clause that says very clearly, each party has to pay an equal share for the tribunal and of course, each party has to cover its own legal fees. The situation was clear: the Russians had signed the treaty so it was law in Russia. But just as I'd feared, when time came to write a check they refused to pay their share.

Why? The Russians refused to pay their half because they said they'd been unfairly dragged into the arbitration and weren't going to support it.

Their refusal forced the tribunal to halt proceedings. Judge Magnusson explained it to me this way: "We expect a deposit of 200,000 Swedish crowns to be deposited from each side. If one of the parties doesn't pay we repeat our request to both parties. If one side still fails to make its deposit, the other side either makes up the fee, or everything comes to a halt. Without full payment the arbitration process will be stopped until the full sum is received. And should the initial funds be exhausted, the tribunal will ask for another payment from each party until the arbitration is concluded and an award can be rendered. So, either you put it all up, Franz, or everything stops here."

Which is exactly what Moscow wanted. I told Judge Magnusson, "Screw them. I'll put up the money."

And I did. I ended up paying for the remainder of the proceedings. Ultimately, it would cost me 1,400,000 Swedish crowns.

The payment received, Judge Magnusson said, "Good. We can proceed immediately."

I soon discovered that 'immediately' was a relative term.

First, a Preliminary Hearing was to be held by the tribunal to decide whether or not to allow the claim to be heard, and if, as a prerequisite, an arbitration clause existed. In our case the agreement to arbitrate was embedded in the German-Russian investment treaty. The last order of the day would be to fix the schedule for the arbitration proceedings. Thus, all formalities would be concluded. According to Ulf Franke, this would take somewhere between six and seven months, after which the Final Hearing—which takes about a week—would take place. There could be one or more additional briefs from each party, before the Main Hearing would take place. During the Main Hearing the merits and the legal questions were to be debated, the witnesses were to be heard and the final arguments were to be made. After this the tribunal would reach a decision in the form of an arbitration award. But, as Ulf Franke had warned me in the very beginning, everything was in the abstract.

One element that would ultimately work in my favor was that Russia had not been involved in any sort of expropriation or investment dispute since the 1920s. This meant they lacked current practical experience. That deficiency showed itself during the Preliminary Hearing, when the Russian government—to be precise the UdPRF—tried to launch a series of pre-emptive attacks on my case.

The first argument the Russians made to get the case quashed was that, as the owner of an American company, I didn't have the right to ask for arbitration. Except no one at UdPRF had done any legal research. If they had, they'd have known I had the right to arbitrate under a Treaty between Germany and Russia that had been signed in 1989 and ratified in 1991. Maybe they hadn't read the Treaty, but I had. And it said *"Any type of investment made by a natural person, with a permanent residence in either one of those countries"* could seek relief. The origin of the corporation didn't matter. The Tribunal Ruled that the case could proceed.

Then, the Russians protested that while I might indeed be the owner of a company, the treaty covered only individuals who made direct investments in their companies. I, they claimed, had made only indirect investments, using my U.S. company as an investment vehicle, something that would prevent me from seeking arbitration. Their reasoning was simple: when UdPRF took over my property, it confiscated all of the company paperwork, including some of the customs receipts for the cash I'd brought into Russia to invest in Kamenny Ostrov.

Luckily, I'd made copies and had them stored both in the U.S. and Germany. I was also able to provide the Swedes with Russian customs receipts and even some originals showing that I'd brought over $1 million in cash into Russia so that I could plow the money into my company. I also had witnesses who could corroborate my direct investment in Kamenny Ostrov.

After Arbitration Institute's notices went out, the Russians responded with not-so-veiled threats. "It is not a good idea to challenge the Russian Federation" was one of their responses. "There will be strong consequences to this sort of brazen action" went another.

It was typical Russian rhetoric and the Swedes just laughed it off because, as one of the Institute people told me, "We're used to this kind of Russian bullshit."

In the abstract, the theory of arbitration is that it is both quicker and less costly than a lawsuit, in that there is generally a lot less paperwork involved. As is almost always the case, real life is a lot more complicated than the abstract. Still, as a Claimant, there are only two major briefs to file. One would be my Statement of Claim, which would be accompanied by written evidence. The Statement of Claim enumerated what I'd lost during the expropriation process: the equipment, the vehicles, the supplies, and materials that UdPRF had seized. It would also include the cost of each, where it had originally been bought, the shipping costs, and so on. The second element of the Statement of Claim was our 25-year lease on the Kamenny Island property. This was significant because I had copies of our registration certificates, which had been signed and registered by Vladimir Putin. When I was expropriated, the lease still had 20 years to run.

Another major document I had to submit as the Claimant was a list of witnesses who would buttress the written evidence I had provided with context and details that hadn't been included in the statement. I needed witnesses who'd been in Russia and had witnessed significant events or were eyewitnesses when the actual expropriation took place. My friend Tom Church, for example, was at Kamenny Ostrov during the October 1995 assault and he testified as to what he'd seen. Jack Gosnell, the former Consul General in St. Petersburg, had been around during the Pinchuk fiasco. My mechanic from Finland, Michael Melrose, testified about the number of cars I'd bought and he'd serviced. Colonel Stanley Olchovik testified. And I brought over a couple of the trainers I'd used so they could testify as to the level of training I provided. I even brought in Benjamin Lehrer, who'd gone undercover on the *Enchanted Isle*—the cruise ship that had been taken over by the Russian Mafiya during the Goodwill Games.

So, that was my end of things. My witness list was just over a dozen individuals.

The role of the Respondent belonged to the Russians. Their job was to file a Response. Often, the Response would be accompanied by a Counter Claim, which means the Respondent will attempt to offset whatever you'd demanded in your Statement of Claim. The Russians took a different tack on witnesses. Many of their witnesses testified by telephone. This became interesting when we could hear on the speaker the Russian lawyers coaching the witnesses on what to say. When that happened, the Arbitration Tribunal interrupted the testimony and noted it. Other Russian witnesses had no personal first-hand knowledge of events, and still, others brought documentation that the tribunal found fragmentary.

After I paid the $1000 filing fee, it didn't take long until each side appointed its arbitrator. Mine was Dr. Jan Peter Waehler, an elderly, Russian speaking German lawyer from Hamburg, who had studied law in Stalin's Russia. He knew all the ins and outs, had handled arbitration disputes in the past, and best of all, could read Russian, which meant he'd understand the arguments the Russians were bringing before they were translated.

Moscow appointed a professor named Zykin. He was such a typical Russian that I thought he flew home every night so he could wash in the waters of the Volga. Professor Zykin was on the permanent list of arbitrators for the Stockholm Institute as well as arbitration institutions in Vienna, Geneva, Moscow, and Paris, and my research indicated he always took the Russian side. Of course he did: his professorial wages were paid by the Russian State, so there was no question about where his loyalty lay.

The fact that he billed himself as a neutral and independent agent while he was being paid by the Russians bothered me. It told me that they weren't above buying expert witnesses, and I made a mental note that in the future, I'd make a point of doing due diligence on every expert witness the Russians put on the stand against me. It was a decision that would serve me very well over the next ten years, because every time—<u>Every. Single. Time.</u>—the Russians presented an expert witness, or one of the courts asked for a Russian expert witness, or called on someone who understands Russian law, we always found a connection to the Kremlin in the sense that those allegedly independent witnesses, experts, and academics depended on the Russian government for their income or their position.

So, it didn't surprise me that Dr. Waehler and Professor Zykin couldn't agree on who would be chairman, so the choice went to Ulf Franke, who chose Judge Magnusson.

With the arbitration panel empaneled, we had the formal exchange of claims, followed by an exchange of briefs. The Russians' main argument was that I had never made an investment in Russia. Which was, of course, crazy because I'd had a huge number of shipping documents on file in my St. Louis and Munich offices, detailing exactly what was shipped to Stone Island in the years before the expropriation. So, when the Russians told the tribunal I couldn't prove my investments, I was able to hand over almost 700 pages of shipping documents, receipts, paid orders, and other incontrovertible evidence.

The score: Sedelmayer 1, Moscow nil.

Then, the Moscow lawyer asserted the company had been established illegally. I thought it was a pretty bizarre charge to make because Vladimir Putin had registered my company—in fact I had the deputy mayor's signature on the document. And not only that: the local tax commission had duly registered the company and I'd received a tax number, which I also submitted. A police document from GUVD attested that "Little Sister" had been a part of a joint venture with me in the Kamenny Ostrov Company—and we had those documents, too. My rebuttal was that none of these government entities would have registered us if we hadn't obtained the proper legal documentation. After all, I had to open a bank account; I had to deposit what we were obliged to contribute into the joint venture with

GUVD, and after that KUGI. And even though UdPRF had confiscated all my records when they'd occupied Stone Island, much to the Russians' chagrin I was able to provide absolute documentation.

The score: Sedelmayer 2, Moscow nil.

So, they changed tack. Madam Koroshilova, the Russian lawyer the Kremlin sent to handle the case, addressed the tribunal: "Well, all this evidence from Herr Sedelmayer might be fine and dandy, and let's assume for a moment it's not fabricated." She gave me and my lawyer a dirty look. "But we will check. We will find out."

When my lawyer objected, the Russian was ready: "We have to consider the fact that Mr. Sedelmayer knew that the GUVD, the Police Department, could not be a commercial partner by law, because it is currently illegal for GUVD to enter into a joint venture with a commercial entity."

Mrs. Koroshilova wasn't lying. But what she stated wasn't true. Because, at the time I'd signed my joint contract with GUVD—the agreement we negotiated in two days because Chief Kramarev and Deputy Chief Pinchuk were anxious to get it done—such deals were legal. In fact, Pinchuk and Kramarev wanted me to sign because they knew the law was going to be changed, and they wanted GUVD's nose under the tent door before anything that could prevent the partnership was final. At which point, Kramarev would allow Pinchuk to take over Kamenny Ostrov, liquidate the company, and keep everything—that's exactly what almost happened in 1992. That was the grand idea of the scheme. But neither Pinchuk nor Kramarev had counted on the fact that I'd defend myself, or that KGB, not OMON, would be providing security at Kamenny Ostrov.

So, she tried another tack. "Herr Sedelmayer, you have told us how much research you do; how diligent you are in your business affairs. If you'd done your research, you would have known that GUVD couldn't legally enter a joint venture. And so it is obvious that you acted negligently."

I thought to myself, '*My God—she really hasn't prepared at all.*'

I looked straight at her. "Madam Koroshilova, Russia has a foreign investment law that deals specifically with the charge you just made."

I watched as she blinked like the proverbial deer in the headlights.

"I will quote it for you.

Quote:

No one bringing in their money in good faith is responsible for changes in Legislation. Changes in legislation is the responsibility of the State."

She said nothing, so I continued. "It was the State that was our partner. If GUVD, a state organ, couldn't legally become a partner in the joint venture, all responsibility for that error lies with the State—with Russia, not with me."

I waited for a response. There was none.

The score: Sedelmayer 3, Moscow nil. The first set was mine.

The one thing the Russians were good at was delaying tactics. The 'in the abstract' time frame of six to seven months Ulf Franke first described to me, turned into five trips to Stockholm drawn out over two years. Two very expensive years.

For my old friend Vladimir Putin, those two years were also years of change. In September of 1996, Mayor Anatoly Sobchak lost the mayor's race to his worst enemy Vladimir Yakovlev, and Putin lost his deputy mayor job overnight. One of the first calls he made was to his new BFF in Moscow, Pavel Borodin. The same Borodin who'd sent me a letter claiming my lease on Kamenny Ostrov was illegal. The same Borodin who'd been described by Putin as "a good guy; a guy we can work with." Borodin must have thought the same about Putin because he hired him straightaway as deputy chief of the UdPRF's International Department.

How did I learn this? It was during the one of the long sessions in Stockholm when I was taking a coffee break and ran into the Kremlin lawyer, Mrs. Koroshilova, in the corridor. We got to talking and it turned out she worked for UdPRF.

That brought a wry smile to my face. "So, who in UdPRF do you work for?"

"I'm in the International Department. I work for Deputy Chief Vladimir Putin," she said. "He's from St. Petersburg. Did you know him?"

"Putin?" I had to laugh. "Yes, I know him. In fact, will you do me a favor?"

"Of course."

"Please extend my warmest regards to him. Tell him Franz says 'Hi.'"

She gave me a quizzical look. "I will."

And she did, too. Because soon thereafter Mrs. Koroshilova took me aside and said with newfound respect, "Mr. Putin sends you greetings and warm regards."

I guessed that Putin still had some positive feelings toward me, because he knew enough about my business to have made the arbitration hearings a lot more uncomfortable, had he wished to do so. But given the way things went, it was obvious that he hadn't given Mrs. Koroshilova any information that would advance Moscow's cause.

And occasionally, over those two years, I asked myself from time to time how he was doing. I still had contacts inside Russia, and so I heard stories. In 1997, I heard he'd started doing some work for the Yeltsin family and that shortly thereafter, Yeltsin made him deputy chief of the Presidential Staff. It was fitting: a perfect position for Putin. He was problem solving and handling crisis management for the Yeltsins much the same as he'd done for Anatoly Sobchak. And, Yeltsin obviously appreciated Putin, because he promoted him repeatedly: in May of 1998 to First Deputy Chief of the Presidential Staff, and then, shortly after the decision in my arbitration case against the Russian Federation, Putin was appointed Director of the FSB, the successor organization to the KGB. It was a post he held until August of 1999.

All the appointments made sense to me. Putin was loyal to the people he worked for. He'd certainly protected Sobchak, who was probably the most corrupt a public official I'd seen until Yeltsin came along. So, Putin was probably doing much the same for Yeltsin. Moreover, Putin was an anomaly among Russian public figures in that he'd never asked for anything in return. Not once in all the time I knew him in St. Petersburg did he ever signal to me or anyone I knew that he wanted anything material in return for his help, his support, or his assistance.

The tribunal's ruling finally came in July of 1998. I'd won game, set, and match. But it wasn't quite the big win I'd hoped for. The problem with our evidence was that we could show that my company went under due to expropriation and we could prove that the Russians had violated the terms of our 25-year lease. But we could not prove that UdPRF had taken the huge inventory of equipment, vehicles, and other supplies from Kamenny Ostrov, because I wasn't present when the Russians ransacked the place and stripped it and our KOC Security Company shortly thereafter. Still, I was the first individuals ever to initiate investment arbitration against Russia, and I was in point of fact the first person ever to win against them.

So, my victory was in some ways Pyrrhic. I ended up receiving just a third of what I'd wanted. The tribunal awarded me $2.35 million plus 10 percent interest and certain costs. But my expenses had been sky-high. Five trips to Stockholm, massive legal fees, and I'd had to pay almost double tribunal fees because the Russians hadn't paid their share.

Still, I'd won. And once the arbitration award decision was delivered in my favor, I assumed the Russians would have to pay up, because not paying would tarnish their image.

Except they reverted to type. The Russians didn't pay. They didn't pay because Moscow didn't give a damn about its image. The only image the Kremlin wanted to project was adamant, uncompromising, authoritarian toughness. The same toughness and brutality they'd shown in Chechnya. It would be the same 'screw the world' attitude they'd demonstrate after Crimea and Eastern Ukraine. In my case it was screw you, Sedelmayer, we're not giving you a dime.

Moscow's reaction was a real wake up call.

Yes, there was a Treaty between Germany and Russia. But, treaties are only as good as the nations that sign them. And, if one of the signees decides they won't abide by the treaty, taking them to court could take not years but decades, not to mention possibly tens of millions of dollars in legal fees. If you don't believe me, just ask the shareholders of Yukos, who spent millions winning a multi-billion dollar arbitration award against the Russian government and haven't ever seen so much as a penny.

That's when I realized arbitration isn't the same as taking someone to court. A court can enforce a settlement. Pay what you owe or you'll face a bailiff who'll seize your property. An arbitration tribunal is in point of fact a private, self-financed institution. It has no enforcement capabilities and at best may call on a state court for interim measures in very, very exceptional circumstances. I had a $2,350,000 judgement, but Moscow was still saying "no."

You fight strength with greater strength. So, I put the Kremlin on notice. I wrote a letter stating that I expected payment or I'd start seizing Russian assets.

The Kremlin responded by suing me over the tribunal's award. UdPRF was going on the offensive. They'd lost the arbitration, so they decided to take me to court in Stockholm.

I couldn't believe it: Moscow had screwed up again. Court was where I could win big. And the power of the state, not some toothless tribunal, would back me up by enforcing the arbitration award I'd secure against Moscow.

Bring it on!

CHAPTER 14

The Rüdiger Protocol

"Rommel, you magnificent bastard, I read your book!!"
—George C. Scott, in "Patton."

Remember the old adage, "Earn while you learn?" Over the next three years—because that is how long the initial court case brought by the Russians ran—I discovered a more accurate version of the phrase: "Spend while you learn."

One of the most basic hurdles was language. During the arbitration we spoke mostly in English, and the evidentiary documents were in German, Russian, or English. But, since Moscow had brought its lawsuit in the Stockholms *Tingsrätt*, which is the equivalent of a circuit court or a city court, everything: the arguments, documents, papers, interrogatories—would all have to be in Swedish.

This meant that all of my evidentiary material—thousands of pages now had to be translated into Swedish. I'd also need a full-time real-time translator in addition to a Swedish attorney, because I didn't speak the language. And every bit of this would come out of my pocket, while the Russians' fees were paid by Moscow.

Things started off badly. The Russians had hired a Swedish attorney named Christer Söderlund. When we finally got to court, my wife, Vlada, took one look at him and whispered, "He looks like a cartoon rat."

Well, he did: Christer Söderlund had a thin face, a long nose, and tight lips, that, when he became fretful or aggressive, pursed up giving him a somewhat rodent-like look. Additionally, lawyer Söderlund may not have been the best attorney in the world, but he sure knew how to drag a case out by introducing tons of irrelevant evidence and proposing ridiculous arguments. Which was, I guess, exactly what Moscow was paying him for (and more on that point later).

But I'm getting ahead of myself. Let's start before the beginning. Because, even prior to the first hearing, Christer Söderlund brought the whole process to a complete halt. In a preliminary letter to the court—before anyone appeared—he claimed Franz Sedelmayer had declared bankruptcy in Germany in 1994 and never made it known to anyone on the arbitration tribunal. Moreover, as I'd declared bankruptcy, I should never have been allowed to start the arbitration process in the first place, let alone participate in the upcoming trial.

The Court took Söderlund's words at face value and enforced what is known as an "Inhibition," meaning that they stopped my ability to enforce my $2.35 million-plus-interest arbitration award.

The decision had no effect in Germany, but it tied my hands in Sweden and also prevented the lawsuit Moscow had initiated—which I was confident of winning—from going forward.

As I hadn't hired a Swedish attorney yet, I immediately flew to Stockholm and showed up at Söderlund's office. It was, as I recall, it was 1998, the day before Halloween and it was late in the day. His offices were mostly deserted and the few employees left were running around in costumes.

He greeted me, looking somewhat surprised, but led me into a conference room. We sat facing one another across the table. He asked, "What can I do for you, Herr Sedelmayer?"

I slapped my hand down on the table for effect and watched him jump in his seat. I growled, "I'm going to ask you something. And I'm only going to ask it once."

He blinked rapidly. His Adam's apple twitched. "Yes?" His expression told me he didn't want to be alone with me.

Too bad. "How dare you smear me in front of the court!"

He started to respond but I didn't allow it. "You accused me of going bankrupt and not reporting it to the arbitration tribunal. That's a lie—a goddamn lie and you know it."

Söderlund's mouth opened but nothing came out. Which was good because I hadn't finished. "You're a frigging attorney. You know the rules of bankruptcy. You know there has to be a record. Yet, you told the court I'd declared bankruptcy four years ago and not reported it. That is a lie on every level. I've never been bankrupt. What you told the court was not true. Moreover, you provided no legitimate evidence."

His eyes were wide as saucers now.

"You better rectify this because I'm going to file a criminal complaint against you for defrauding a court of law."

His Adam's apple was going up and down like a fishing pole bobber. He finally managed to stammer, "Bu-bu-bu-but I was acting in good faith."

"Good faith? Based on what?"

"An individual named F. Sedelmayer declared bankruptcy in Germany four years ago. I assumed it was you."

"Assumed? You did no research?"

Söderlund's silence was eloquent. What this idiot had done was surf the records until he found someone with the same name as I who'd gone bankrupt, then took the information to the judge. It didn't matter that the F. Sedelmayer in question was older than I, didn't live in Munich, and had a completely different occupation than I. Söderlund wrote the "Sedelmayer is bankrupt" letter to the judge and the judge believed him.

So, I did my own footwork and investigating and turned the evidence over to a competent Swedish attorney who easily proved beyond all doubt that it was another Sedelmayer, not I, who'd gone bankrupt. But even after we forced Söderlund to notify the court he'd been mistaken, the court refused to lift the Inhibition to enforce the arbitration award. In point of fact it wasn't lifted until five years later—2003—by the appellate court that issued the decision in my favor.

My takeaway from both the arbitration process and the Söderlund episode was clear: when you're engaged in a complex case, a good lawyer will do well for you if he has all his ducks in a row. But getting those ducks in a row takes time, effort, and above all money—hundreds, even thousands of billable hours of work. And, as my funds and resources were limited because I'd recently lost all my assets and a considerable amount of cash in Russia, I started prepping cases myself, assuming the roles of troubleshooter, historian, researcher, and investigator.

During the arbitration, for example, my lawyers relied on my ability to provide exactly the evidence they needed both quickly and accurately. Doing so was financially efficient for me, of course, especially when compared with what I'd pay for an associate, who had no idea what I'd been through or where the evidence lay, trying to find the proverbial needle in the haystack. Indeed, I assisted my attorneys because I understood the subtleties and the backstory of my case, which helped them to provide a winning narrative.

Working as an active partner with my attorneys became the template for the more than 100 cases that would follow. I'm convinced the concept works, because we haven't lost a single important case so far. The few cases we did lose were all limited to immunity from execution, and even in those, I managed to break the wall and introduced new case law other claimants now rely on. In fact, these days, when I'm advising clients on dispute management and enforcement strategies, I advise them not to just hand their cases over to a lawyer and walk away, but to become involved on a day-to-day basis. The bottom line is that you know your case better than any lawyer and you have a lot more to lose, too.

The Russians faced a different set of problems. The paperwork about my expropriation was spread between at least a dozen or more different departments, bureaus, agencies and offices in Moscow and St. Petersburg. Combine that organizational maze with inefficiency and incompetence, and the result was bureaucratic and legal chaos. And so, instead of finding and filing paperwork that would buttress its case, Moscow compensated by hiring expert witnesses. In the Stockholm case, they based their arguments on a thick, long-winded expert opinion authored by a prominent German professor by the name of Rüdiger Wolfrum.

Prominent is actually an understatement. Rüdiger Wolfrum is a world-renown professor of international public law. For years, he has been associated with Heidelberg's prestigious Max Planck Institute for Comparative Public Law and International Law. In 1996, he was appointed a justice at, and in 2005, became president of the International Tribunal for the Law of the Sea. He was a member of the United Nations Committee on the Elimination of Racial Discrimination. In other words, in the legal world Rüdiger Wolfrum was a Big Kahuna.

And yet, instead of submitting his opinion to the court, Lawyer Söderlund simply dropped the thick document on his attorney's table during the Court hearing, as if seeing Wolfrum's name would influence the judges to rule in their favor before they'd even read it. As a matter of fact, when my Swedish lawyers Dag Wérsen and Jonas Löttiger saw Wolfrum's name on the document, they made it clear to me: "Franz, we're going to lose this case if you don't find someone with an equal standing. This guy's world-class—how the Russians got him to do this heaven knows. So, to have any chance of winning we have to present solid counter-opinions from some equally heavy hitters."

Please note that my lawyers said this BEFORE they or anyone else had read a single sentence of Rüdiger Wolfrum's magnum opus.

I even raised that point with them.

Dag said, "Franz, it could all be baloney, but the Judge might just look at it and say, 'Well, this guy has a big name and a world class reputation,' and give him the benefit of the doubt."

He had a point. But here's a fact: by nature I am a skeptical individual. By birth I am a Bavarian, and yes, I inherited the Teutonic love of detail, accuracy, and precision. And so, I consequently accept very little at face value. I probe. I examine. I explore.

I tend, for example, not to find my lawyers by asking friends if they know a good lawyer. The best way to find a good lawyer—or any other expert in any field—is by checking on the Internet and seeing what subjects in which the individual is an expert, what his career track has been, and what connections he has or had.

So, I decided to investigate EM. Prof. Dr. DRES. h. c. Rüdiger Wolfrum. In my particular case I wanted to learn whether EM. Prof. Dr. DRES. h. c. Rüdiger Wolfrum ever had any connections—financial, academic, or personal to Russia.

And guess what: I discovered that he had a close and financial relationship with Mother Russia—a relationship that he had not disclosed in the curriculum vitae that accompanied his expert opinion. But there's more. When I sat down and actually read the Professor Doktor Wolfrum's report; read it slowly and very carefully, I discovered he'd made an elemental error.

It is said that the legal profession is not an exact science, but it is a science that has to be based on fact. What Rüdiger Wolfrum had done was to base his findings, which were legal in character, on facts that were not true. Obviously, instead of questioning the validity of the premises upon which he'd been asked to write an opinion, he had simply accepted them as true. And then he'd proceeded to develop a case against me.

His entire argument came down to one false premise: *Mr. Sedelmayer is not entitled to compensation under the terms of the treaty because he invested in Russia through a U.S. corporation, had his domicile there, and therefore was not an investor.*

That was the nucleus of his finding, which wasn't scientific at all. Professor Doktor Wolfrum was doing nothing more than expressing an opinion on behalf of his client. In fact, his argument was so simplistic I asked myself more than once whether he had written it himself or whether he'd hired a student or teaching assistant to do it for him.

If he was smart, he'd see the error of his ways and either withdraw his paper, or revise it. So, I wrote him a letter. I told him I was very disappointed that he'd produced a 'scientific' opinion that would not hold water. I told him that in any reputable scientific, legal, or historical paper, the facts have to be properly footnoted; documented—and that he had failed to do so. I added that I was profoundly saddened because he was not just any professor: he was also the head of the Max Planck Institute for Comparative Public Law and International Law in Heidelberg.

I then listed the most important objections I'd found, all of which had to do with the specifics of the case. Then I wrote—I'll paraphrase myself here. Look, Wolfrum, you're a distinguished lawyer and an academic. You know exactly how easy it is to lose a hard-earned reputation. So, you should remember that taking on a case like mine just for money can tar you with the appearance of being a what we Germans call a *Mietmaul* (rented mouth). And you know what rented mouths are? They're individuals who don't express their own opinions or tell the truth, but who get paid to say whatever the people paying them tell them to say.

If I were you, I wrote, if I were interested in my own reputation in my circle, I would definitely recommend you withdraw your 'expert opinion,' because I'm going to have to go after you, both in court during the case and also against you as a person afterwards. Because what you're writing here is slander. It is nothing to do with anything factual.

I mentioned that my research indicated the German federal government and several German states paid 97.5 percent of the Max Planck Institute's budget. How, I asked, could Wolfrum in good conscience write a report on his Institute's letterhead when that report would benefit a foreign government? Moreover, by writing the report on his Max Planck letterhead, his opinion was not just the private legal opinion of expert witness Professor Doktor Rüdiger Wolfrum, it was by inference the opinion of the Max Planck Institute and by association, the very German government that financed the Institute.

I asked—politely, I might add—that I would like to know whether the payment you receive from Moscow will go to the Institute or to you? If you wrote it on your Institute letterhead, shouldn't the money go to the Institute? Certainly, it shouldn't go into your own pocket.

Finally, I told him that I'd give him a week to 10 days in which to withdraw his legal opinion and either write one that would hold water or withdraw from the case. If he didn't, I said, I'd reserve the right to sue him.

"But before I do," I wrote, "please inform me where you'd like the lawsuit sent: Germany, or Russia?"

So that was the beginning. If Rüdiger Wolfrum had only understood what I was trying to tell him, he would have withdrawn his legal opinion and Moscow might have folded its case right then. But he didn't withdraw, and the case went on for four more years. Only in the last year did we actually have witnesses. The rest of the time was spent fighting the legal equivalent of trench warfare: memos, briefs, accusations, and counter accusations, and all the while my lawyers were billing me by the hour. My costs rose exponentially. But I wasn't about to give in. The only thing that gave me joy was the knowledge that Moscow was probably paying out a lot more than I was.

And the drawn-out process also gave me time to recruit my own expert witnesses. My two top experts on international law were professors Bruno Simma and Rudolf Geiger. Professor Simma became a member of the United Nations International Court of Justice (ICJ). He dealt with legal disputes submitted by sovereign states, the United Nations, and handled questions over territorial disputes, human rights, the effects of international treaties—all core matters of international law. Before that he had represented Germany against the United States in the LaGrand case before the ICJ and won. Bruno Simma's book on International Law was known internationally as the gold standard on the subject. He also held the Chair of International Law at the University of Munich.

Professor Geiger, recently retired, had been a judge at one of Germany's most prominent appellate courts in Munich, and taught law at several tier-one universities. He'd even spent time right after the wall came down, rebuilding the legal structure and law faculties in the former German Democratic Republic (East Germany), and also held the Chair for European Law at Leipzig University.

Professors Simma and Geiger wrote me a series of fabulous legal opinions that dealt in minute, footnoted detail with subjects from the effects of treaties on individuals, to the application of the German-Russian Treaty of 1989 to my case in particular, to questions of residence. They also proved beyond a shadow of a doubt that the clear language of a treaty is binding and is not subject to interpretation or modification.

They defined "direct investment" and "indirect investment" in precise legal terms, cementing once and for all that what I had done during my seven years in Russia was direct investment, and not as Moscow claimed, indirect investment. For example, a direct investment, it turns out, is not just the fact that you put your money on the table. Legally, direct investment means that you, not someone else, make the business decisions and you control your money. Investing with a stockbroker is an indirect investment. What I did in St. Petersburg was direct investment because I controlled my funds one hundred percent of the time.

Moscow's flawed claim was that I'd put my personal money into a U.S.

corporation that subsequently became the partner of a Russian entity in Kamenny Ostrov. Moscow and its experts argued that not I, but my U.S. corporation, had invested in the project and that because there was no investment protection treaty between the Russian Federation and the United States, I wasn't protected.

And Moscow's argument was partially correct: Americans who lost their assets in those days in Russia had no recourse except to go to the Russian courts, where they inevitably lost. But I, my professors argued, was a German citizen who owned an American company that invested with a Russian partner. I used my own German-based funds, and I could show direct control of the company and direct control of all the funds. I could show my cash flow to Kamenny Ostrov. In evidence, I submitted a copy of the lawsuit filed by the City of St. Petersburg, mentioning my name specifically and signed by none other than Vladimir Vladimirovich Putin on my behalf, stating that I had done all my investments properly. Simultaneously, I also submitted a copy of the letter Pavel Borodin of the *Upravlenie* had written me, telling me that my investment in Kamenny Ostrov was illegal. My lawyers argued that it was impossible for an individual investor to find justice if the Russian Federation does one thing one day and the next day it makes a 180 degree change in policy. And, I was pleased to see that those two pieces of contradictory evidence didn't sit very well with the Court.

I know I'm repeating myself, but those five long years were trench warfare. You had to grind it out, brief by brief. Every time Moscow brought something up, no matter how ridiculous it might have been, it had to be smacked down. And the work had to be done right; it had to be done thoroughly, methodically, systematically, scrupulously. We were forced to answer anything and everything the Russians brought up, because not answering meant accepting Moscow's position, which would lose me the case.

So on it went. And on. And on. And on. All because Professor

Doktor Rüdiger Wolfrum, despite the fact that he knew he'd fabricated an expert opinion on behalf of people who didn't give a damn about the truth or the facts, chose not to withdraw that flawed, dishonest opinion.

❖

Fast forward to 2002. It's now four years later and we finally got a hearing. So the witnesses assembled—mine, and the Russian witnesses. Incredibly, they were all deposited in the same witness room.

So, there was Rüdiger Wolfrum, along with two of my witnesses: Professor Rudolph Geiger and Professor Bruno Simma. Of course, they all knew each other on a first-name basis, and this was a big deal in German academia because it signified they were colleagues—equals. It also should be said, however, that Bruno Simma and Rüdiger Wolfrum were long-term rivals.

According to what I was told later, Wolfrum looked at his colleagues, shook his head, and said something to the effect of, "You know, this Sedelmayer, he wrote me a letter once and I've never had a letter like it in all my professional life. Who does he think he is?"

Bruno looked at him and said, "Look, Rüdiger, I know Sedelmayer. In fact I worked with him on this case. And I've read your opinion and I'm sorry to have to tell you it's so weak I'd be surprised if you'd actually written it yourself."

Wolfrum objected: "But of course I wrote it."

And Bruno snorted, "That makes it even worse."

Rüdiger's eyes narrowed. "Well, let's see how it all plays out today."

Bruno slowly shook his head from side to side because he realized Wolfrum wasn't getting it. He gave it one last shot. "Rüdiger, about Sedelmayer?"

"Yes?"

"He's a very stubborn guy. I'm telling you as an old friend, if I were you I would just withdraw this thing and get it over with, because you're not going to walk out of here unscathed."

"Don't be ridiculous." Wolfrum shook his head. "He's a layman. What does he know?"

"No—I can guarantee you: Sedelmayer will go after you because what you have done is just a little bit over the top." Bruno Simma paused to see if his words were having any effect on his long-time rival. "Rüdiger—I'm telling you this in a friendly manner. After all, we're all colleagues here."

But it was, he told me later, like talking to the wall.

So we put Professor Doktor Rüdiger Wolfrum on the stand. And my lawyers got the chance to cross examine him. He made a flimsy defense of his expert opinion—you could see the judge wasn't impressed.

And then we got into other matters. When I'd investigated Wolfrum I learned that he'd presented the Swedish court with his curriculum vitae. But, I discovered it was an incomplete CV, because I compared what he'd given to the court with what was online at the Max Planck Institute. On the Institute's website I found that Rüdiger Wolfrum mentioned receiving an honorable doctorate from Russia's Institute of State and Law. He'd also worked with the Volkswagen System to teach at various universities in Russia and was active at the Institute of State and Law, which was financed by UdPRF—the property office of the President of the Russian Federation.

I knew people like Rüdiger Wolfrum—and guys like him, they don't work for free. In fact, my further investigation uncovered that he was a regular speaker in Russia—so regular that one could argue that he basically worked for the Russian government, because he most certainly was compensated by the Russian government for his services as a speaker.

Then, I'd started digging into the finances of the Max Planck Institute. By law, it's registered as a tax-free association, which meant they had to publish yearly statements about their funding, expenses, and product—

similar but more complete than the IRS 990 forms required for 501(c)(3) nonprofit organizations in the United States.

So, when I saw the figures that covered that year in which Rüdiger had written his expert opinion, there was no mention that the Max Planck Institute had received any money for preparing it. In fact, there was no mention of the opinion at all. But that was crazy: the expert opinion had been written on Wolfrum's Max Planck Institute letterhead, which made it an official document of the Institute. By law, it had to be in the yearly paperwork.

So, Dag Wersén confronted him. "Professor Wolfrum, is this the CV that you provided to the Court when you submitted your expert opinion?"

Rüdiger looked at the papers. "Yes, of course."

Dag handed him a second CV. "Here is a printout of your CV from the Max Planck Institute. It indicates that you have a relationship with the government of the Russian Federation. Is there any reason your relationship with the Russian government is not included in the version you submitted to the court?"

Wolfrum blinked. "I didn't think it was important."

"Would you read us the section about your relationships in Russia?"

Wolfrum gritted his teeth and read the damning material.

I watched my lawyer sweat him. I was transfixed. It was like a scene out of a "*Law & Order*" episode.

Dag bore in. "Don't you think it's important to let us know you were very active in Russia over the last five or six years?"

The judge broke in: "Mr. Wersén, what is this about?"

Dag never lost a beat. "Your honor, this is about the fact that this witness was lying to the Court by hiding the fact that he is connected to the Russians."

Wolfrum tried to explain himself. "I didn't think it would affect my actions. Besides, I've never been paid by Russia."

"Really?" Dag paused so the judge could consider what followed in the light of what had just transpired. "Professor Wolfrum, are you sure about this?"

Wolfrum's head bobbed up and down. "Absolutely. I'm doing this out of the goodness of my heart."

"If you say so," said Dag Wersén. "Now, I'd like to ask the court to remind the witness he has been sworn—he's testifying under oath. So considering the evidence that's just been presented, the witness has obviously perjured…"

That was as far as Dag got.

Wolfrum raised his hand. "Your honor, I would like to withdraw my legal opinion and be excused."

And with that he stood up, walked off the stand, and straight out of the courtroom.

As he passed me he cursed in German, "You goddamn son of a bitch."

I started to give as good as I'd gotten, but Jonas Löttiger's hand pressed around my arm. He whispered, "Shut up, Franz—the judge speaks German, let it go. You won."

And indeed I had.

In a matter of weeks, the score would read Sedelmayer 4, Moscow nil.

And so, the case was closed.

But it wasn't finished.

In Sweden, if you win your case, you get your court costs back. Travel expenses, lawyers' fees, witness fees, legal experts—all of that gets reimbursed. And those cost statements are public information.

Wolfrum had claimed he'd never received a penny from the Russians. Well, not to put too fine a point on it, he lied. When Moscow's Swedish lawyer Christer Söderlund handed in his expense sheets, they included a cost position for a Rüdiger Wolfrum having received a sum totaling 229,688 Swedish crowns, equivalent to about $25,000 in those days—for his services to the Russian Federation.

So much for the son of a bitch not being paid. Moreover, he'd not only denied the fact that he collected money for himself, he'd put his ridiculous opinion on his Max Planck Institute letterhead, thus making it appear that the Institute stood behind what he'd written.

That, too, was a lie.

One of the things I have learned over the years is that when you uncover dishonesty on such a large scale, it's never a mistake to make the news about it public. So, I sent copies of the Stockholm judgment to all the courts and institutes with which Professor Doktor Rüdiger Wolfrum was involved, accompanied by a copy of my letter asking him to retract his opinion.

There's also a final footnote about Christer Söderlund. On the last day of the hearing, he bought Dag Wersén and me coffee in the court's cafeteria and apologized for the way he had conducted himself throughout the case. A few weeks later, the Kremlin fired him and categorically refused to pay his bills, which had piled up over the previous years. As much as I despised Söderlund's unscrupulous methods, I couldn't bring myself to feel *Schadenfreude*.

I haven't heard back from either Wolfrum or Söderlund since.

Which is why I consider Stockholm "case closed."

And by the way, because of what I learned about dealing with the Russians after five years of legal trench warfare and countless billable hours in Stockholm, every penny was worth it.

CHAPTER 15

Greetings from the Chan-Zell-Or

"Question: "How many politicians does it take to change a lightbulb?"
Answer: "None: They're too busy screwing the people to be bothered with lightbulbs."
— American Joke

Let me speak plainly. Extracting payment from Moscow for what Moscow stole from me has been tough, painstaking, demanding work. In the two-plus decades since Kamenny Ostrov was expropriated, I have pushed myself through roughly 140 court cases. I've spent countless hours on planes, trains, and automobiles coming or going from hearings, depositions, or seizures. I've had to put up with deadbeat adversaries who lied, cheated, made up, and even forged evidence. I've had my wife and my lawyer threatened. Serious stuff all. But once every great while during my odyssey, something so totally and comically absurd took place that I had to stand back and say to myself, "I've been teleported into an alternative universe."

In my case, the best transporting to an alternative universe took place in 2006 at an international air show and trade fair in Berlin. It was—and still is—formally known as the ILA Berlin Air Show and as an aviation and aerospace event, it ranks just behind France's Le Bourget and Britain's

Farnborough air shows in popularity and deal making. It takes place in even-numbered years, has been attended by as many as a quarter-million people, and runs for four days. And at every ILA, the German hosts have a partner country with whom they pair to do the show.

And just by coincidence, 2006 was the year the German partner country was…(cue the trumpets)…the Russian Federation.

This was, I believed, good news: the Russians would be bringing a sizeable amount of state property with them. Moreover, it would be legal to enforce a court ordered writ of execution and have a bailiff seize the goods for me in partial payment to what Moscow still owed but hadn't paid. And since they were coming to me in Germany, all I'd have to do is show up. Plus, even if I wasn't able to seize anything, I'd still get media attention—ILA was a magnet for the world press—so I'd be able to spread the word about my case and how dishonorable Moscow was about paying its debts.

Bottom line? The Russians were providing what's known as a 'soft target.' Either I'd get cash out of this, or a boatload of publicity. It all made perfect sense. Of course, the one element I hadn't factored in was my own government.

That was about to change.

About six weeks before ILA the phone rang just as I was about to leave the house to bring my daughter home from kindergarten.

"Hello?"

"This is Dr. Benterbusch speaking. I'm calling from the German Chancellor's Office and I would like to speak to Mr. Sedelmayer."

"He is speaking to you, Dr. Benterbusch. What can I do for you today?"

"Yes," Dr. Benterbusch said, "There are things I must discuss with you."

There was something weird about this call. First of all, Dr. Benterbusch was obviously on a speakerphone. There was an audible echo on the line and I could hear people murmuring in the background.

"Discuss. That's fine," I said. "But the problem is I have to pick up my child from the kindergarten and I don't have time to talk to you now."

I heard Dr. Benterbusch say, "He doesn't understand with whom he is speaking," as if he was explaining to someone in the room. Then his voice picked up again. "You don't understand, I'm calling you from the Chancellor's Office. The <u>Chan</u>-zell-or's Office." He said the three syllables slowly, as if I were an idiot.

"I got it," I said. "The <u>Chan</u>-zell-or's Office. But I don't think you unn-derr-<u>stand</u>—I have a child to pick up."

There was silence on the line and then I heard him whisper, "He claims he has a child to pick up."

I said, "How about tomorrow? I'd be willing to schedule a phone call tomorrow."

"Tomorrow, then. Three in the afternoon," Dr. Benterbusch growled. Obviously, he was not a happy camper.

"Three works for me," I said. And I hung up before he could say anything else.

I wasn't being rude, just realistic. I'd been engaged in arbitrations and lawsuits for 10 years by 2006, and since the great majority of them pitted me—an individual—against the President of the Russian Federation, at that time my old compadre and drinking buddy Vladimir Putin. Putin's people played rough, so I wasn't cowed by a call from some self-important bureaucrat in the Chan-zell-or's office.

❖

He called the next day, right at three, on the same echo-intense speakerphone. "Herr Sedelmayer," he said, "Dr. Benterbusch from the Chancellor's office here."

"Yes?"

"Mr. Sedelmayer, the reason for my call is to ensure that we will be keeping the peace at the ILA air show that is coming up in Berlin."

"Ah," I said.

Now I knew precisely why he was on the phone. He was the Chancellor's G.O.C.R.I.R.: the German Official in Charge of Running Interference for the Russians.

"Thank you for your call, Dr. Benterbusch. I was planning on going to Berlin but I hadn't been aware we are in imminent danger of a war. However, I am grateful to learn that you will be keeping the peace. Many thanks for the heads-up."

Dr. Benterbusch harrumphed and cleared his throat. Obviously, he did not appreciate irony. He continued as if he hadn't heard me. "To be specific, Herr Sedelmayer, the <u>Chanz</u>ellor does not want you to enforce your claims against the Russian Federation at ILA."

"Dr. Benterbusch," I said, "I think the <u>Chan</u>-zell-or had a brilliant idea."

"You do?"

"Yes—absolutely brilliant. So here's the question: will she be cutting me a check for what the Russians owe me, or are you going to be bringing me cash?"

"This is not funny, Mr. Sedelmayer."

"I agree, Dr. Benterbusch. This is serious. Deadly serious. I am a business professional. So, here is my professional bottom line. Please listen closely. I will exercise my rights as I see fit and I will not accept any interference from the German government, especially since the German government has never even lifted a finger to assist me in my dispute against Moscow. In fact, as I gather from your phone call, she is actually trying to assist the Russians."

I heard nothing but silence on the line. I wondered how many people were listening.

It didn't matter. "My *personal* bottom line, Dr. Benterbusch, is that I consider your call an outrageous and hostile act from my own government. And I will treat it as such."

It gave me great joy to slam the receiver down.

Six weeks later, I went to Berlin. Because I knew my appearance was not going to be well-received and that my own government was out to screw me, I'd arranged for a news team from ZDF, the German State TV broadcaster, to accompany me. I knew ZDF correspondent Eberhard Bitz because he'd covered my campaign against Moscow on several other occasions and now wanted to get the story on to the prime evening news. I'd also warned him that the Chancellor's office didn't want me around and was probably going to try to make life tough. But Eberhard was always up for a challenge, so in addition to his usual cameras and mikes, he brought a satchel of undercover equipment—a minicam built into a pair of eyeglasses was one of the more sophisticated gadgets in his bag of tricks—that would allow him to get 'up close and personal' to the action without giving away the fact that he was filming everything.

Our first stop was the at the court in Königs Wusterhausen, southeast of Berlin's city center but close to the airport at Schönefeld, which was the site of the show and trade fair. At one point—poetic, I thought—Königs Wusterhausen had been the headquarters of the Red Army in Europe. First,

I located the bailiff responsible for the Air Show. He recruited another bailiff from his office and I sent them over to Schönefeld to do a reconnaissance while I got the paperwork completed at the president of the court's office.

Before you can start an enforcement action against a foreign sovereign on German soil, you first have to get the permission of the court's president. I suggested to the bailiffs that they reconnoiter for an hour, and then meet me back at the president's office to collect the paperwork. Then we'd go and start appropriating what they'd found for me.

"Yes, sir, Mr. Sedelmayer. You got it."

"Great. Happy hunting!"

Bailiffs on the prowl, I took Eberhard and his crew inside, asked to see the president of the court. And to my surprise, instead of the usual hem-and-hawing and 'come back later,' the President of the Court, a gray-haired, slightly pudgy gentleman in his mid-60s came down the stairs from his office suite, smiled and said, "No problem. It'll take an hour. Come back with the bailiffs for the paperwork."

We waited outside the courthouse for a while. I tried to call the bailiffs but couldn't reach them—their cell phones were off. Then I walked over to the bailiffs' office but no one had heard from them either. So, I cooled my heels and waited. It was probably close to three hours later that I finally decided to go back to the president of the court's chambers. Perhaps he knew where the bailiffs were. I went into the court house, followed by the news team. The video was rolling and the cameraman was using his undercover eyeglasses camera.

The President of the Court immediately came down from his office and waved me over. "Mr. Sedelmayer, Mr. Sedelmayer…"

"Yes?"

"I'd like to talk to you." The president pointed up the stairs, so I followed him to his third floor suite. The door was open and I could see inside toward his study. I took a peek. There were a bunch of people sitting there—they looked like court personnel or lawyers

I nodded at the news crew. "Okay, guys, let's go talk to these people."

But the president put his arm around my shoulder and said, "No-no-no, Mr. Sedelmayer. Not them—just you."

And he started to walk me toward his study.

Except the cameraman hadn't heard the president. He got in front of us—all the better to get good video of the president and me walking into the study.

In a desperate ploy to stay on top of things, the president yelled and screamed at the news crew and actually attacked the cameraman with his fists, pummeling him about the head and, in the process, breaking the undercover camera.

Eberhard and the other crewmembers rushed through the doorway to protect their colleague and there was a lot of shoving and pushing and name-calling. I wasn't about to stand for this craziness. I wanted my paperwork. I put my fingers in my mouth and whistled—loudly. "Hey-hey-hey! Stop this crap!"

That made people stop and look up.

"C'mon—everybody cut it out," I shouted.

This was absurd. A bar brawl in a court president's office, all because I was trying to enforce a legal court decision and my own frigging government didn't want me to succeed.

I caught Eberhard's eye. "Let's just get outta here, because this is absolute bullshit." I jerked my thumb in the cameraman's direction. "And if you want to call the police and file a criminal complaint against these people, I think that would be just fine, too."

The president started to object.

I gave him a dirty look. "Because, thank God, we have everything on tape."

The president went white and grabbed his chest. I thought he was going to faint.

We went back into the hallway just as the two missing bailiffs came up the stairs. They looked at me helplessly, said, "Excuse us, Mr. Sedelmayer," trudged into the president's chambers, and closed the door behind them.

They hadn't been in there 30 seconds when we heard more shouting.

Three minutes later the bailiffs emerged. Now they were ashen-faced.

I looked at them. "What happened?"

"We didn't find anything."

"No—I mean in there—" I pointed toward the president's chambers. "And what do you mean you haven't found anything?"

They shrugged.

I wasn't about to let them get away with shrugs.

"First of all, I'm the one who hired you. Enforcements come under private contracts, so you're not working for the president. He can't decide whether an enforcement case has legal merits or not. His only job is to see if there are any formal issues to allow or forbid the enforcement against a foreign sovereign for obvious reasons of immunity. He gave you a green light and now you must act. So do your fucking job! You work for me. I'm the guy who pays your fee. And, what I pay you for is to assist me to make sure nothing is being manipulated here. And now you tell me, 'We didn't find anything?' What in God's name do you mean, you didn't find anything?

The lead bailiff said, "Well, we met this lawyer from the organizers. He took us to a warehouse. He told us, 'If the Russians have any stuff here, it'll be in this warehouse.' But the warehouse was empty, so there's nothing to seize."

I looked back and forth at their faces. Their expressions told me they knew that I knew that they were feeding me the bullshit they'd been ordered to feed me by the people behind the door they'd just come through.

My fucking government was betraying me to Moscow. That's what it came down to. My fucking government had become an agent of the Russian Federation.

I look down at the head bailiff. "Are you stupid? Or do you think I'm stupid?"

No answer.

"This is baloney," I said. "This is not East Germany anymore, my friend. Welcome to the West. Yeah—the West, where the individual and not the collective rules. Where the people don't work for the government, but government works for the people."

I looked at their faces. Frankly, I thought they were going to cry. "Okay, now that you understand we're in Germany, not Russia, you need to hand over the enforcement documents—my writ of execution."

They were silent.

"I know you have them."

Finally, the lead bailiff said, "We've been ordered to send them to you through the mail. To Munich."

"You want me to take them from you?" I gave him a menacing look and held my hand out palm up.

The bailiff extracted the papers from his jacket pocket and handed them to me. "We're sorry, Mr. Sedelmayer."

I waved them off. They were useless. I looked at Eberhard. "We should be going, too."

We went back to the hotel, sat in the bar, and I cooled down over a couple of beers. And about halfway through the second one, Eberhard said, "Y'know, Franz," he said, "Those two bailiffs?"

"Yeah? What about them."

"It's not their fault."

"Why?"

"Because they work for that jackass president of the court."

"But I'm the one that pays them."

"Yes you do. But you're here for what? Three days? They have to see that idiot of a president every single day. He can make them suffer."

"So what? They still wouldn't do anything."

"I bet I could convince them."

"To what?" I looked over at him dubiously. "Actually do what I paid them for?"

"Yes."

"It wouldn't work."

"Yes it would. Look—I'm a reporter. One of my jobs is to convince people who don't want to talk about something to talk about it. I think I could convince them to help you."

I looked at him. There was nothing to lose. If he was right, I'd be back in business. "You're willing to give it a try?"

"Absolutely. Just give me his phone number. But first, order us another round, will you?"

So, Eberhard got the lead bailiff on the phone. Actually, he took an effective approach. He told the bailiff he was a reporter, and that the guy probably knew that what had gone on was a disgrace, something the bailiff didn't disagree with. And then Eberhard told him that the footage was going to make him and his buddy look like fools—all because of the stupid president.

"Look, I really don't want to put this report on the air the way it ended earlier. My guess is you were under pressure from those saboteurs at the courthouse. But y'know what: I looked everything up. You bailiffs have your own authority. And if the law says Sedelmayer can legally seize stuff from the Russians, then that's the way it is. Especially after they gave you express permission to execute the enforcement against the Russians. Look—the president of the court's just trying to keep out of the line of Sedelmayer's fire and stay in the Chancellor's good graces at the same time. But guess what: the Chancellor's got nothing to say here, whatsoever. Wake up, man!"

Eberhard winked at me. "The law's the law, right? Don't you have to act according to the law?"

The reporter listened to something the bailiff was saying. "That's right—you do have absolute legal authority to seize Russian government property. You even have it in writing."

Eberhard talked with him a bit longer. It turned out the bailiff was in his early 30s and hadn't had a lot of experience, and yes, he admitted he'd been bullied by the president and knew the officials from the Chancellor's office had been all over the president for days. Ultimately, he agreed to recruit a couple of his colleagues and he promised he'd meet us at the hotel, so we could drive to ILA together the following morning, so that ZDF would get what it needed for its report.

Eberhard snapped his phone shut and laid it on the table, a huge smile on his face. "Now—finally I'll get a decent ending to my segment."

Well, he did. But it wasn't the ending he or I expected.

I drove over to Schönefeld the following morning with my father. I'd invited him to come with me from Munich so he could witness a seizure or two. I was driving my parents' car, a Mercedes with Munich plates. We eased into the line for the parking area where a policeman was checking all the cars. Which, I thought, was a good thing. Planes, defense industry goods, all sorts of stuff was on display, and what with Al Qaeda and the other terrorist groups you couldn't be too careful.

I pulled up and rolled the window down. The policeman said, "You're Mr. Sedelmayer, aren't you?"

I blinked. "Yes. How did you know?"

The cop said. "Don't worry—we have all the Sedelmayer license plates."

That gave me pause. They'd been waiting for me.

I pulled over and had a chat with him. It turned out I'd been the subject of a security meeting two weeks earlier—a month after my nasty call from the charming Dr. Benterbusch. And the bottom line was that the Chancellor's Office had made sure the cops had been given all my family's license plate numbers so they could spot us, identify us, and prevent me from seizing assets. When I say cops, I mean all the 500 or so who provided ILA security!

I was outraged. I was more than outraged: I was furious. The Chancellor's Office was using the German police to protect the Russians from a German citizen who had won multiple court cases against Moscow and was legally entitled to seize Russian property.

Not only was that incredibly wrong, but it was against the law. Under German law neither the police nor the legislature nor any executive organ of the German State can interfere with due process of law. It's unheard of. It's anti-constitutional. It's ridiculous. More to the point, it's a crime. It's punishable by prison.

So, I told the cop, "Look, officer, I'm not alone. I have bailiffs in tow, and I have a camera team from ZDF as well."

The cop looked at me strangely. Not hostile, but strange. And finally he said, "Okay, how about everybody pulls over and parks on the side here while I radio for instructions?"

I said, "That's fine with me. And while you're on the radio please ask your superiors why you stopped me, because what you're doing is illegal and I will file a criminal complaint against the lot of you."

It didn't take long for more cops to arrive. So, now we had a bunch of curious bystanders watching the cops and watching us, and all the time Eberhard and his ZDF crew were taping away.

And then a couple of other cars—the kinds of dark ones with multiple antennas on them pulled up and guys in civilian clothes get out, and one of them came up to where I'm standing with Eberhard and he growled, "I need to see everybody's ID."

Eberhard cocked his head to the side. "Why do you need mine? I'm a journalist." He shook the press card and ILA ID that he wore around his neck in the guy's face. "I'm accredited here."

The guy looked at Eberhard and said, "Okay. If you don't want to show me your ID, it's alright," and he disappeared.

Then, the other cops had a long discussion about which Franz Sedelmayer to take into custody. After all, there were two of us: me and my dad. And because I was in my 40s, and he was in his 60s and he obviously looked more like Boss Sedelmayer than I did, one of the cops looked back and forth between us and finally said, "Okay—let's arrest the old guy."

So, that's what they did. They let the bailiffs go; they let the ZDF crew go, and they let me go. That left my father sitting in his Mercedes, surrounded by cops.

So, what did he do?

He put on an act that was frigging Oscarworthy.

You could probably hear him half a mile away. "What the hell do you think you're doing? Why do you think you can hold me? This isn't Moscow, it's Berlin, you idiots! We're not in East Germany or Nazi Germany—this isn't a bloody dictatorship!"

Believe me when I say the police had their hands full with him. But full or not they kept him surrounded, making sure he wouldn't go anywhere. And me? I melted into the crowd.

❖

I finally found my bailiffs—there were four of them—and when I found them they were in deep discussion and literally encircled by some 50 Russians talking to a lawyer from the air show about the schedule. It was somehow agreed that all attaching of property would have to be done on Friday, which was the final day of the air show.

Frankly, I didn't give a damn about the schedule. After all, it had been a decade since my first arbitration had commenced and Moscow still owed me millions. The *When* would come when it did; the *What* was a lot more germane. Besides, I knew that seizures were going to be a long shot at ILA. What I'd really get out of the air show was publicity. In fact, by its clumsy very public attempts to have me muzzled, the German Chan-zell-or's Office was actually doing me a huge favor.

Still, I started looking at the possibilities. Initially, I thought about seizing the exhibits of the Russian Space Agency (Moscow's NASA equivalent) because they'd brought satellite models and rocket models and space suits, the sorts of things that would make collectors happy and bring good money—we're talking the five and six figures—at auction. Also, seizing space swag makes great video, which would make the ZDF crew happy.

And, there was another part of this puzzle that worked in my favor, something neither the Chan-zell-or's Office nor I knew: the Russians thought I was going to seize the $30 million prototype of their newest Tupolev Tu-204-300 aircraft. It was roughly the size of an Airbus 320, and the plane on which they'd flown the whole Russian delegation in from Moscow just a day earlier.

I had never considered seizing the Tupolev because the plane was off limits: as a prototype it still belonged to the factory that had built it, not the Russian government. But it was still worth taking a look at. So, I walked over to the flight line where it was parked. A guy's gotta dream, right?

Then reality struck. Almost immediately, I was approached by two individuals in civilian clothes.

One asked, "Are you Mr. Sedelmayer?"

I said, "Yes."

He said, "Please come with us."

"Why?" I said, "I'm a visitor, I have a ticket."

He said, "Do you have an exhibitor credential or a press pass? Because this area is for exhibitors or press only. We can't have you standing here."

I looked at them "Who is we? You're police officers, right?"

"That's not of your concern!

"Well here's the thing: if you're not police officers, I'm not coming with you."

We went back and forth until one of them broke out his ID. Then another chap, a private security guard showed up, covering his badge number with his hand, and they started herding me toward the gate.

My reaction was to start taking pictures of everybody—which was not appreciated. But we moved and we moved and finally we were all outside the gate to the flight line.

I thought we'd come to the end of this comedy episode.

But we hadn't. The next thing I knew there were blue lights and sirens. A police car pulled up, stopped next to me, and a uniformed officer jumped out. "Mr. Sedelmayer."

"Yes?"

"I'm Kommissar Wassermann, my boss sent me to deal with your situation because we understand that you want to file a criminal complaint."

"That's true, Kommissar."

"Well, I'm here to take care of that. You can file your complaint at the station. He pointed toward the door of the police car. "Let's go. Jump right in."

"I'm grateful, Kommissar, but I'd like to file my complaint right here and right now."

"Ah," he said, "unfortunately that will not be possible. I have specific instructions. I have to take you to the police station. It is 20 kilometers from here and we really do have to leave right now."

I started to argue my point when Eberhard and his ZDF crew showed up. They started taping, which the Kommissar hated but could not stop.

As if that wasn't enough, the ruling party's foreign-policy spokesman walked by on his way to the flight line. Eberhard Bitz knew him and called: "Sir, Sir, come on over. You've got to meet Franz Sedelmayer, who's here to seize a lot of Russian stuff including their planes!"

At the sound of my name the foreign-policy spokesman's eyes just about popped out of his skull. But I have to say he had great self-control, because he realized the ZDF camera was rolling and he was being recorded. So, he quickly regained his composure, wagged his hand in Eberhard's direction, said something to the effect of, "Lovely to see you again, Herr Bitz, but I'm very late for an appointment," and, waving his hand at the camera, he disappeared into the crowd as quickly as he could.

Ultimately, I did go with the Kommissar, both to find my father and to launch an official complaint. I did both, then headed back to Schönefeld. Meanwhile—I didn't know this at the time—the Russian delegation was getting paranoid. They had no idea what I was going to seize. All they knew was that the bailiffs and I were coming back on Friday. So, at some point early Wednesday afternoon, the Russian powers decided to take the whole trade delegation, and as much of the goods as they could carry, and fly everything back to Moscow aboard the Tupolev. We must, the Russians said, deny the plane to Sedelmayer.

Their hurried packing up and unscheduled departure, of course, turned into a field day for the press. The story went global, and virtually every one of them mentioned my name and cited my long-term case against the Russian Federation. There were also TV news crews everywhere, and the

Russians' actions were televised live in Moscow. I learned this because my wife was at home watching the four Russian channels we got in Munich. Every one of them covered the story live.

The best report—I still have the YouTube footage—was from NTV's senior foreign correspondent in Germany, a Russian correspondent, who did his stand-up in front of a patch of bare concrete apron. "See that empty space behind me? That is where the Tupolev 204-300 prototype used to stand before the plane, carrying our Russian delegation, left for Moscow… Franz Sedelmayer sent bailiffs to take down the registration number of the plane and wanted to seize it, but they managed to get away in time. It was no problem and Sedelmayer did not succeed."

Then, the network cut to its correspondent at the Moscow airport, who asked the head of the delegation just as he came off the Tupolev, why the delegation had come back two days ahead of schedule.

"Well, um, it was great flying weather," he said, looking lamely at the camera. "So we came back early."

Those remarks alone took the score to Sedelmayer 5, Moscow nil, even though I didn't seize a single damn thing.

CHAPTER 16

The Law According to Vranyo

"If accused: admit nothing, deny everything, file countercharges."—Seen on a counterfeit CIA coffee mug at KGB headquarters

I've been involved in roughly 140 court cases with Moscow, and everything Moscow does; every ploy, every strategy, every argument they present—every single one has been based on a lie.

The culture of *vranyo*—lying—is central to the Russian soul; a vestige of the Soviet Union and communist rule. And whether it's foreign policy, domestic affairs, military operations, or the justice system, the lie is the chief and often the only strategy by which they operate.

Think about recent history.

Vranyo is the basis of Russia's geopolitical tactics in its dealings with the West. Russia assured the United States it would ensure that Syria gave up all its chemical and biological weapons.

Vranyo.

Russia ensured nothing of the sort. We found that out in April of 2017.

Russian diplomats insisted there was no Russian military involvement in the takeover of Crimea.

Vranyo.

Russian government spokesmen have long denied any official Russian involvement in the 2006 polonium poisoning murder of former FSB officer Alexander Litvinenko.

Vranyo.

When Russian leaders engage in *vranyo*, you have to accept that in every facet of your relationship with the Russian Federation, the culture of lying extends from top to bottom.

Vranyo affects the legal system as well. Whenever I spoke to people who'd engaged in litigation with the Russians, it was always the same story; the same pattern. Russian lawsuits were consistently based on false allegations and false representations. There was always the fact that they owed money to one party or other and hadn't paid. But they'd lied about it. There was always the fact that they were not compensating anybody for their losses, whether it was through expropriation, nationalization, or corruption. And they'd lie about it.

Even some of the foreign lawyers working for the Russians got pulled into the culture of *vranyo*. I realized that when UdPRF's Swedish lawyer Christer Söderlund presented a bold-faced lie to the court about my going bankrupt. Why did he lie? Because his Russian bosses told him to. And so, a large part of my prep for every court appearance and every stage of every case, has been to spend some time trying to anticipate how the Russians were going to play fast and loose with the facts, or attempt to bribe the judge or the magistrate, or put me or my allies in some sort of compromising position.

Sometimes, Moscow just flat-out makes stuff up. At one point UdPRF, through the GUVD, sent a telex to Interpol inquiring whether I was under investigation, then they told a Swedish judge that Interpol was contemplating an investigation of me. Of course the telex copy they submitted to the tribunal had been truncated, so the judges could see they'd contacted Interpol but were unable to see what the specific request had actually been about.

In 2003, shortly after I'd seized Russian property in Cologne (more about this later), the Russians told the U.S. Department of Justice that I was probably engaging in smuggling operations and other unlawful acts through my St. Louis, Missouri-based corporation. It took the FBI months of interviewing my company's personnel until it finally realized that the Russians had lied. They'd filed their legal aid request in the hope of obtaining evidence to use in the numerous civil court cases they'd filed against me in Sweden and Germany.

But that's how Moscow does business. And it wasn't that the KGB was after me. It wasn't. UdPRF was. In fact, it's a little known fact that the UdPRF, not the KGB or FSB or even SVR (Russia's foreign intelligence service) is responsible for much of what Russians call *kompromat*, which is the use of compromising material against a target. (The so-called Steele Dossier of opposition research against candidate Donald Trump was compiled by former SIS officer Christopher Steele at the behest of a shadowy U.S. opposition research company, Fusion GPS. Fusion hired Steele's firm, London-based Orbis Business Intelligence, to dig up dirt on Trump. The Steele Dossier, a collection of raw intelligence data, much of which has not been confirmed, or proven, made a splash during the 2016 presidential campaign. Because so much of its most damaging and salacious content cannot be independently confirmed, the document is a textbook example of the sort of *kompromat* originated by the KGB but refined by UdPRF).

It makes sense: UdPRF—the Blandly titled Office of Presidential Affairs—has unbelievably deep pockets and a long reach when it comes to black funds. After all, it is the entity that handles all of the assets of the office of the President both inside and outside Russia. We're talking about a conglomerate, which by its own admisson, is holding about $600 billion— yeah, that's with a 'b' worth of land, warehouses, construction companies, air and shipping lines, publishers and printing houses, vehicle fleets, yachts, and even restaurants, hotels, and hospitals.

The UdPRF is also used for other miscellaneous activities, some of which seem to have very little to do with the Russian state. The UdPRF recently refurbished the Volkhonsky House, an historic office building in central Moscow, owned by a private entity but controlled by Vladimir Putin's first wife Ludmila, and another Putin confidant. UdPRF has also overseen the construction of a billion dollar residence at Cape Idokopas, near Sochi on the Black Sea. Its nickname? "Putin's Palace".

If you work for the Russian Federation in an official capacity, UdPRF is the office that supplies all the *kruglak*—the perks bestowed on loyal apparatchiks. Your dacha, your apartment, your furniture, your vacations down in Sochi, and your car and driver all come from UdPRF. It even provides tailored shirts, bespoke suits, Swiss watches, and Italian shoes for Russian officials. And if you don't behave you lose it all.

Why was this so important for me to understand?

It was mission critical because if UdPRF decides to put pressure on a German administrative judge in Cologne who happens to be in charge of one of the many *Sedelmayer vs. Russian Federation* foreclosures I've initiated, I'd better know precisely how Moscow puts pressure on people. In my experience it was typical, for example, for the German Chancellor's office or the minister of justice to be visited by the Russian ambassador or the Chargé, who might in a friendly way inquire about the upcoming case, and perhaps slip to the chancellor or one of her deputies some nasty information about me in the chance they might want to pass it on to some appropriate individual.

Or, the ambassador might even play a little hardball and suggest that the Chancellor's office might want to take up some interest in the case because its outcome could affect the relationship between Russia and Germany. Possible dialog? "*Of course, Mrs. Merkel, we know that neither you nor we want under any circumstances to alter our many agreements about how Germany receives most of its natural gas from Gazprom and*

Rosneft at what we consider bargain basement prices."

Think of it as a scene out of "The Godfather." The Russian ambassador would simply be making Madam Chan-zell-or an offer she and her office couldn't refuse.

❖

Speaking of "Godfather" tactics, in 2003, I received an offer Moscow thought I couldn't refuse. How would I feel, I was asked by a Russian negotiator in Cologne, about putting the whole *Sedelmayer vs. Russian Federation* mess behind me? After all, wasn't President Putin a forgiving man? Hadn't he and I worked together well in St. Petersburg? Hadn't he sent a Russian delegation to Munich at my direct request to negotiate about a Russian compound I'd put a lien against? Wouldn't it just be easier to solve things once and for all?

Warily, I inquired about the conditions. They appeared simple enough. Come to Moscow. Sign papers ending your lawsuit and we will transfer $10 million U.S. currency—real *valuta* into your account. The slate will be wiped clean. No more lawsuits from you; no more countersuits from us.

My lawyer, Wolfgang Heinicke, was against it. "Bad deal, Franz," he told me.

Instinctively I agreed with him, but I wanted to hear his reasoning.

"First of all," he said, "You'd be under Moscow's control."

"And second?"

"Second, you'd be under Moscow's control. You have no protection in Moscow, Franz. They could arrest you for jaywalking. They can throw you in Lubyanka, toss the key into the Moskva River, and I could do nothing."

"Still, if it's a possibility that we can end this..."

Heinicke frowned. "What about that article?"

"Which one?"

"That English language Russian magazine that came out last year or maybe early this year—there was an article about you. Remember how Putin was quoted?"

"Yeah, I do." My former friend the president of the Russian Federation had told the magazine, "Before Sedelmayer gets paid, sauerkraut will shoot out of my butt."

Yes, he really said that.

I looked at Wolfgang. "So what?"

"So what? If you go to Moscow, your pal Putin will probably find some way to shoot sauerkraut out of your butt. That's what."

The lawyer caught my expression and gave me a wry glance. "Okay, okay. Look, if there's a way to do this we'll find one. After all, we've been doing this long enough."

And we had. When I'd first engaged him, Wolfgang Heinicke was our family lawyer and he hadn't done arbitration enforcement or asset recovery cases. So we'd learned the ropes together, and we made, I thought then and still do now—a pretty damn good pair of legal warriors. The Butch Cassidy and Sundance Kid of asset recovery as I jokingly put it.

But Wolfgang had a point. One thing I knew about Vladimir Putin was that he held grudges. And people—even Westerners—had been known to disappear in Russia. Dissidents and journalists had been mysteriously murdered; oligarchs had been arrested and sent to Siberia. And I'd been a thorn in Putin's side for almost a decade now.

Would I make an inviting target if I went back to Russia? I answered my own question in one word: probably.

I rapped my knuckles on Wolfgang's desk. "Okay, I don't go. So how do we handle it?"

"I'll go."

"You?"

"I'm just the lawyer. I can't sign anything binding without your permission. All I can do is look over the settlement papers. If they make sense I'll call you and fax you the draft. If you give me express permission then I'll sign, they'll pay, and it's all over. If it looks bad, I'll say 'sorry, no deal' and come straight home. I can probably do it in a couple of days."

I agreed. So, Wolfgang made the arrangements and flew to Moscow. The flight from Munich is roughly three hours each way. He'd arrive in the late afternoon; spend a night and do his business the next day, catch an early evening flight out and given the one-hour time change, be home in plenty of time for a late dinner.

UdPRF's people picked him up from the hotel with all the bells and whistles: a motorcade with blue lights and sirens. They drove him to the UdPRF offices, walked him inside, and then locked him inside an office that had a desk, a chair, and a sheet of paper that they instructed him to sign. They accused me of being a criminal. They told him I was under investigation for tax evasion in St. Petersburg; they said I was liable for $65 million in fines and could expect a jail term. They told Wolfgang that if he signed the paper both the Russian charges and the Sedelmayer charges would cancel each other out. No $10 mil or real estate for me; no $65 mil and Sedelmayer jail time for Russia.

The paper said, *Sedelmayer agrees to forfeit any and all of his claims against the Russian Federation.*

But it was all *vranyo*. The tax evasion charges had been trumped up—and Wolfgang Heinicke knew it. So he told them up front, "I'm not signing this. This isn't what you brought me here to do."

But of course it was exactly what they'd brought him to Moscow to do. And so they kept him in that room for hours. No phone calls. No food. No water. No toilet.

Wolfgang was rattled. But he neither budged nor cracked. Whenever they'd tell him to sign the document he'd answer, "Go screw yourself. I'm not signing this garbage." And all the time he was thinking, '*What are they going to do? If they actually hold me here, it's going to be a huge scandal.*'

When cajoling didn't work, Wolfgang's minders started screaming at him. They threatened all sorts of dire possibilities. "You'll just disappear." "No one knows where you are." "We could hold you for a year and you wouldn't be missed." "Keep doing what you're doing and you'll never go home."

But he held firm. Scared as he was he stared them down: "Do what you want. Do what you want. I don't care. I'm here. I'm an attorney. I'm representing a client, and I want to see you arrest me."

In the end they realized he wasn't going to budge. And so, they took him back to the airport and walked him onto the Munich flight—which they'd held at the gate for hours—and he flew out.

Wolfgang called me as soon as he got home to let me know how things had gone. I wasn't surprised that they'd lied about the settlement. But the fact that they now had me under investigation gave me real pause. It meant I could not safely return to Russia—ever.

Wolfgang had come to a similar decision: "I will do many things for you Mr. Sedelmayer," he told me. "But going back to Moscow will not be one of them. Once was plenty."

By 2006, *Sedelmayer vs. Russian Federation* had been going on for 10 biblically lean years. In 1998 I'd been awarded $2.35 million in Sweden. But Moscow simply disregarded the award and filed countersuits claiming sovereign immunity, misrepresentation, or fraud. I won every challenge but still hadn't received a penny of what I was owed. In 2004, I'd attached a 7-story Russian-owned building in Lidingö, a Swedish town northeast of Stockholm, as payment when Moscow refused to honor the award. That building was still in flux after several Russian challenges. I was confident that within the next three to four years I'd prevail in Stockholm and collect what I was owed plus interests and costs—somewhere in the $4.7-$5 million area. But right then, after a decade of lawsuits, claims, challenges, interrogatories, depositions, challenges, complaints, counter-counter-complaints and counter-counter-complaint litigations I'd collected exactly...$0.00.

Zilch.

How could things take that long? Well, Cologne was typical. The Cologne case started in 2003. I'm looking—optimistically, I must add—for a final decision and the release of the leftover funds from the very last auction sometime in the summer of 2017.

Yes: that is a long time frame. But one of the things one has to understand about taking on the Russian Federation is that nothing happens overnight. You've got to play the long game.

I'd known that if I wanted to collect the *valuta* the Russian Federation owed me, I'd have to find property that belonged to the Russian Federation, but wasn't protected by sovereign immunity, and seize it. I liked the idea of seizing property as opposed to other alternatives because once I obtained a property legally, I could either rent it or I could auction it off. I'd tried other strategies: for example, seizing the money Lufthansa paid the Russian government for overflight fees. But that tactic couldn't be legally accomplished.

And then, one day late in 2002, I got a call from one of my old friends who was working in the State Intelligence organization for North Rhine-Westphalia, which is in Düsseldorf. (FYI, each Federal State in Germany has its own intelligence-gathering organization.) For decades, his office had been assigned to keep an eye on the USSR trade mission located on Friedrich-Engels-Straße in Cologne. The Soviet trade mission was a 12,000-square meter compound that had held at one point one hundred families. There were three buildings and its own infrastructure with restaurants, a big gym—the works. There were a large number of undercover KGB personnel at the trade mission, which is why my friend kept tabs on it. In any case, after the Wall came down and the USSR imploded and the seat of government was moved from Bonn to Berlin, the KGB moved on to greener pastures and the Russians closed the Cologne site down.

My friend said, "You told me you were looking for Russian assets? How did you ever miss this one? It's perfect."

It certainly was worth a trip to Cologne. So I drove up, checked out the land registration records at the Cologne courthouse, and discovered that the trade mission site was still registered in the name of USSR. That was a problem. My claim was against the Russian Federation, not the USSR. Until the site was re-registered as property of the Russian Federation I couldn't seize it. But yes, it was definitely worth keeping an eye on.

About five months later I discovered a letter to the Cologne court from an attorney in Koblenz requesting a title change from the USSR to the Russian Federation.

Two days after it was re-registered I obtained a copy of the register document, then immediately filed a lien against the property. The Cologne court promptly attached the trade mission site and informed me that they were preparing a diplomatic note to be sent to the Russian Embassy in Berlin, notifying the Russian Federation that I had introduced a lien against their property and intended to auction it off.

Now, I'd been through this process before. I knew the Russians were pros at evading court documents. If the papers couldn't be served the process of enforcement could not go forward and I'd be unable to auction off the property. So the question was: how could I ensure that the papers were served in a way that Moscow couldn't argue that they'd never received them.

I thought about possible tactics. The staff at the embassy in Berlin would claim they'd never been served, or had been served improperly—they'd done it before. The only way to force them to accept the fact that they'd been served was to get the paperwork in front of someone so high up that it couldn't be ignored. Once they'd acknowledged my claim, they'd react and force court hearings. But that didn't matter to me, because I'd win in court and when I won I'd actually get some money out of it.

So the problem was: how to get the Russians to accept service of the paperwork and then react.

Y'know, I thought to myself, how about the president of the Russian Federation, my old friend Vladimir Putin. Volodya might want to pay me off just for old time's sake. Even if he didn't, he'd have to pay attention to my claim.

The more I thought about it the better the idea seemed to me. The only problem was how to get my paperwork onto his desk. I'd written a congratulatory note to Putin after he'd been named prime minister but hadn't received an answer. I'd sent another when he was elected president. Again, no response. My verdict: the notes weren't getting through. Obviously, they were being diverted at the staff level. I needed to get my message directly onto Putin's desk. But how?

I started making phone calls. And sometimes it pays to have high friends in low places. In my case, I knew an individual who'd maintained contact with Putin all through the incredible odyssey after he'd left St. Petersburg in 1996. And after a bit of badgering, my source slipped me the direct-dial number for the presidential telefax that sat inside Putin's office.

I asked my source: "Are you absolutely sure the line goes directly to Volodya?

"Yes I am. The answer I received last week could only have come from the President and him alone."

I sat down to write President Putin a note. I wondered if I'd get an answer. It had been seven years and a whole lot of water under the bridge—an effing flood to be honest—since we'd last communicated.

❖

In 1996, I'd found it ironic that Putin's first job in Moscow had been at UdPRF and even more so that he worked for Pavel Borodin, the man who'd expropriated Stone Island, as head of UdPRF's international division. From UdPRF he was plucked by Boris Yeltsin to become one of the president's deputy chiefs of staff, running an auditing group. He'd been recommended by, among others, the oligarch Boris Berezovsky, who thought that Putin, whom he'd known in St. Petersburg, was both loyal and manageable. His loyalty was quickly noticed by Yeltsin: by May of 1998, Putin had been promoted to First Deputy Chief of Staff in charge of Russian Regions.

But not for long. In July 1998, Putin was selected as Director of the FSB, the successor agency to the KGB. His ascent had been astonishing; dazzling; meteoric.

Putin himself has been quoted as saying the FSB appointment came as a complete surprise. "They had given me no inkling that I was even being considered for such an appointment. The president simply signed a decree," is what he wrote in his autobiography, "First Person."

Others have differing opinions. One story circulating at the time had the billionaire Oligarch Boris Berezovsky being asked in June, 1998, by Valentin Yumashov, Yeltsin's son-in-law, what he thought of Vladimir Putin. The oligarch, who'd known Putin since his time as deputy mayor of St. Petersburg and Berezovsky had an automobile business there, asked why Yumashov wanted to know about Putin all of a sudden.

Because, Yumashov said, Putin was being considered for the FSB directorship.

Why did Boris Yeltsin ever think that Putin, a 'grey man' with no background at the top echelons of power, could successfully assume what was one of the half-dozen most important and powerful posts in the Russian Federation? It came down to one word: loyalty. Putin was loyal to his superiors. Even better: he wasn't corrupt. Unlike oligarchs like Berezovsky, unlike the Yeltsin family itself, unlike the vast majority of Russia's power structure, Putin had resisted the greed that came with power. He may have enabled; he may have shielded. But he hadn't taken anything.

In all the time I knew him he'd taken no bribes and he'd asked for no special favors. Yet, he had a long and proven history of loyalty and the protection of those who did. That was the key. Putin was loyal. He was loyal to his shadow and gatekeeper, Igor Ivanovich Sechin. He was loyal to his former KGB colleagues. And he'd been incredibly loyal to his boss, Mayor Anatoly Sobchak. He'd risked his career to save Sobchak during the 1991 coup attempt against Gorbachev. Indeed, in St. Petersburg he'd built a protective wall around Sobchak and his wife Ludmila Narusova even as they'd cached millions of illicit dollars in Paris. He'd stood by as organized crime took over much of St. Petersburg's business because he followed the GUVD dictum that he wasn't in power to stop crime, just control it. Which, I believed, was why he'd allowed GUVD to pursue illegal activities. In fact, it occurred to me that if I hadn't stopped Leonid Pinchuk's attempt to take over Kamenny Ostrov in 1992, Putin would have most certainly let it happen.

It made perfect sense to me that Putin had been put up for the job of FSB director. He was an outsider; not a member of one of the current Kremlin tongs vying for power and influence. And because he was loyal, he'd be loyal to the Yeltsins. And indeed, one of Putin's first acts as FSB Director was to quash an investigation of the Yeltsins by Russia's Prosecutor General Yuri Skuratov. FSB vouched for the authenticity of a fuzzy video of a man said to be Skuratov in bed with a prostitute. FSB's conclusion ruined Skuratov's credibility. He resigned and the Yeltsins remained unindicted.

So it made sense that Boris Yeltsin, alcoholic, corrupt, and growing more distant every day, would need a Putin to protect him, and so he brought the new FSB director even closer. In March 1999, Yeltsin appointed Putin secretary of the Russian Security Council.

That job didn't last very long either. On August 9, 1999, Putin was named acting prime minister. Television coverage of the new PM showed the 2003 footage of a macho Putin at Kamenny Ostrov the day we'd launched the KGB's GRAD team. That very same day Yeltsin said he'd like to see Putin succeed him as president and Putin announced that he would indeed run.

Yeltsin's decision was a shock to most Kremlinologists, who thought Yeltsin would select as his heir Boris Nemtzov. Nemtzov had negotiated the end of the first Chechen War and had served as Yeltsin's deputy prime minister. But Yeltsin needed a loyalist to protect him and his family and Nemtzov was an activist reformer, not a go-along-to-get-along loyalist.

Which is why on December 31, 1999, President Boris Yeltsin abruptly resigned and named Vladimir Putin as acting president. It was an act of self-preservation. Putin's first official act was a Presidential Decree entitled

"On Guarantees for Former President of the
Russian Federation
and Members of His Family."

The decree pardoned the Yeltsin family from "all corruption charges against the outgoing President and his relatives."

On March 26, 2000, Putin was elected president of the Russian Federation with just over 50 percent of the vote. I'd written to congratulate him when he was appointed deputy prime minister—but hadn't heard back. I did the same after his election.

Once again, there'd been no answer.

As I said earlier, there'd been a lot of water under the Putin/Sedelmayer bridge, not all of it potable.

Maybe brevity would be best. I copied the land registration report and its attachments showing the separate pieces of property. And then I wrote a simple cover note:

> *Dear Mr. Putin:*
> *This is for your information.*
> *All the best,*
> *Franz Sedelmayer.*

I put everything into the fax and pressed the 'transmit' button.

Putin was true to form. I never heard a word from him.

But within a week a delegation of Russian negotiators showed up in Munich to go nose to nose with Heinicke and me about the former Soviet trade mission site.

❖

I'd attached the property in 2003. It was 2008 and a long series of court appearances before the German Constitutional Court ruled that I could actually obtain rent money from one of the buildings that had been rented out and I was also allowed to put it up for auction. The first payment wasn't a lot of money: 25,000 euros.

But the sum didn't matter. What mattered is that I'd broken the ice. Before those 25,000 euros no one—and I mean nobody—had ever extracted any *valuta* from the Russian Federation. And happiness turned to exhilaration when the receiver—the individual who'd been holding the rent payments in escrow—turned over another 470,000 euros in rent payments and auction fees to me. It wasn't enough to pay all my attorneys back, but I was able to pay down a substantial amount.

Of course the Russians changed their tactics. I'd not only won, but I'd collected *valuta*, and Moscow was mad. Once again, they went on offense, concocting a fraudulent suit alleging I'd defrauded GUVD. The suit they brought against me was for more than 20 million euros.

When Wolfgang Heinicke showed me the paperwork all I could do was laugh. He looked at me quizzically. "Wolfgang, there's nothing to worry about. How can I be concerned about twenty million euros when I'm scrambling to come up with the two or three grand I need to pay you? C'mon..."

But it was still bothersome. Gnawing. And Moscow knew it. And so they brought nuisance suit after nuisance suit—almost a dozen in all. And each one for grotesquely large sums of money. But from these legal mosquito bites—and we swatted them all away—I learned a valuable lesson. It was to stay focused on the real goal, which was prying what Moscow owed me out of Moscow's hands no matter what.

I'm not saying it wasn't difficult. When you go to court and your opponent's lawyer accuses you of high crimes and misdemeanors, insults your character, lies about your business dealings, and characterizes you as a felon, you're not going to like it. You know what's being said and what's in the written lawsuit isn't true but it's still frigging upsetting.

During the first couple of cases it took me a good 10 days or so to cool off and focus myself so that I could actually work on the problems at hand and obliterate the charges. And yes, I had to do it. I, and not Wolfgang or any of my other attorneys. What many individuals and companies never learn about going up against the Russian Federation is that your lawyers cannot ever substitute for you, because your lawyers don't know all the details of your case the way you do—or at least the way you should.

You have to stay on top of every detail yourself. You simply cannot leave everything to your lawyers.

In fact, every case brought by an individual or a company against Moscow that has been turned over to the lawyers has been won by Moscow, not by the plaintiffs. If you sue, you have to do the work, because if you don't and you leave it to them, you're going to lose the case. That's the secret. Leave it all to the lawyers and you'll lose. Why is that? The answer is because enforcement is all about the details, and what I've discovered is that because I know every molecule of my case, I'm better at picking over details than most lawyers.

In the Cologne case for example, I discovered by going over the picayune details of Russian law that whenever the Russian Federation is sued in a foreign court it must issue a decree that allows them to hire and retain lawyers in that foreign country.

So in 2016, Heinicke and I asked Moscow's German lawyers in Cologne to produce the decree to prove that they legally represented Moscow. They couldn't produce one—probably because they'd never been given one.

Fast forward to 2017. The Russians finally said they could produce the decree. We went back to court. One of the lawyers, a woman attorney, held up a document. "We have the decree, your honor." She laid a fuzzy photocopy on the judge's desk.

One of the judges lifted the document with two fingers and peered at it. "Hmm," he said, "It looks new. And there's no signature."

I said, "No signature, your honor? Is there a stamp?" I knew all too well that all Russian official documents have stamps.

I asked the judge, "May I have a look?"

"Of course."

I examined the photocopy. I said, "My case is from 2003. This document is dated May of 2006."

The judges glanced at one another. One of them said, "We're going to have a conference about this evidence," and they headed to their chambers. About 10 minutes later they returned. The judge who'd done the original examination said something to the effect of, "We have a very hard time with this document because first of all it's a photocopy and second it hasn't been notarized. Moreover, the original document seems not to carry a signature. Further, we can't read it because it's in Russian and there has not been provided a bona fide, notarized translation. We don't, therefore, deem it a valid piece of evidence."

He looked at Moscow's lead German attorney. "Mr. Piltz, where did you get it from?"

Piltz shrugged. "Me? I got it from her." He pointed at the woman attorney. "The first time I saw it was 20 minutes ago."

The Judge looked at the woman. "Mrs. So-and-so, where did you get it from?"

"Me?" she said, "I got it from him," pointing to a Russian academic who Moscow had sent to Cologne as an expert witness.

The Judge asked the Russian if he spoke German. When the professor said he did, the judge asked where he'd obtained the decree.

"It's from the Kremlin, your honor."

"I figured as much," said the judge. "But from whom in the Kremlin?"

"I don't know, your honor."

"Well, where did you go in the Kremlin to get the decree?"

The Russian hemmed and hawed.

"You just told me you obtained the decree from the Kremlin. Did you go to the Kremlin?"

"Not directly, your honor."

"'Not directly.' Then where did you get it?"

"I went to a private company, and the director of the company gave me the decree."

The judge was very patient with him. "And who gave it to you?"

"I forgot his name, your honor."

The judge shook his head. "We don't have to discuss this any further." He paused. "Here are our findings. Finding One: there's an arbitration agreement in place, which Russia is bound by. Finding Two: we cannot accept the validity of this piece of paper at this time."

In 1998, my arbitration award had been set at $2,350,000. As of 2017, I have collected more than $5,000,000 from the Russian Federation, and I won the majority of cases.

So, has it been worth it for the Russians? IMHO no. They could've simply paid the original debt and everything would've gone away. But they didn't. They played tough; they played the bully. But in the end, all they showed was weakness.

Moscow's weakness—and Vladimir Putin's I am sad to have to say—is the result of an authoritarian, dictatorial system of his own making; a system that is incapable of admitting it could ever be wrong; a system that bases its whole existence on *vranyo*.

That system was how Moscow approached my case from the get-go. And that system is why Moscow ultimately lost.

CHAPTER 17

The Rules of War In Putingrad

"I have some rules of my own.
 One of them is never to regret anything."
 - Vladimir Putin as quoted in his book "First Person."

When you're working to pry what's owed you out of the Russian Federation, and you know what the RF's modus operandi is—*vranyo* coupled with intimidation—effective enforcement, by which I mean getting paid, often becomes more a matter of investigation and dogged persistence than it does a matter of law. At least that's the way it worked for me.

I needed lawyers of course. Wolfgang Heinicke was an invaluable partner. So were Jonas Löttiger, Hans Forssell, Reiner Heyer and scholars like Andreas Paulus, among others. But in working toward a denouement that resulted in actually receiving *valuta*, I had to start thinking more like a detective or an investigator—think Harry Bosch or Sam Spade—than a lawyer. Lawyers like to win cases. Detectives? They like to put bad guys behind bars. There's a difference. Winning a case doesn't necessarily mean winning money. Winning an enforcement means the other guy pays up. Case closed.

So, I changed my own modus operandi. I thought differently and I planned differently because I was investigating, tracking, pursuing, gathering intelligence, eliciting information, and searching for patterns. I started asking 'just the facts, ma'am' kinds of questions. What's available? How much is it worth? What's it being used for? Is it seize-worthy? Only after I'd determined that something was worth acquiring did I start looking at the case law and decide whether or not to actually attach it.

And, to prevent being blindsided or charting the wrong course, I started operating under what's known in some military units as "The Law of the Five P's:" Proper Planning Prevents Poor Performance.

Planning is everything. In the Yukos case, for example, the claimants, all the former Yukos shareholders, *inter alia*, received a bombastic $50 billion award. But when it came to attaching property to enforce the judgement, they had no plan. They simply went out and attached everything they could find. I guess they were hoping for shock and awe, which makes perfect sense if you know that you can retain those assets over a significant period of time.

In 2016, I gave a speech in London to an audience of seasoned litigators and arbitrators, one day before a district court in the Netherlands killed the $50 billion Yukos award. The court found the arbitration tribunal had no jurisdiction to rule on the case. I reminded the audience about two identical Swedish voidance proceedings, also concerning Yukos arbitration awards rendered against Russia, which had previously come to the very same conclusions as the Dutch court. The underlying multilateral Energy Charter Treaty only contained a provisionary arbitration clause. The Russians had signed it in the 1990s when they needed foreign investment to jumpstart their derelict oil and gas sector, Russia's no. 1 export commodities. But the Russian parliament never ratified the treaty. So when the suit was brought, the Russians simply claimed there was no international institution of law competent to rule on questions of compensation with the exception of Russian courts.

Any litigator worth his salt would have built a series of defensive walls in order to handle the case with sufficient time and allow for careful preparation of the battlefield. But, for reasons unknown, the Yukos claimants allowed themselves to be rushed by the Russians and let the court limit everything to one legal question: the arbitration agreement. Their decision was fatal. Time works in the claimant's favor; every extra day you get helps you build your case. In *Sedelmayer vs. Russian Federation*, for example, the initial proceedings in Sweden lasted from 1998 to 2002 and were only finalized by a Supreme Court decision in 2005. Yes, it took a long time — seven years. But I won every single round.

The 2016 Dutch judgment instantly killed off the attachment proceedings and all the frozen assets were returned to Russian control. Why did this happen? Because instead of concentrating on the vital court proceedings in the Hague with a view to void the award, the Yukos shareholders got carried away with enforcement.

What did this self-inflicted error cost Yukos shareholders? As I write these lines in May of 2017, the Russian Federation is selling off most of its assets in the West to avoid the Yukos claimants and other creditors. Yukos shareholders might very well win the next court rounds in the Netherlands. As a matter of fact, I would be thrilled if they do. But the question remains: where can they go to enforce? There will be no assets left for them to attach.

Bottom line? The claimants' lawyers won the battle—a $50 billion award. But they lost the war. Yukos shareholders have nothing to show for all their legal fees.

What first-timers and many good and great law firms either forget, or don't know in the first place, is that when it comes to successful enforcement, you have to take it one step at a time. Small steps. Building blocks. When you enforce against a government, it's not enough to send a letter: "*Please attach this or enforce that.*" You have to go and hand in the application personally. You have to shake hands with the judge, with the administrator, and with the bailiff who will be helping you enforce the judgement. You have to become familiar with their turf and their operational methods so you understand how the paper flow works.

And then you have to tell them — and make sure that they understand: "I'm here to help with any problem that might arise. I'll be back next week too, because I want to see how it went."

And, you have to go back that next week. And, you have to examine the file and ask how the enforcement process is proceeding. And, if it's not proceeding at a satisfactory pace, you have to nudge these people along, encourage them, support them, and when necessary prod them.

Prod? Yes. Because — and it took me a while to learn this — these bailiffs, and judges and administrators, they're sometimes nervous about doing what you are asking them to do.

Why nervous?

Because the Russians like to use intimidation. Sometimes it's implied; sometimes it is not. And if you read the papers, you know that individuals who go up against the Russian Federation have been known to turn up dead. So, some judges, bailiffs, or administrators are going to feel personally threatened simply because you're asking them to help you go after Moscow's assets.

At times, I've told nervous bureaucrats, bailiffs, registrars, and administrators, "If you cannot do what has to be done because you are personally afraid, then please hand the job off to someone who'll get the job done. I don't want to have any quarrels with you. But at the same time I won't allow your fear or unease to deny me what's rightfully mine."

An example: I once went to the Land Registry in the City Court of Cologne. The registry was buried so deep in the basement I thought I was heading to the morgue. I knocked on the door. "Hello. My name is Sedelmayer."

The registrar looked up at me "I know about you. You're the guy who's suing the Russians. Right?"

"Yes, ma'am."

She said, "Do you know you could get me shot?"

"Shot? Why?"

"Because you're going to ask me for documents that the Russians don't want you to have, and if they find out I gave them to you they'll shoot me. You should be ashamed of yourself."

I squinted at her to see if she was joking. But she wasn't. She was serious.

Ultimately, I was able to convince the registrar that no Russians would come looking for her and she pulled the files for me. But it took a while. And while I thanked her I also told her, "You're making too much of this. You don't have to worry. If there were any real danger to giving me what I'm asking for, I wouldn't have asked you to do it in the first place."

That registrar wasn't alone. She—and many of the administrators, clerks, and bailiffs I dealt with—had the same sorts of latent fears about what the Russians would do to them if they helped me. Their fears may have been irrational. But they were nonetheless real.

Of course their fears were real: bailiffs, registrars, and administrators read the newspapers. They knew that the Russian Federation is capable of violence. And they knew that Vladimir Putin's Russia does everything it can do to block, thwart, and avoid paying settlements, and that it goes after its enemies. They know that just below the surface, the potential for violence from Moscow exists.

❖

Thinking about the Law of the Five P's, I can remember another case where lack of a game plan hurt a claimant's ability to collect. Back in 1998, the *Wall Street Journal* published the first major article about *Sedelmayer vs. Russian Federation*, describing the dispute between the Russians and me. And, in the same article, the *Journal* told the story of a similar case about a venture called the Moscow Country Club. The Moscow Country Club was the creation of an American entrepreneur who put together a group of investors, then partnered with the Russian Ministry of Foreign Affairs. They built a resort, golf course, and country club for diplomats on property owned by the Ministry. And, very much like the Subway joint venture back in St. Petersburg, as soon as the golf course was finished and the hotel had been refurbished and renovated, and the resort was completely outfitted, the Russian partners had said, "Thank you very much, now get the heck out of Dodge before someone gets hurt."

The major shareholder and his attorney were both from California. Their contract included a commercial arbitration clause, and they obtained their award around the same time I did in 1998. However, they'd approached their case differently from the way I'd approached mine. I'd sued the Russian Federation. They'd brought their action against a state corporation owned and operated by the Ministry of Foreign Affairs—the entity that had been used as the umbrella corporation for the venture—as opposed to the Russian Federation or the Ministry of Foreign Affairs itself. And so, although they'd been awarded damages, the Russians weren't paying, arguing that the company was incapable of paying, and neither the Ministry of Foreign Affairs nor the Russian Federation, had any responsibility.

It wasn't quite the same as my case, but it was close. And it, like mine, was built on a lie. So, in 1998, I telephoned the main American lawyer. His name was Larry Shine. He was from Sacramento, California, and he was young, ambitious, and confident.

We chatted about the article and listened to each other's horror stories about doing business in Russia. And then I suggested that we might join forces.

I said, "Larry, why don't we work together on enforcing these awards?"

He said, "Why, Franz?"

I said, "Well, we're in the same boat. You've collected an award and I've collected an award, but neither of us is getting any *valuta*. You're not getting paid; I'm not getting paid. So, since we're going to be running simultaneous enforcements, wouldn't it be better to do it together? We'd save time and effort—and probably spend less than working separately."

Larry thought about it for a few minutes. But his answer was, "Thanks, but no thanks, Franz. Don't worry about us—we've got everything under control."

And that was that. I wished him good luck and rang off.

Fast forward to 2011. I was in Florida with my wife, Vlada, for about ten days of vacation, and, in the middle of sun, sand, surf, and adult beverages topped with little umbrellas, my cell phone rang.

I picked it up. "Hey, Franz, this is Larry Shine."

It took me a few seconds to place the name. "Hello, Larry." How the hell did he get my number?

"Hi, how are you? Long time no hear."

Long time indeed. I calculated. "Thirteen years. A long time. By the way, did you guys ever collect your money from the Russians?"

There was a pause. "Ahh, no, Franz, we didn't."

"But you were so confident."

"Yeah, we were. But they never paid us."

"I know what that's like. What happened?"

"So, when collecting from the company didn't work, we tried to enforce the award against the State—the Russian Federation, but..."

I jumped in. "Let me guess. They probably said, 'Sorry, the state corporation is not the Russian Federation, it's just the state corporation.'"

"You hit it on the nose."

Of course I had. Because I'd known all along that the company was just one of the shells in a shell game. Bottom line? They'd wasted lots of money, lots of time, and barked up the wrong tree, because the arbitration hadn't been done correctly right from the get-go.

❖

After we'd hung up, I thought to myself, maybe there's money in advising people how to actually get paid after they've been awarded an arbitration settlement from countries like the Russian Federation. Because I knew from bitter experience that winning a case is one thing; collecting the money is something completely different.

Yes, you could win. The tribunal could listen to the case and rule in your favor. "Poor guy," says the judge, "What happened to you? They took everything away from you? Well, that's wrong. So, here's a judgment of $5 million, or $10 million, or $50 million—or even $50 billion."

And you walk out of the tribunal with that wonderful piece of paper in your hand that says you've just been awarded $50 billion.

And then the Russians say, "Okay, smart guy, try and collect. Because we're not paying."

And guess what: in every single case, with the exception of mine, the Russians were right. They didn't pay. Claimants never collected a single kopek. My analysis went something like this. Claimants didn't know what to do because they hadn't done any homework or research. They'd simply hire a lawyer and sue—without any idea where or how to enforce a judgment or arbitration award if they prevailed.

They also didn't understand who they were suing. Because suing the

Russian Federation is a different universe from suing a corporation or a dishonest partner. The Russian Federation is a sovereign state. It has immunity from virtually any claim unless it consents to proceedings under law or international treaty. And the vast majority of businessmen and entrepreneurs have never had to face issues of immunity, because they'd never sued a sovereign state. Sovereign states additionally have what's known as Immunity from Execution, which means that their property can't be attached. But there is one loophole. It's called mixed use. If you can prove that the Russian Federation uses a state-owned building, vessel, or airplane for commercial purposes, then it becomes fair game. That's what I discovered by doing my homework, and that's how I was able to foreclose on Russian properties in Sweden and Germany.

Another problem I identified not just with the Moscow Country Club, but other unsuccessful cases against the Russian Federation, was that no one—neither the attorneys nor the principals—had done very much homework before they initiated arbitration. That was a huge mistake. Pre-arbitration homework is critical. Because, as the Moscow Country Club people discovered, they arbitrated against the wrong entity. They should have joined the Russian Federation or the Ministry of Foreign Affairs. They didn't—and so they lost before the fight even started.

Which led me, in 2012, to create MARC, my Multinational Asset Recovery Company, based in St. Louis, Missouri. With MARC, I have the capability to help both companies and individuals who have run into problems bringing court and arbitration action, as well as collecting the awards they're owed by governments, and/or local partners, in countries where the laws can be stacked against foreign investors and entrepreneurs.

I also discovered that there are a large number of claimants who drop their case simply because they've run out of money. Arbitration is expensive. You've already lost your investment. And if, after arbitration, the defendant, be it an individual or a sovereign nation, refuses to pay, you can run out of money before you conclude all the court cases.

All that certainly was and is the case with Russia. And it is why MARC does not recommend investing in Russia. Not these days. Not with Vladimir Vladimirovich Putin as president.

Because one of the truths I have confirmed over the past seventeen years, is that Russia, under Vladimir Putin, has become a horrible place for foreign investment. In 1989, when I went to Leningrad, possibilities did actually exist. Today, as a single entrepreneur, I wouldn't invest a dime in Russia. The only companies able to invest there now are multinational corporations so big that if they lose five or ten million dollars, it doesn't matter because they'll make it up elsewhere. But when you talk about what I and many others had—small and mid-sized companies—there's no way I'd take the risk to invest in Russia, because in point of fact there is no way to recover debt.

It all goes back to Putin. Instead of reforming the broken system from the 1990s, he's done everything to institutionalize an already inhospitable atmosphere for Western business. He's created a system that is weighted against honesty, openness, candor, and fairness. He's created a system that rewards *vranyo*, criminality, corruption, and favoritism.

Under Putin, Russia has become a bully state in which the weak have nothing and the bullies have everything. And the threat of violence? It's always there—just under the surface. Every time I think about doing business in Putin's Russia, the theme from the movie "Jaws" plays in my head.

Back in the 1990s, I formed my KOC security company to help Western investors deal with the local mobs who tried to take away their business or a chunk of the business. I was able to help suppress the organized crime takeover of the Enchanted Isle during the Goodwill Games, for example, and also stop the theft and pilfering during the Banque Credit Lyonnais Russie renovations. And one of the things I learned was that the mobsters didn't fight one another. They preferred soft targets. There was enough money floating round for them all, so they made agreements and by and large stuck to them. Honor among thieves.

It seems to me that Vladimir Putin has done much the same over the course of his presidency. He's certainly created wealth for his friends, associates, and old KGB colleagues. But if you don't go along, if you protest, or make waves, or investigate, there's a chance in Vladimir Putin's Russia that you will end up dead.

CHAPTER 18
Death and Putin

"Even in the valley of the shadow of death,
two and two do not make six."—Leo Tolstoy

When I look back on my time in St. Petersburg and remember the people I met, lived, and worked with it is always with great joy. Never again in my lifetime will I see such dramatic and progressive historical change. For almost seven years I witnessed days of awe, surprise, and hope. I found the love of my life in Russia. Indeed, Russia and its people became a part of me and I do not regret one single thing about my time there. Yes, Russia was corrupt. Yes, building Kamenny Ostrov was a challenge and often a battle. And yes, in the end, Boris Yeltsin's corrupt government expropriated everything I'd struggled to build.

Even so, it was all worth it. In fact, I've always tried to pass the positive thoughts and emotions about my time in St. Petersburg on to my two children, who sadly have never had the opportunity to see transitional Russia as young adults.

My only regret is that I wish the Vladimir Putin, with whom I worked so closely, the Volodya in whom I confided over beer and German food; the plugged-in, savvy deputy mayor who supported me and my business, had not become the individual who has made Russia into the *bardack* (mess) it is today. Putin's Russia is a Russia in which the strong prosper and the weak struggle; a Russia in which it is sometimes hard to tell the difference between the state security apparatus and organized crime; a Russia that has made militant nationalism and indiscriminate, confrontational counterterrorism the substitutes for patriotism and love of country; a Russia that lurches toward financial ruin while Putin's friends grow obscenely rich.

Indeed, what pains me as much as anything is my conviction that Putin's pals could have struck it rich without turning Russia into a kleptocracy. But they couldn't stop at just striking it rich—they simply had to take it all. And so, not only did Putin swerve Russia from a nascent democracy into a kleptocracy, he and his pals did it by substituting a 21st century form of authoritarianism that has almost completely obliterated Russia's burgeoning experiment in fundamental democratic rights and freedoms.

It is as if the moment he became president, Putin immediately chose to ignore the bitter lessons taught by the 70 years of inhumane communist dictatorship. Lessons, by the way, he knew all too well how to avoid.

How can I say that with certainty? Because during our time together in Leningrad and St. Petersburg, Putin and I talked at length about exactly those subjects, and about the people who stood on both sides of the political divide.

If the bad deeds done over the last 18 years had been solely material in nature they would be much easier to understand. But it gets worse. In the absence of a regulated communist agenda and in the presence of graft and corruption, Putin's totalitarian regime has morphed into something that essentially tinges on fascism. Certainly, Putin has helped to encourage racism and homophobia, both of which are fueled jointly by the Russian state and the Orthodox Church, whose unholy alliance seems to be incapable of any compassion and tolerance for those who need it the most.

Moreover, fear of losing his singular control has caused Putin to attempt to regulate even such ephemeral activities as comedy, music, alternative religions, and the arts. Absurd charges such as blasphemy and the incitement of racial hatred are used as a pretense to ignore, exclude, and dismiss creative, independent, and critical minds.

Think about this: under the presidency of Vladimir Vladimirovich Putin, Russians have been charged with blasphemy!

Blasphemy?

The Wahabi Saudis, who want only to chop off hands, arms, legs, and heads charge people with blasphemy. The Taliban, who want to take Afghanistan back into the Stone Age, charge people with blasphemy. ISIS, which teaches eight-year-olds how to behead nonbelievers, charged Charlie Hebdo with blasphemy. And we all know how that turned out.

Of course, charging people with blasphemy used to be routine. But that was in the 15th century, when people believed in witchcraft and thought the earth was flat.

But in 21st century Russia?

Has Volodya lost his mind? Or is he simply attempting—and all too often succeeding—in summoning up the darkest, most racist, most sexist, most malicious and malevolent aspects of the Russian soul and encouraging those repulsive, appalling and vile qualities as the new status quo because the current status quo, the Putin status quo, sucks.

And suck it does. Over the last 18 years—and especially since Putin returned to the presidency in 2012—Russians' lives certainly have not gotten a lot better. Oil prices have collapsed; Western sanctions have been imposed because of Putin's aggressive actions in Georgia, Eastern Ukraine, and Crimea.

For ordinary Russians, the quality of life has deteriorated exponentially. To counter his failures and the fiscal contractions caused by sanctions, Volodya has tried to claim *Krymnash* (Crimea is Ours!) as a proud symbol of his expansionism and reviving Russia's Imperial sphere of influence.

Instead, fortuitously, the phrase has become a sardonic meme in online cartoons and graffiti sprayed on walls all over Russia: "I may be homeless, but *Krymnash!*" "The toilets don't work, but *Krymnash!*" "The ruble has fallen, but *Krymnash.*"

How did this happen? It happened in part because Putin skillfully betrayed his people by using the democratic process to come to power and then began slowly, inexorably, to chip away at what was supposed to become a free and just society. Unencumbered by Marxist-Leninist ideology, he transformed the executive organs of the state judiciary, the parliament, the security apparatus, the office of the president to tools of oppression against Russians, who only want to speak their minds and live their lives without the state dictating what they can and cannot do and say in everyday life. He encouraged chaos; he understood the importance of bribery and blackmail; he never retreated, never paused or stopped and always kept the West, most of which had retreated into a nanny-nation form of socialism, off-balance.

In today's Russia, loyalty to country has become secondary to loyalty to Volodya. Putin has recently even created his own Praetorian Guard—a paramilitary unit of over 400,000 men loyal to him alone. And even as domestic repression has increased exponentially, Russian destabilization programs against foreign governments have also expanded. Did Putin insinuate himself into the 2016 U.S. election process? It's still moot, but my sense is that he probably did. Did he influence the 2017 French elections? One can certainly say it appears that he tried, but failed. Has he caused shudders and ripples in the former Soviet republics and Western Europe? Absolutely.

Putin's *vranyo*-based Russia is cynical; provocative; insidious. It can also be lethal.

Lethal? The regrettable answer is yes.

One reason: it has become much easier in the past few years to utter the words "Russia" and "death" in the same sentence. One basis for this is that unexpected and unexplained deaths have become a lot more commonplace in Russia over the 18 years since Vladimir Vladimirovich Putin came to power. Dozens of individuals have died under mysterious circumstances. In many of the cases, the victims had a personal or professional relationship with him. Some worked for him; some he worked for. Some knew him as a colleague at the KGB; others knew him as president or prime minister.

Some, like GRU General Igor Sergun had died from a sudden heart attack. Some, like the Oligarch Boris Berezovsky, who was instrumental in getting Putin appointed head of the FSB but later fell out with him, and Ivan Safronov, a retired Russian Space Force colonel who blew the whistle on illegal Russian arms sales to Iran and Syria, allegedly committed suicide. Some, like the investigative journalist Anna Politkovskaya, the human rights lawyer Stanislav Markelov, the opposition leader and Putin critic Boris Nemtsov, and Andrei Kozlov, vice chairman of the Russian Central Bank, were shot to death. Others, like the lawyer Sergei Magnitsky, were beaten to death. Still others, like journalist Yuri Shchekochikhin and former KGB officers Oleg Gordievsky and Alexander Litvinenko were poisoned. Gordievsky survived; Litvinenko and Shchekochikhin did not.

Still, others passed away mysteriously, as did Putin's former press minister Mikhail Lesin, who died of unexplained blunt force trauma in a hotel room in Washington D.C. And on December 26, 2016, Oleg Yerovinkin, a former KGB and FSB general and a close associate of Volodya's one-time gatekeeper and deputy prime minister, Igor Ivanovich Sechin, who is the current head of the huge state-owned oil company Rosneft, was discovered dead in the back seat of his Lexus. Cause of death: unknown. But Kremlinologists were quick to identify Yerovinkin as a liaison/cutout between Rosneft boss Sechin and his BFF Vladimir Putin. That was significant, because Russian bloggers had already identified Gen. Yerovinkin of being one of the sources feeding derogatory information—some of it *kompromat;* some of it *dezinformatsya*—on U.S. presidential candidate Donald J. Trump to former MI6 officer Christopher Steele for what has become known as the Trump Dossier. Did Putin or Putin's office control, shape, or even create the raw intelligence Steele received? If so, that would be known in the spy world as a brilliant example of covert action. And Yerovinkin's death put the lid on the kettle. Whatever he knew he took to the grave—and it's unlikely that either Putin or Sechin will go on television and tell how it all happened to Megan Kelly, *60 Minutes*, or even Oliver Stone.

Putin and death. All of the victims mentioned above either knew secrets about, worked with, or opposed Vladimir Putin. Some were involved with episodes or actions that might show Putin in an unfavorable light. It would not be paranoid of me to state that the sheer number of Putin-connected victims, killed not just in Russia, but Western Europe and even the United States, has raised lots of questions—but received very few answers—among Kremlin watchers both in Russia and in the West.

There are two murders that—to me on a personal level—most represent Putin's connection to death. One was the killing of Boris Nemtsov, a political protégé of Boris Yeltsin, political reformer, and opposition leader who was shot to death in 2015 on a bridge within view of the Kremlin. The other is former KGB Lieutenant Colonel Alexander Litvinenko, who complained to Putin about KGB corruption, was ultimately poisoned with polonium and died a lingering, painful death in London in 2006. Both of these individuals were political threats to Putin's presidency, and by extension, to Putin's circle of self-enriching friends and associates.

Boris Nemtsov was by training a physicist, but by choice a young, aggressive, and liberal reformer. He'd been in politics ever since the USSR disintegrated. He made a name for himself by privatizing local industries, not allowing oligarchs to manipulate public auctions, and rooting out corruption. He played a vital role as a peacemaker and negotiator in the first Chechen war. He was recruited by President Yeltsin and became deputy prime minister of Russia in March of 1997. Yeltsin, even after Nemtzov had left the government, promoted him publicly as his only choice for successor.

Even as Boris Nemtsov's star rose, so did my then-friend Vladimir Putin's. The month Yeltsin mentioned Nemtzov as his successor, he appointed Putin deputy chief of the presidential administration. The two knew one another as colleagues, and, reportedly, as friends. They even lived in the same *kruglak*-supplied Moscow apartment house. But whereas Nemtzov left the cabinet in 1998, Putin would go on to become the head of the Russian FSB and Prime Minister.

And in an unforeseen turn of events, it would not be Boris Nemtzov, the reformer and political gadfly who would replace Boris Yeltsin, but Vladimir Putin, the man who ran the security services; the man who kept Yeltsin's secrets. Indeed, the reason for Putin's appointment became abundantly clear when the newly appointed president signed a pardon for Yeltsin and his entire family within hours of his appointment. If Nemtzov had been at the helm such a pardon would have been extremely unlikely.

Shortly after Putin's election in 2000, Nemtzov joined the opposition. Over the next decade his attacks on Putin and Putin's friends grew more and more intense. Putin, frustrated because he couldn't prosecute Nemtzov on any criminal violation, decided to throw him in jail for demonstrating against the regime, so he'd be hauled off on such charges as unlawful assembly or disruption. Even so, Nemtzov continued his protests.

The stakes rose exponentially when, early in 2014, Putin decided to annex Crimea and to invade eastern Ukraine. For Putin, the campaign in Crimea and eastern Ukraine was the single most important strategic undertaking of his presidency. He used speed, surprise, stealth, *vranyo*, *dezinformatsya*, even *kompromat*, claiming the uprisings were caused by locals— Crimean and Eastern Ukraine nationals, not Russian troops.

Then, in July, a Malaysia Airlines passenger jet carrying 295 passengers on a flight from Amsterdam to Kuala Lumpur, was brought down by a missile in eastern Ukraine. Putin insisted it had been targeted by Ukrainian nationalists, not Russian-supported rebels. Putin's lies were quickly exposed by Boris Nemtzov, who claimed he had undeniable proof that Russian troops were fighting in eastern Ukraine, and evidence would show it was a Russian missile that brought the Malaysian aircraft down. The Kremlin took note.

On February 27, 2015, while crossing the Bolshoy Moskvoretsky Bridge within sight of the Kremlin, Nemtzov was shot to death. That particular area of Moscow is under permanent surveillance, by foot and vehicular patrols and 24/7 video. But on February 27, the day the assassination took place, there were no police, no vehicles, and by some incredible coincidence all the closed circuit TV cameras were inoperable. According to the authorities they'd been shut down for repairs.

Putin put himself in charge of the investigation. In short order, several Chechens were conveniently identified, arrested, and convicted of the murder. But to everyday Russians, Nemtsov's obscenely public murder signaled to everyone, whether they were in the opposition or a supporter of the government, no one was safe from retribution if the president felt he was being threatened. And not even Nemtsov's family was spared. His daughter and mother were forced to leave Russia and seek asylum in Germany because of threats to them. I saw them in Munich at the premier of a documentary about Nemtsov's life. They left me with no doubts: they will pursue the case until their loved one's death has been solved — not to Volodya's sweep-it-under-the-rug satisfaction — but to theirs.

❖

Alexander Litvinenko was a dogged KGB investigator. He'd been recruited straight out of the army and worked on organized crime, terrorism, and corruption cases. He was what the KGB called an "oper", which meant he was an investigator who sometimes operated undercover in order to get close to the targets of an investigation.

In 1994, Litvinenko met and soon became friends with an oligarch named Boris Berezovsky, who had been targeted for assassination by a corrupt group of Moscow police officers. He and Berezovsky became close. By 1998, Litvinenko had been recruited as a member of URPO—the elite Division of Operations against Criminal Organizations—a 'black' unit of the FSB, KGB's successor organization.

In March of that year, Litvinenko was stunned to receive orders from his superiors at URPO to assassinate Boris Berezovsky. What he was being asked to do was murder and Litvinenko refused to cooperate. He informed Berezovsky of the plot and also let his superiors know he believed the order to be illegal.

In July of 1998, Vladimir Putin was appointed head of the FSB. Although Litvinenko did not know it, Berezovsky had pushed Putin's candidacy. Litvinenko took his story to the new director, who not only did not act on it, but dealt with Litvinenko as a hostile whistleblower, who was betraying the brotherhood of the security services by publicly bringing up what Putin thought should be kept as internal affairs.

Rebuffed by Putin, Litvinenko and five of his fellow URPO officers held a press conference in November of 1998. That act alone condemned Sacha in Putin's eyes as a traitor to the system. He was arrested and imprisoned on trumped-up charges. In 2000, after his release but before a second trial, Sacha Litvinenko, his wife Marina, and his young son Anatoly defected from Russia and found asylum in Great Britain, where he eventually went to work with the British intelligence services MI5 and MI6.

On November 1st, 2006, after meeting with two former Russian security officials, Sacha Litvinenko started feeling poorly. He was hospitalized. Over the next three weeks, owing to the persistence of his wife, Marina, who instinctively understood that Sasha was not just ill but he'd been poisoned, Litvinenko gave a series of detailed interviews to police detectives. The investigation discovered that the former KGB officer had been poisoned with radionuclide polonium-210, a rare and highly toxic element in his body. Traces of polonium were also tracked to the two former KGB officers with whom Litvinenko had met.

Litvinenko died on November 23, 2006. The next day, a posthumous statement attributed to him was released by his friend human rights activist Alex Goldfarb, who'd met Litvinenko at the behest of Boris Berezovsky and had helped spirit the Litvinenkos out of Russia and find them asylum in Great Britain. Litvinenko's statement charged Putin with being behind his murder.

Over the next decade, Marina Litvinenko fought to keep the inquiry over her husband's murder alive in the English court system. It wasn't easy. The governments of England and Germany were more than reluctant to implicate Russia, let alone Vladimir Putin. To force the British to launch a public inquiry in England, Marina had to bring expensive legal action not against Russia, but against the United Kingdom. Through sheer will, determination, and grit she ultimately prevailed. One look into her eyes across a dinner table and you understand that she is a force of nature.

I stand in awe of Marina!

Was Vladimir Putin directly involved in these two murders? That question will most likely never be answered. On a personal level, when I think of Putin during our time together in St. Petersburg, it is beyond me to believe Putin could order such killings. But as I look at events today, approaching the question with German logic and organization, it is not irrational that I myself conclude that Putin and his cronies were the only ones benefiting from Nemtzov's and Litvinenko's needless deaths—and by creating such an atmosphere, they had to have some responsibility for them.

❖

An interviewer once asked me if Putin has any weak spots. My answer was yes—one huge weak spot. Putin cannot stand when people make fun of him. If "Saturday Night Live" were broadcast from Moscow and Alec Baldwin did to Putin what he does to Donald Trump, I'm convinced that Baldwin's corpse would be found one night in his hotel room. That is how seriously Vladimir Putin takes himself.

It didn't used to be that way. But life does change. And, as his career changed, expanded, morphed, Putin has become a changed man. From being a local fixer for the mayor to becoming a president, life has changed for him, his family, his friends... and also his enemies.

And who are Putin's enemies today?

Obviously to Volodya the list is endless: anyone who opposes his system of governance; members of the opposition, journalists, and business people qualify. So do ordinary citizens who dare protest in the streets and end up in jail. They're being sentenced to years of *gulag* at a rate not seen since Stalin's days. There's a Russian saying attributed to Putin that's been making the rounds lately. It defines the current situation in Russia succinctly: "For my enemies, the law, for my friends, everything!"

As for me, I sit in Munich, watch the news, read the blogs, shake my head in disbelief, and wish for the Volodya I knew in St. Petersburg. Unfortunately for me—and the rest of the world as well—that particular Volodya is as dead as Boris Nemtsov or Sacha Litvinenko. He's been replaced by an evil meme; a greedy zombie; a caricature of the Manly Man: Putin the Great bareback on a horse; Putin the Brave in scuba gear; Putin the Deadly on the shooting range; Putin the Athlete playing ice hockey with the national team; Putin the Ninja in the dojo, tossing opponents left and right.

It is, of course, all an act. And, I believe that more and more Russians are learning that it's an act—which will, at some point, have dire consequences for Vladimir Vladimirovich. Because Putin, unfortunately, doesn't have a Putin watching his back the way Anatoly Sobchak and Boris Yeltsin had a Putin watching theirs. Volodya's in it all alone. And that could be dangerous. For him—and for Russia.

I had a dream a couple of weeks before I finished this book. I dreamt I ran into Vladimir Vladimirovich in Munich. In my dream, he was much younger than he is now, and his eyes twinkled the way they used to when he visited Kamenny Ostrov and we'd talk politics and German history and literature, and shared gossip about the assholes at GUVD. He was dressed in *Lederhosen*, an Alpine hat, a *Prien* vest over a blue plaid shirt and cleat-soled *Haferlschuhe*, as if for Oktoberfest, and we strolled amongst knots of tourists past the *Hauptbahnhof*, wandered up Landsberger Strasse, and ambled toward the Augustinerbräu for a beer.

Outside the Augustiner sat a white Ford Explorer with Missouri plates, with red and blue lights flashing and a Kamenny Ostrov Security Company sign on the door. Leonid Pinchuk was sticking a ticket under the windshield wiper, but Putin grabbed the ticket out of his hands and tore it up. We went inside and sat down at a long beer table, where we were served by Igor Ivanovich Sechin, wearing a white shirt with the sleeves rolled up. He brought us full liter steins of Augustiner's magnificent *Edelstoff* export beer coming straight from a *Hirsch*, a huge 200 liter wooden barrel. And, in my dream, we raised our steins and toasted "*Prost*" to Boris Yeltsin, who was sitting across the room along with his daughter Tatanya and Anatoly

Sobchak, and they were all eating white Munich sausages with sweet mustard and pretzels and paying for the food from a two-foot stack of hundred dollar bills sitting in the middle of the table.

Putin exclaimed how good the beer was when it was fresh from the tap, and I noticed that he was wearing an immense Super Bowl Ring. I asked him where he got it and he laughed and said, "I'm *nachalnik*."

And so we drank again, raising our glasses in salute to Sacha Litvinenko and Boris Nemtsov, who were standing by the door. They were dressed like early French revolutionaries in *sans culottes* and deep in conversation. And then, smiling, I lit a small cigar and I asked Putin the same question he'd asked me back in 1992, the first time that we met.

I said, "So, Volodya, remember when you asked me what I'd done for St. Petersburg? Now it's my turn. Tell me: what have *you* ever done for your country?"

And the young Putin grinned the same way he'd grinned when he watched the demonstration of the new GRAD swat team I'd built for him, and he looked straight into my eyes, set his beer stein down with a *thwock* and said, still grinning, "What have *I* done for *my* country Franz? I have fucked it up. I have fucked it up good."

And that's when I woke up.

GLOSSARY

Arbitration –

Private dispute resolution mechanism through and by a private tribunal, usually made up of three arbitrators to rule on disputes outside state courts. However, state courts may review the judgment–called arbitration award– as goes for the validity of the arbitration clause and thus the competence of the tribunal, as well as for potential violations of law or misconduct of the tribunal.

Ataman –

Cossack commander.

Augustiner Bräu –

Munich's oldest brewery, founded 1328, and producer of Munich's best beer; Edelstoff.

Banya (Russian) –

Sauna house.

Bardack (Russian) –

Mess, whorehouse or circus (depending on the severity of the situation).

Bilateral Investment Treaties (BITs) –

Are international, bilateral and sometimes multilateral agreements that regulate the terms and conditions for private investment by foreign companies or individuals on the territory of the other state. In case of an expropriation or measures with similar effect, the injured investor may bring arbitration in a third country, and/or pursue proceedings before state courts on the territory of the state responsible for the takings, or may at times even rely on his own government to do that for him, with a view to effect proper compensation.

BFF –

Best Friend(s) Forever

BND –

Bundesnachrichtendienst, Germany's foreign intelligence agency.

CIA –

Central Intelligence Agency of the U.S.

Chutzpah –

Audacity; pushiness.

Claimant –

Plaintiff, also creditor.

Commercial use –

A legal term to describe the use of assets, bank accounts, buildings, land vehicles and vessels for purely commercial purposes by a foreign sovereign.

Daj (Russian) –

Gimme (give me!).

Detachment (A) Alpha –

Undercover Special Forces (U.S. Army) unit that worked in Berlin as part of the intelligence community's covert action program and as a counterterrorist asset in Europe.

Dezinformatsiya (Russian) –

Disinformation campaigns used by both Soviet and Russian intelligence to plant false information in the West through the use of agents of influence, the financing of Russian and international media, and, nowadays, internet trolls and hackers.

Diplomatic Immunity–

Form of legal immunity that ensures individual diplomats are given safe passage, are not subject to arrest, prosecution, civil litigation, taxation and enforcement action. Also their private residence is inviolable, as are the diplomat's family members.

Dikiy Dikiy Vostok (Russian) –

The Wild, Wild East.

Dummkopf (German) –

Dumbbell.

FSB –

Russia's Federal Security Service, or domestic counterintelligence service; successor to the KGB.

G.O.C.R.I.R. –

German Official in Charge of Running Interference for the Russians.

GRAD –

Russian counterterrorist SWAT team of the FSB.

Gastralyori (Russian)–

Guest criminal.

German Appellate Court –

Oberlandesgericht, Kammergericht. German bailiff – Gerichtsvollzieher.

German Chancellor –

Chancellor of the Federal Republic of Germany i.e. Angela Merkel.

German Circuit Court –

Landgericht.

German City Court –

Amtsgericht.

German Constitutional Court –

Bundesverfassungsgericht.

German Enforcement Authority –

Amtsgericht, Vollstreckungsgericht.

German Supreme Court –

Bundesgerichtshof.

GKI –

Russia's State Property Committee.

Glasnost (Russian) –

Transparency; Gorbachev's attempt to create accountability in the Soviet society.

Gruppa Zahvata (Russian) –

Soviet SWAT team (ex. Team Special for KGB, Spetsnaz for KGB and Red Army).

GSG-9 –

Germany's premier police border guard, counterterrorist and hostage rescue unit.

GUVD –

Here: Leningrad Police Department. Now St. Petersburg Police Department. Jurisdiction covers the city and the Leningrad region.

Haferlschuh (German) –

Traditional shoe model in the alpine regions of Bavaria.

Hauptbahnhof (German) –

Main or central train station.

HAZO –

Procurement Department of the GUVD.

Hirsch (German) –

A 200 liter beer keg.

Idyot (Russian) –

Idiot.

Immunity from execution –

Assets, bank accounts, vehicles, vessels, buildings and land are immune from enforcement when exclusively in use for a sovereign, non-commercial purpose.

Kamenny Ostrov (Russian) –

Stone Island, one of three islands sitting in the delta where the mouth of the Neva River meets the Gulf of Finland.

Kamenny Ostrov Company –

Sedelmayer's joint venture with GUVD and later KUGI

KGB –

Former Soviet Intelligence Agency. (Also used as a generic term to describe FSB and SVR because the organizations underwent several name changes since 1991.)

KOC –

Kamenny Ostrov Security Company, and Sedelmayer's guarding structure, "AO KOC".

KUGI –

Local branches of GKI (Russian State Property Committee).

Lumpenproletariat –

Working class members too pathetic to take part in a revolutionary struggle.

Mixed Use –

A legal term to describe the use of assets, buildings, land vehicles and vessels for sovereign and commercial purposes, by a foreign sovereign.

OMON –

Leningrad (now St. Petersburg) riot police unit.

Pfennig –

Decimal subunit of the (former) Deutsche Mark .

Prien vest –

Traditional vest of the Chiemgau region in Bavaria.

Prost (German) –

Cheers.

Refusenik –
A political activist; also used as an unofficial term for individuals, typically but not exclusively Soviet Jews, who were denied permission to emigrate by the Soviet authorities.

Respondent –
Defendant.

RSO –
Regional Security Officer.

Salo (Russian) –
Bacon.

Sans-culottes (French) –
Literally, "without breeches". The term refers to the Jacobin clothing of the lower-classes in late 18th century France, a great many of whom became radical participants in the French Revolution. Culottes were the fashionable silk knee-breeches of the nobility whereas the working class wore sansculottes, or trousers, instead.

SAS –
Special Air Service, army unit of United Kingdom Special Forces.

Scheisse (German) –
Shit.

SEAL –
Special Warfare unit of the U.S. Navy.

Shratz-I-Den'gi (Russian) –
Chow and money.

Smetana (Russian) –
Sour cream.

Sovereign Immunity –
Legal term to describe the inviolability of buildings, land, vessels and vehicles by a foreign state, when used for sovereign purposes from seizure,

access, law suits, taxation and enforcement actions. Also in use for international organizations like the U.N.

Stone Island –

Kamenny Ostrov, one of three islands sitting in the delta where the mouth of the Neva River meets the Gulf of Finland.

Stone Island Company –

Sedelmayer's joint venture with GUVD "AO Kamenny Ostrov" later replaced with the partner KUGI.

SVR –

Russia's foreign intelligence agency (in the book at times referred to as KGB as a generic term, because the organizations underwent several name changes during the time period covered).

SWAT –

Special Weapons And Tactics, term for law enforcement units which use specialized or military equipment and tactics in the U.S.

Swedish appellate court –

Hovrätt.

Swedish Circuit Court –

Tingsrätt.

Swedish City Court –

Tingsrätt.

Swedish Constitutional Court –

Högsta domstolen.

Swedish enforcement authority –

Kronofogden.

Swedish Supreme Court –

Högsta domstolen.

T&E –

Testing and Evaluation.

Tochno (Russian) –
Precisely.
Tovarich (Russian) –
Comrade.

UdPRF –
Office of Affairs of the President of the Russian Federation, successor of UsPRF.
Upravlenie (Russian) –
Office of Affairs of the President of the Russian Federation.
URPO –
FSB's elite Division of Operations against Criminal Organizations.
UsPRF –
Office of Affairs of the Communist Party, now renamed UdPRF, Office of Affairs of the President of the Russian Federation.

Valuta –
Hard currencies: euros, U.S. dollars, Swiss francs, British pounds, etc.
Ventilateur (French) –
Fan.
Vranyo (Russian) –
A little or big white lie.

Weisswurst (German) –
Literally, "white sausage". A traditional Bavarian sausage made from minced veal and pork back bacon, usually flavored with parsley, lemon, onions, and mace. Commonly served with sweet mustard, pretzels, and good beer.

Zakhodi (Russian) –
Come on in.

Special Acknowledgements

A word of thanks to all my friends from the international press, who patiently have covered me and my travails over so many years. It was a great experience and lots of fun working with you all!

And with the greatest respect, I would like to point out that Russian journalists have without fail covered my dispute truthfully and always reported impartially about Sedelmayer vs. Russia. They have bravely defied—often at great personal risk—the ever-growing repression the Russian press faces under Vladimir Putin.

I cannot thank you enough! Together, we will all see the light at the end of the tunnel.

F.J.S.

Photocredits

Page 161, 181; Laetitia Vancon
Page 163; Andreas Labes
Page 177; Julian Baumann
Page 178, 179; Filip Normann

DATE DUE

WITHDRAWN